Called to Transformation
Ecumenical Diakonia

World Council of Churches

actalliance

Called to Transformation – Ecumenical *Diakonia*

WCC Publications is the book publishing programme of the World Council of Churches. The WCC is a worldwide fellowship of 352 member churches which represents more than half a billion Christians around the world. The WCC calls its member churches to seek unity, a common public witness and service to others in a world where hope and solidarity are the seeds for justice and peace. The WCC works with people of all faiths seeking reconciliation with the goal of justice, peace, and a more equitable world.

Opinions expressed in WCC Publications are those of the authors.

Production: Lyn van Rooyen, coordinator
WCC Publications
Cover design: Beth Oberholtzer
Book design and typesetting: Beth Oberholtzer
Photo credits: See page 139
ISBN (PDF)w: 978-2-8254-1806-2
ISBN (Print): 978-2-8254-1814-7

World Council of Churches
150 route de Ferney, P.O. Box 2100
1211 Geneva 2, Switzerland
www.oikoumene.org

Contents

Preface

Acts 6 describes the calling of the first deacons – Stephen, Philip, Prochorus, Nicanor, Timon, Parmenas and Nicolaus. Almost two thousand years later, this call to care in Christ's name is just as relevant, essential and urgent. Discerning how best to do so in changing times is what led to the writing of this document.

"Called to Transformation – Ecumenical Diakonia" has its origins in a conference held in Malawi in 2014, working on clarification on the relationship between churches and specialized ministries. Since then, there have been further developments – not least the launch of the United Nations Sustainable Development Goals (SDGs) in 2015 and the COVID-19 pandemic since 2020. Both require churches and their diaconal agencies to respond and engage. To be effective, such engagement requires co-ordination, co-operation and mutual aid – delivered in a spirit of prayer and Christian loving kindness – hence the emphasis on ecumenical *diakonia*.

This document aims to outline theological and practical service for *diakonia*. It is offered as a resource to facilitate learning and encourage good practices. It highlights the prophetic *diakonia* that addresses peace building, climate justice, gender justice, racial justice, health and healing. It also aim to address the diverse practices of *diakonia* and the theological background of *diakonia* as well as addressing misleading theologies.

The main document was prepared prior to the outbreak of the COVID-19 pandemic. Rather than change the document, the Executive Committee of the World Council of Churches felt that an addendum on the diaconal response to COVID-19 should be commissioned. Both the main document and the addendum can be read here together. I would like to thank everyone involved in the preparation of both.

Witness and service are crucial for the Church: mission, *diakonia* and ecumenism belong together and to the heart of what it means to be Church. The World Council of Churches and ACT Alliance have worked together to produce this resource, which we offer for the churches and their diaconal ministries throughout the World. We hope that it will lead to the sharing of ideas across confessions and borders to serve people in need.

Rev. Professor Dr Ioan Sauca
Acting General Secretary
World Council of Churches

Preface

It is with appreciation and joy that we present the document "Called to Transformation – Ecumenical *Diakonia*", which is the result of a joint effort of the ACT Alliance and the World Council of Churches (WCC) to clarify our joint understanding of ecumenical *diakonia* and articulate who we are and what we do. It outlines theological components and builds on the practice of churches and ecumenical organizations through the years. It demonstrates the convergence between churches and specialized ministries to guide our actions, practices and policy development. It is also intended to strengthen the institutional capacity of our respective constituencies.

Understanding ecumenical *diakonia* in diverse confessional contexts (chapter 8) and in diverse geographical contexts (chapter 9) is critical in times of pandemic, conflict, exclusion and climate crisis. Our joint commitment to *diakonia* bodes well for strengthened cooperation between WCC member churches and ACT members, whilst still preserving the shared understanding that binds our different constituencies together across contexts.

This document provides a new 'base-line' for joint reflection and practice of *diakonia* – one that articulates our centuries old church tradition in the contemporary framework of the UN's Sustainable Development Goals (chapter 5.3) and the commitment to 'localisation', promotion of local leadership and community led responses.

The document equips us for the necessary engagement with 'networks of cooperation' (chapter 10.7) – and helps us to develop a language to sensitize an international development and humanitarian system that has long been faith-illiterate but that is fortunately now changing with the discussion on 'religion and development'.

Diakonia is 'an integral part of the church's being and mission' (4.4). There is no church without *diakonia*, and no *diakonia* without 'the distinctiveness of its faith-based action'. In this context, there is no contradiction between a faith-based and a rights-based approach in *diakonia*, as they are mutually reinforcing: "faith-based and rights-based actions affirm each other".

Ecumenical *diakonia* affirms the fundamental importance of gender justice, recognizing that it is indispensable for development and poverty reduction. "Every human being holds the right to live in dignity and in freedom, and to be subjects in their own lives."

The understanding of our 'calling to transformation' comes with the insight that this call (vocatio) includes the need for us to engage with the poor, marginalized and excluded in advocacy (ad-vocatio) and if necessary, provocation (pro-vocatio): "*diakonia* will provoke resistance and contradiction, however always convinced that it will be transformative, calling into new ways of seeing, acting and judging".

The ACT Alliance thanks all involved in preparing the document and appreciates the collaboration with the WCC in articulating and sharing this document for continuous improvement of effective cooperation in service of people in need and in pursuit of justice.

Rudelmar Bueno de Faria
General Secretary
ACT Alliance

Executive summary

Photo: Paul Jeffrey/Life on Earth

The idea of developing this text on ecumenical *diakonia* surfaced in September 2014 during the International Consultation organized by the World Council of Churches (WCC) and ACT Alliance on the Relationship between Churches and Specialized Ministries, held in Malawi. The purpose of the document is to clarify the understanding of ecumenical *diakonia* and provide a common platform for acting and reflecting together. It outlines the theological components of *diakonia* and offers practical content for those engaged in such service. It is intended to be used for formation and training in ecumenical *diakonia*, to strengthen the institutional capacity of churches' respective constituencies, and to foster dialogue and cooperation between churches, ecumenical partners and the WCC.

The process of developing the document was accompanied by a working group with membership from the WCC and ACT Alliance, and initially accompanied by the Lutheran World Federation (LWF). As affirmed by the WCC Executive Committee at its meeting in Trondheim, Norway (June 2016), the document:

- Considers the longstanding experiences of diaconal practice and reflection within the ecumenical movement, in particular by the WCC and the LWF;
- Considers the specific contribution of professional diaconal agencies in their role as members of the ACT Alliance;
- Responds to relevant social and political issues in today's world that challenge churches and related agencies in their diaconal action;
- Provides theological insight that underscores the trinitarian and ecclesiological founding of *diakonia* and that can orient churches and related agencies in their diaconal practices;
- Proposes concrete steps to be taken in order to strengthen the diaconal capacity of the churches in cooperation with their ecumenical partners.

The document conceptualizes ecumenical *diakonia* from two perspectives. The first links to a theological understanding of *diakonia* as a dimension integral to the nature and mission of the church. This perspective shows that *diakonia* is a key expression of the strong link between what the churches are and do. Reflection on ecumenical *diakonia* requires understanding both dimensions: the churches' being and their joint action as a worldwide communion of Christians and institutions.

The second perspective is practical, describing how churches are engaged in diaconal action across confessional and geographical boundaries. The presentation in this document focuses on the ecumenical movement and its role in promoting and coordinating diaconal work. The World Council of Churches has played a pivotal role from its founding in 1948. Since then, the WCC has engaged in a vast number of programmes and projects with a clear diaconal profile, even without always using the term *diakonia*. As part of this diaconal praxis, the WCC has stimulated its member churches to engage in ecumenical *diakonia* and to strengthen their diaconal capacities. In partnership with the LWF, the WCC contributed to the founding of ACT Alliance with the goal of establishing a coordinated platform for ecumenical *diakonia*, expressing the joint vision of the ecumenical movement with its member churches and related agencies to assist people in need and to work for a better world.

Diakonia aims to respond to contextual challenges when moving in changing landscapes. This document includes analysis of the social and political environment in which ecumenical *diakonia* is engaged. It refers to basic trends in today's world that challenge diaconal action, and at the same time offer opportunities for innovative practice. It also reflects on the changing ecumenical landscape that affects ecumenical *diakonia*.

The document contains ten chapters. The first chapter presents background information and introduces a definition of ecumenical *diakonia*. It outlines some major trends in the contemporary context that are challenging active diaconal agents to reflect on the distinctiveness of faith- and rights-based action and how best to be innovative in their practice.

Chapter 2 introduces the history of ecumenical *diakonia*. It demonstrates that this history starts in the faith and practice of the early church and its commitment to serve people in need. Such practice continued in different forms throughout the history of the church as an integral part of missionary outreach. It then focuses on the development of *diakonia* within the ecumenical movement, its beginning as interchurch aid in the aftermath of the world wars, later widening its mandate to include development work and to engage in public advocacy. The second chapter concludes by presenting the formation of the ACT Alliance and its vision of providing coordination and cooperation within the area of ecumenical *diakonia*.

Chapter 3 presents the place of *diakonia* within today's polycentric ecumenical movement. Its main point of reference is the WCC's 10th Assembly at Busan in 2013 and its outcome, in particular the challenge to reflect on *diakonia* from the perspective of the margins, and as part of the invitation to a pilgrimage of justice and peace.

Chapter 4 provides some basic theological reflection on *diakonia*. It sketches the use of the term "*diakonia*" and related vocabulary in the New Testament, and presents the term in trinitarian, ecclesial and missiological perspectives. It then reviews the role of *diakonia* as a dimension of Christian discipleship and concludes by discussing the relationship between *diakonia* and proclamation.

Chapter 5 begins by describing the changing landscape of diaconal action and the new faces of poverty in today's world. It presents the UN Sustainable Development Goals as a relevant platform for diaconal engagement. The chapter indicates some specific themes as priority areas for diaconal action, such as migration and refugees, economic justice, climate justice, gender justice and health justice.

Chapter 6 reflects on the distinctiveness of diaconal practice, how its identity as both faith- and rights-based action forms its mission, objectives and methods. It presents diaconal assets, both tangible and intangible resources that are at hand for diaconal action, and indicates the advantages of developing a diaconal language. Finally, it points to the importance of building diaconal capacity and presents core elements of diaconal professionalism.

Chapter 7 presents contemporary challenges and opportunities, wrapping up what we have learned in the previous chapters. It deals with the challenge of shrinking financial resources and the importance of innovative practices in sharing resources, as well as highlighting the importance of partnerships and of building networks. Finally, it underscores advocacy as an integral dimension of diaconal work, affirming its prophetic vocation.

Chapter 8 looks at ecumenical *diakonia* in different confessional contexts, showing areas of similarity and dissimilarity amongst the confessions, thus leading towards greater mutual understanding and learning.

Chapter 9 describes ecumenical *diakonia* in different regional contexts, based on practices as well as socio-economic, social-political, environmental and other challenges in each area covered by the Regional Ecumenical Organisations (REOs).

Chapter 10 concludes this study by indicating the way forward. It invites the ecumenical movement, its member churches and related agencies to affirm the vision and the mandate of ecumenical *diakonia*, and finally proposes measures for strengthening the structures of shared action and networks of cooperation.

CHAPTER 1

Introduction

Photo: Paul Jeffrey/Life on Earth

1.1. Background

The idea of developing a document on ecumenical *diakonia* surfaced during the International Consultation on the Relationship between Churches and Specialized Ministries held in Malawi in September 2014. The report proposed as a specific point of action:

> For the WCC and ACT Alliance jointly to develop, by the end of 2016, a document that clarifies our joint understanding of ecumenical *diakonia*, and articulates who we are and what we do. This document should help clarify the understanding of ecumenical *diakonia*. This document should outline the theological components and be practical in terms of content. It should also build on the learning exercise/review conducted in 2015. It is intended to be used for formation and training in ecumenical *diakonia* to strengthen the institutional capacity of our respective constituencies.

This corresponded to the findings at Ecumenical Conversations 21 during the WCC's 10th Assembly at Busan, Republic of Korea, in 2013:

> The participants affirm that churches, ecumenical partners and the WCC must respond to the current context by developing a common diaconal language. We are faith-based and rights-based and we need to identify what this means in practice including defining both our mandate, our core values and our diaconal assets.

The present document seeks to understand and respond to these concerns; it intends to develop a common understanding of ecumenical *diakonia* that fosters the dialogue and cooperation between churches, ecumenical partners and the WCC.

The WCC executive committee at its meeting in Trondheim, Norway, in June 2016, approved the general direction of this document and affirmed the purpose, which is to develop an understanding of ecumenical *diakonia* that:

- Takes into account the longstanding experiences of diaconal practice and reflection within the ecumenical movement, in particular by the WCC and the LWF
- Considers the specific contribution of professional diaconal agencies in their role as members of the ACT Alliance
- Responds to relevant social and political issues in today's world that challenge churches and related agencies in their diaconal action
- Provides theological insight that underscores the trinitarian and ecclesiological founding of *diakonia* and that can orient churches and related agencies in their diaconal practices
- Proposes concrete steps to be taken in order to strengthen the diaconal capacity of the churches in cooperation with their ecumenical partners.

1.2. How to read this document

The background described in the preceding paragraph forms the context that this document intends to address: the international arena where the WCC, the LWF and ACT Alliance have cooperated closely together in establishing agendas and activities that promote human dignity, justice and peace, at the same time recognizing the wider network of confessional families, ecumenical partners and diaconal organisations in this endeavour. The document seeks to address burning issues related to this global arena, including tensions, challenges and opportunities, describing the joint efforts of the wide ecumenical movement as 'ecumenical *diakonia*'.

On the other hand, the document also aims to reflect the same issues in local contexts, where churches are engaged in different kinds of diaconal or social ministry. The diversity of contexts makes it impossible for this document to give a clear answer to all issues that deserve attention, although some basic themes hopefully will be recognized in all contexts. It is proposed that the process of reception will address this matter, providing proper space for local experiences and challenges. The companion study document is intended to facilitate this process. As this happens, it will be easier to see how this process shall be followed up and how practical tools of implementation should be put in place. The aspect of capacity-building and training in *diakonia* could be one such issue.

At this stage of introducing the document, it must be admitted that both "ecumenical" and "*diakonia*" are demanding terms to work with. Both concepts are value-laden; they express a vision for the global church and her mission in the world. At the same time, they are disputed. To be ecumenical is not as obvious as it may appear in this and other texts coming from the ecumenical movement. The ecumenical movement is marked not only by joint interests but also by tension and conflict. This reality constantly challenges the concept of ecumenical *diakonia*.

Similarly, the concept of *diakonia* is disputed. It is mainly used in some denominations, and it is better known in some regions of the world than in others. Many agencies involved in diaconal work prefer not to use the term, but rather use social or development work, thinking that the term *diakonia* does not communicate well in the secular world, or that it would signal a "churchy" move away from professional working methods.

It must be recognized that it was the modern diaconal movement that emerged in Germany in the 1830s that paved the way for understanding *diakonia* as the social ministry of the church. As will be explained in chapter 4, there are biblical and theological arguments for elaborating a theology of *diakonia*, but not simply by repeating terms as they are used in the New Testament. To reflect on *diakonia* is therefore an invitation to give new expression to the vocation to be part of God's mission to the world, and to understand this call (*vocatio*) as advocacy (*ad-vocatio*) and if necessary provocation (*pro-vocatio*); the first affirming the situation and the wellbeing of the other as fundamental for how discipleship is performed, the other acknowledging that this way of doing *diakonia* will provoke resistance and contradiction, however always convinced that it will be transformative, calling into being (which is the original meaning of provoke) new ways of seeing, judging and acting.

1.3. What do we understand by ecumenical *diakonia*?

This document conceptualizes ecumenical *diakonia* from two perspectives. The first links to a theological understanding of *diakonia*, based on a reflection that seeks to understand *diakonia* as an integral dimension of the nature and the mission of the church. This perspective reflects *diakonia* as a biblical and theological concept; it intends to identify motifs and normative elements that guide the understanding and practice of *diakonia*. One such motif is the image of human beings created in the image of God, another is the vocation to compassion and justice, a third links *diakonia* to the human vocation to serve as stewards of creation, and might be described as ecological *diakonia*, expressed in both prophetic and practical dimensions.

This perspective states that *diakonia* expresses a strong link between what the churches *are* and *do*. Reflection on ecumenical *diakonia* requires an understanding of both dimensions, their being and their joint action as a worldwide communion of churches and Christians. The ecumenical movement is carried by the conviction that unity and sharing are intimately interrelated as God's gracious gift and vocation. At the same time, this commitment to unity and sharing cannot be limited to the life of the churches and their wellbeing. It is a calling to serve in the world, participating in God's mission of healing and reconciliation, and of lifting up signs of hope, announcing by word and deed God's reign, its justice and peace.

The second perspective is practical, describing how churches across confessional and geographical borders are engaged in diaconal action. The presentation given here focuses on the ecumenical movement and its role in promoting and coordinating diaconal work. The World Council of Churches had a pivotal role from its founding in 1948, when it established a Division of Inter-

Church Aid and Service to Refugees. Since then, WCC has been engaged in a vast number of programmes and projects with a clear diaconal profile, even without always using the term *diakonia*. As part of this diaconal praxis, WCC has stimulated its member churches to engage in ecumenical *diakonia* and to strengthen their diaconal capacities. The Lutheran World Federation has also been strongly involved in ecumenical *diakonia*, in particular through its Lutheran World Service. Both the WCC and LWF contributed greatly to the founding of the ACT Alliance with the goal of establishing a coordinated platform for ecumenical *diakonia*, expressing the joint vision of the ecumenical movement with the member churches and their related agencies assisting people in need and working for a better world.

The Constitution of the World Council of Churches defines *diakonia* (service) as an integral dimension of its vision and life; Article III states,

> The primary purpose of the fellowship of churches in the World Council of Churches is to call one another to visible unity in one faith and in one eucharistic fellowship, expressed in worship and common life in Christ, through witness and service to the world, and to advance towards that unity in order that the world may believe.

It further reads:

> In seeking *koinonia* in faith and life, witness and service, the churches through the Council will: . . . express their commitment to *diakonia* in serving human need, breaking down barriers between people, promoting one human family in justice and peace, and upholding the integrity of creation, so that all may experience the fullness of life.

Here the terms "*diakonia*" and "service" are used interchangeably, which is quite common in the ecumenical movement's texts. However, there are differences between the two; "*diakonia*" has stronger theological connotations, while "service" points in the direction of concrete action. This may give the impression that *diakonia* is an internal Christian concept, not easily applicable in the public arena where services are performed. On the other hand, the term "service" may also have problematic connotations, especially if associated to a pattern of action that separates donors and beneficiaries, or that ignores the social and political context in which the service is delivered.

This document presents ecumenical *diakonia* as faith-based and rights-based action; the following chapters will elaborate on the meaning of these terms and their critical function as regards the challenges and opportunities in today's world. To be rights-based refers on the one hand to the biblical concept of justice and the prophetic heritage of unmasking systemic injustice and defending the rights of the poor. On the other hand, it refers to human rights and their central role in the formation of a just society. The commitment to human rights has convinced actors of ecumenical *diakonia* to include advocacy in their work with the task of bringing duty-bearers to account. This also helps us to see how *diakonia* is different from benevolent action, and that it does not aim to replace responsibilities of other stakeholders, including governments.

This understanding of *diakonia* as faith- and rights-based action opens us to defining activities as ecumenical *diakonia* in cases when this term is not used; it also allows for designating the ACT Alliance as a consortium of diaconal agents, which is evidenced by the fact that the alliance and many of its members now are in the process of including the *diakonia*-terminology in their vernacular.

The *Dictionary of the Ecumenical Movement* defines *diakonia* as "the responsible service of the gospel by deeds and by words performed by Christians in response to the needs of people." This wording indicates three components in the understanding of *diakonia*: it is action, or performing services, by using deeds and words; Christian faith motivates this action and views it as an expression of Christian discipleship; diaconal intervention reflects social reality and seeks in its performance to alleviate human suffering and promote justice, peace and human dignity.

This definition opens up the possibility of viewing ecumenical *diakonia* as one specific expression of *diakonia* that in its wider sense is a mandate given to all churches, at local and national level, and to every Christian as an integral part of discipleship. As all baptized are called to be "a holy priesthood" (1 Pet. 2:5), they are called to participate in God's mission of healing and reconciliation, to serve one's neighbour and be committed to causes of justice and peace. This vocation may be presented as "the diaconate of all believers," based on the view that God's Spirit graciously empowers and equips for discipleship, from the youngest to the oldest, men and women (Acts 2:17). From this follows that the diaconal vocation in the first place relates to everyday life: the family that cares for its members and in particular children and the elderly, the neighbourhood and the workplace, civil society and other arenas for social action. Diaconal activities organized by local congregations and other church structures, including professional diaconal agents, depend on and are largely borne by the diaconate of all believers. This is also the case for ecumenical *diakonia*, which makes it so important to affirm and strengthen this basic expression of diaconal capacity and commitment.

This study demonstrates that there are many different shapes and institutional forms of engagement in Christian social service or *diakonia*, depending on the cultural, political and social environments churches have to exist in – all of which have the same validity and legitimacy and are not to be put in any hierarchical order of importance:

There are churches performing diaconal services:

a) Only within local churches/congregations, as an individual or group commitment to limited, and often voluntary, service to the needy
b) Within and via the first expressions of institutionalized centres of Christian community life and service, outside the local parishes (such as religious communities in ecclesial traditions, such as monasteries, sisterhoods, brotherhoods and spiritual centres)
c) Both in local church voluntary services, as well as in specialized ministries on the regional level (diaconal professional agencies), but only funded by local church funds
d) Both in local church voluntary services, as well as in specialized ministries on the regional level (diaconal professional agencies), funded by both church funds and contributions from other church partners outside the country (interchurch aid)
e) Both in local church voluntary services, as well as in specialized ministries on the regional level (diaconal professional agencies), and also diaconal lobbying and advocacy activities on the national and international levels, funded by both church funds and contributions coming from state authorities.

The key point in visualizing this or similar phases in the development of diaconal competences and different degrees of professionalization is that none of these phases can be regarded as the normative model for the other, and none of these can claim to be on top of a normative hierarchy theologically.

1.4. The context of this document

Diakonia aims to respond to contextual challenges when moving in changing landscapes. Reflection on *diakonia* therefore includes an analysis of the social and political environment in which it is performing its work. In what follows, we shall point to some basic trends in today's world that challenge diaconal action, and at the same time offer opportunities for innovative practice. Finally, we shall briefly look at the changing ecumenical landscape that simultaneously affects ecumenical *diakonia*.

Changing development paradigm. The traditional development model of offering aid to "developing" countries focusing on economic growth is being replaced by a new approach that integrates more dimensions. The UN Sustainable Development Goals (SDGs) seek global answers to global challenges, and they invite not only governments but also civil society and faith-based actors to contribute to their realization. The SDG Agenda 2030 represents a new public platform for diaconal engagement. It challenges ecumenical *diakonia* to develop strategies for action, and to equip local churches and other partners to assume an active role in relation to the SDG agenda.

Shrinking space of civil society. There is a growing concern that civil society is under ever more pressure worldwide. This trend manifests itself through systematic restrictions and repression affecting civil rights organizations and human rights defenders in an increasing number of countries. Repressive NGO regulations have become an operational challenge for the independent work of diaconal agents and their international partners. In addition, other laws, such as antiterrorism, safety, security, internet and media laws, constrict the civil society's scope of action. All this has led to seriously changing the working conditions of diaconal agents for the worse.

Rise of nationalism. In many parts of the world, new forms of political nationalism are emerging, often expressing national selfishness and policies that aim at dismantling principles of global solidarity. In some cases, this growing nationalism emerges together with the weakening role of the state and growing mistrust in the established political order. It is often linked to xenophobia, leading to racism and hate speech. This ideological trend challenges ecumenical *diakonia* to engage in public debate, to promote its view on human dignity, and to construct civil order based on the common good and human rights.

Religion and development. There is growing recognition of the role of religion in development, and of religious leaders as agents of change. This role is, however, ambiguous: in some cases, religious faith and leaders add fuel to violent action and hinder development. Ecumenical *diakonia* is challenged, together with other social and development agents, to increase competence in working with faith communities and their leaders. Such ability includes a proper critique of religion, including our own, discerning its positive and negative roles in promoting human dignity and the common good. It also requires capacity-building for diaconal work.

Deepening socio-economic inequalities. Economic injustice continues to grow, both within countries and globally. In January 2017, Oxfam published a report indicating that the world's eight richest men own the same wealth as the 3.6 billion people who make up the poorest half of humanity. This growing inequality has many negative consequences; it excludes large populations from common goods and services that should secure their fundamental rights and welfare. Economic justice therefore will require increased attention by diaconal actors and must be high on the agenda of ecumenical *diakonia*.

The landscape of suffering, injustice and war. Agents of ecumenical *diakonia* share the commitment to respond to human suffering at times of crisis and war. Politicization of aid and deteriorating security environment have impacted the conditions for this engagement. Actors need to balance the need to help the suffering with the duty of care of their staff members. Humanitarian principles and international human rights law as a common framework guiding the engagement are increasingly being challenged. Simultaneously, there is an increasing expectation that the responses are being carried out by local actors without adequate financial support from the international community. This potentially can lead to a situation where the root causes of poverty and suffering are not addressed, with the focus shifting away from sustainable long-term development and political problems remain unsolved.

Forced migration. The number of people forced to leave their homes in the hope of a better future in a new place, often in another country, is higher than ever before. Social and political unrest is one major driving force; another is the consequences of climate change. Whether refugees, asylum seekers, forcibly displaced persons or those considered "economic refugees," they are facing situations marked by uncertainties and lack of rights. Many have been exploited by criminal traffickers; when arriving, they experience discrimination, xenophobia and racism. Their situation challenges ecumenical *diakonia* to innovative action, to engage in advocacy and in promoting inclusiveness in church and society.

Children and youth. More than a quarter of the global population is aged under 15; in situations of crisis and conflict, they are among the most vulnerable. To invest in the welfare of children and young people will guarantee a more positive development of societies. Churches and diaconal agents can take a leading role in advocating on behalf of children, which clearly corresponds to the Christian view on family and society as a safe space for children and as an arena for developing their talents. UNICEF has opted for the view that children should not been seen simply as a "vulnerable group" but rather as actors in their own right who can transform a nation's development trajectory if prioritized in politics and budgets.

Ecological crisis. Climate change and other ecological issues are causing unprecedented ecological destruction, in many cases leading to food insecurity and lack of clean water. On the one hand, important results have been achieved, mainly thanks to the work of United Nations Framework Convention on Climate Change (UNFCCC), not least its COP 21 meeting in Paris in 2015. On the other hand, populist politicians who reject that climate change is caused by humans are gaining power in many countries, undermining the political support to implement the measures taken. Climate justice therefore continues to be a core issue for ecumenical *diakonia*, i.e. new forms of "*ecodiakonia*" both at the level of advocacy and public witness, and in promoting and implementing a resilience agenda at the local level.

The landscape of the ecumenical movement is also changing. While in the past it may have been conceived as vertical with a strong centre, it today sees itself as polycentric, affirming a horizontal model of relations and cooperation. It also recognizes the wider context of Christian churches and communities and is committed to establishing new forms of relationships affirming the churches' joint vocation to witness and service.

The following themes indicate some contemporary challenges and opportunities:

Advocacy and prophetic* diakonia *as signs of hope. The advocacy of the churches can be based only on a Christian faith that has a prophetic, critical approach aiming at transformation and hope. The ecumenical movement is called to be a fellowship of living hope, always "prepared to make a defence to anyone who calls you to account for the hope that is in you" (1 Peter 3:15). This must be done in mutual accountability, in terms of self-critique and critical analysis, and in signs of hope, as well as common action. Within this understanding, ecumenical *diakonia* must also be able to give account of its hope, and of how its work offers signs of hope. In doing this, it should affirm every person's right to hope, contributing to constructing a world that "leaves nobody behind," as the vision of Agenda 2030 states.

***Public theology and* diakonia.** There is a growing awareness that public witness and advocacy are integral parts of the church's mission and of diaconal work. It has stimulated the creation and promotion of different forms of "public theology." Its aim is to strengthen the churches in their public responsibility and diaconal work, responding to contexts of increasing religion-based extremism, violence and corruption.

In 2017, churches commemorated the 500 years since the publication of Luther's 95 Theses. That event marked the beginning of the Lutheran Reformation, which envisaged renewing the church based on the centrality of God's liberating grace in Jesus Christ and the vocation to serve one's neighbour. This Reformation introduced new practices of addressing the issue of poverty, and it called on political authorities to provide care and education for those in need. Its doctrine of the universal priesthood of all believers states that all baptized persons are empowered to participate in God's mission and that a prime arena for service is one's secular profession, contributing to common good. It makes sense to reformulate this theology of vocation as the diaconate of all believers.

The Pilgrimage of Justice and Peace. The WCC Busan Assembly in 2013 called churches and all people of good will to embark on a "pilgrimage of justice and peace." Objectives include calling churches to move outside their comfort zones and respond to the burning issues of today's world, and to lift up signs up hope. The pilgrimage is affirming the experience that unity and service strengthen each other mutually, and the view that the ecumenical mission cannot be restricted to the wellbeing of the churches; its mandate is to participate in God's mission, the goal of which is the healing of the world and the coming of God's reign. The vocation to *diakonia* thus constitutes an integral part when unfolding the Pilgrimage of Justice and Peace in the life of the churches. At the same time, the pilgrimage inspires ecumenical *diakonia* to renew its commitment to justice and peace in partnership with churches and people of good will.

1.5. Existing texts on ecumenical *diakonia*

Diakonia has long been a topic for reflection in the ecumenical movement; this section presents some of the existing texts. The present document is largely based on them. In addition, it is informed by key articles in *Dictionary of the Ecumenical Movement*, and the presentation on "*Diakonia* in the Ecumenical Movement" by the late Richard D.N. Dickinson in *A History of the Ecumenical Movement*.

In 1961 the WCC Assembly in New Delhi highlighted the programmatic importance of service as one of the three pillars of the ecumenical movement (along with unity and witness). In 1964, Faith and Order organized a consultation in Geneva on the ministry of the deacon. The report elaborates not only on the role of this ministry, but also on its relation to *diakonia*, "the service to those who are in want," and then states that the "Church cannot be truly the Church of Jesus Christ without giving itself to such *diakonia*." The document *Baptism, Eucharist and Ministry* also prepared by the Faith and Order Commission, largely reflects this understanding.

The WCC Commission on Inter-Church Aid, Refugee and World Service (CICARWS) took a leading role in promoting a creative reflection on *diakonia* within the ecumenical family. It organized various consultations, often from a more practical perspective, with the aim of connecting critical theological reflection to innovative practice. In 1966, the WCC convened a world consultation on interchurch aid, refugee and world service in Swanwick, UK, that added the idea of social advancement or social action to the prevailing concept of social relief work and service.

After the Nairobi assembly in 1976, the WCC initiated a study project on Ecumenical Sharing of Resources (ESR) that addressed emerging critical questions about the selfhood and identity of churches regarded as "receiving" churches and their partnership with "sending" or "giving" churches. This study project led to the publication of a study guide titled *Empty Hands: An Agenda for the Churches* in 1980, and later to the global consultation on *koinonia* held in El Escorial, Spain, in 1987 which was the culmination of the ESR process.

The consultation on "Contemporary Understandings of *Diakonia*", held in Geneva in 1982, in many ways marks a milestone. It harvested impulses from the ESR process, and in addition from another consultation that CICARWS had organized, in Chania, Crete, in 1978, under the theme "An Orthodox Approach to *Diakonia*." The material from these meetings strongly inspired the WCC's 6th Assembly at Vancouver in 1983 and its view on *diakonia* "as the church's ministry of sharing, healing and reconciliation."

Another important event organized by CICARWS was the global consultation at Larnaca, Cyprus, in 1986. This time, a major number of participants represented churches from the global South; they gave stronger emphasis to the role of the local church and to the prophetic dimension of diaconal action.

After 1991, the WCC's Unit IV, and in particular its *Diakonia* & Solidarity team, received the mandate to work further with the issues raised by the Larnaca consultation. In 2002, Chris Ferguson and Ofelia Ortega produced a document titled *Ecumenical Diakonia*, which, however, remains unpublished in English. Another publication from that same year, *From Inter-church Aid to Jubilee*, gave a historical presentation of ecumenical *diakonia*. In addition, the WCC has published two booklets that relate issues of poverty and development to *diakonia*: *Poverty: A Scandal Challenging the Churches—Current Contexts and Approaches in Diakonia and Development, A Study Guide* (2004), and *Diakonia: Creating Harmony, Seeking Justice and Practicing Compassion* (2005). In 2010, William Temu drafted a document titled *Mapping Prophetic Diakonia*. It presents the various kinds of diaconal work across the World Council of Churches fellowship. The report was submitted to the Global Consultation on Prophetic *Diakonia*, which took place at Utrecht, The Netherlands, in December that year; it remains unpublished.

In preparation for the WCC's 10th Assembly in Busan, three WCC programmes, Solidarity and *Diakonia*, Just and Inclusive Communities, and Mission and Evangelism, jointly organized a conference on *diakonia* in Colombo, Sri Lanka, in June 2013. The document from this meeting, *Theological Perspectives on Diakonia in the Twenty-First Century*, was included in the *Resource Book* for the Busan assembly. After the assembly, *The Ecumenical Review* edited a whole issue under the title *New Perspectives on Diakonia*, with reports and commentaries.

In addition, the Lutheran World Federation (LWF) has contributed to reflections on ecumenical *diakonia*. In preparing for the 10th LWF Assembly in Winnipeg (2003), a consultation was held in Johannesburg, South Africa, in November 2002, under the heading *Prophetic Diakonia: "For the Healing of the World."* The Winnipeg assembly recommended further work on *diakonia*, which the LWF Department of Mission and Development followed up through a programme called "Understanding *Diakonia* and Its Guiding Principles." The programme organized several workshops in different parts of the world, and a final consultation in Addis Ababa, Ethiopia, in October 2008. The findings are collected in the book *Serving the Whole Person*; they are also reflected in the document *Diakonia in Context*, that was received by the LWF Council in 2009. LWF has also had a study process related to the understanding and role of the ministry of deacon, reported in the publication *The Diaconal Ministry of the Church*.

1.6. Outline of the document

This first chapter presented the background of this document and introduced a definition of ecumenical *diakonia*. It has also outlined some major trends in the contemporary context in which ecumenical *diakonia* is performing its work yet challenges diaconal agents to reflect on the distinctiveness of faith- and rights-based action and to be innovative in their practice. Finally, it has brought a list of texts on *diakonia* that have been produced within the framework of the ecumenical movement, in particular the WCC and LWF.

Chapter 2 introduces *the history of ecumenical diakonia*. It starts with the early church and its commitment to serving people in need, a practice that has being continued in different forms throughout the history of the church, and as an integral part of missionary outreach. It then focuses on the development of *diakonia* within the ecumenical movement, its beginning as interchurch aid in the aftermath of the world wars, later widening its mandate also to include development work and to engaging in public advocacy. It points at important steps in deepening the understanding of ecumenical *diakonia*, with a growing awareness of its ecclesial and prophetic dimension, and, at the same time, the importance of professional competence. The chapter concludes by presenting the formation of the ACT Alliance and its vision of providing coordination and cooperation within the area of ecumenical *diakonia*.

Chapter 3 presents *diakonia in today's polycentric ecumenical movement*. Its main point of reference is the WCC Busan assembly in 2013 and its outcome. That assembly was challenged to reflect *diakonia* from the perspective of the margins, and it concluded its work by inviting all people of good will to a pilgrimage of justice and peace.

Chapter 4 provides *theological reflection on diakonia*. It sketches the use of the term "*diakonia*" and its related terms in the New Testament and presents the concept in a trinitarian, ecclesial and missiological perspective. It then views *diakonia* as a dimension of Christian discipleship and concludes by discussing the relationship between *diakonia* and proclamation.

Chapter 5 starts by describing *the changing landscape of diaconal action* and the new faces of poverty in today's world. It presents the UN Sustainable Development Goals as a relevant platform for diaconal engagement. The chapter indicates some specific themes as priority areas for diaconal action, such as migration and refugees, economic justice, climate justice, gender justice and health justice.

Chapter 6 reflects on *the distinctiveness of diaconal practice*, and how its identity as faith- and rights-based action forms its mission, objectives and methods. It further presents diaconal assets, both tangible and intangible resources that are at hand for diaconal action, and indicates the advantages of developing a diaconal language. Finally, it points to the importance of building diaconal capacity and presents core elements to be included in the professional profile of diaconal activity.

Chapter 7 presents *contemporary challenges and opportunities*, wrapping up the learning from the previous chapters. Its first part deals with the challenge of shrinking financial resources and the importance of innovative practice in sharing resources. The second part looks at partnerships and the importance of building networks, with secular organizations and with people of other faiths. The third part underscores advocacy as an integral dimension of diaconal work, affirming its prophetic vocation.

Chapter 8 attempts to discern different confessional contexts, showing similarities and dissimilarities in the approach to *diakonia* throughout Christianity.

Chapter 9 attempts to show how different socio-economic, socio-political, environmental, historic and cultural challenges can all affect approaches to *diakonia*. Issues such as conflict, political ideologies, natural disasters, wealth, poverty, the legacies of colonialism, and the legal status of churches are just some of the issues can have a direct bearing on diaconal provision.

Chapter 10 concludes the document by indicating *the way forward*. It invites the ecumenical movement, its member churches and related agencies, to affirm the vision and the mandate of ecumenical *diakonia* and proposes measures for strengthening the structures of shared action and networks of cooperation. An addition, it proposes building diaconal capacity and, lastly, including codes of conduct in diaconal work.

CHAPTER 2

The History of Ecumenical *Diakonia*

Photo: Albin Hillert/WCC

2.1. Introduction

This chapter offers a historical outline of the history of ecumenical *diakonia*, starting with the early church and its care for people in need. It passes to the missionary era and its witness to holistic mission, in particular through its long tradition of medical mission.

From the very beginning of the ecumenical movement, *diakonia* has been an integral part of its mandate and work; interchurch aid thus became a central task of the WCC from its founding in 1948. Since then, new challenges and perspectives have shaped ecumenical *diakonia*, both in its practice and understanding. The 1960s introduced the quest for professionalization and for engagement in development work; at the same time, they raised issues of justice and of solidarity with oppressed people and their movements of liberation. Later discussion emphasized the ecclesial dimension of *diakonia*, and in particular the role of the local church in the performance of *diakonia*. It underscored *diakonia* as an integral part of the holistic mission of the church, particularly when acknowledging the distinctiveness of diaconal work. Within the ecumenical movement today, *diakonia* is affirmed to be both faith-based and rights-based.

The founding of the ACT Alliance has provided a new opportunity for coordinating ecumenical *diakonia*, for holding together bilateral and multilateral forms of partnership, which include respect and space for local churches and their diaconal resources. At the same time, and through its organizational bonds with the WCC and the LWF, the ACT Alliance gives visibility to the diaconal commitment of the ecumenical movement.

2.2. The Early Church

According to the gospel narratives, Jesus mandated his disciples to continue his ministry of caring for people in need. "As you go, proclaim this message: 'The kingdom of heaven has come near.' Heal the sick, raise the dead, cleanse those who have leprosy, drive out demons. Freely you have received; freely give." (Matt 10:7-8).

"But Jesus called them to Himself and said, 'You know that the rulers of the Gentiles lord it over them, and those who are great exercise authority over them. Yet it shall not be so among you; but whoever desires to become great among you, let him be your servant. And whoever desires to be first among you, let him be your slave--just as the Son of Man did not come to be served, but to serve, and give His life a ransom for many" (Matthew 20:25-28).

The early church integrated this mandate into her being and mission. Acts 2:44-45 reports of the congregation established in Jerusalem on the day of Pentecost that "all who believed were together and had all things in common; they would sell their possessions and goods and distribute the proceeds to all, as any had need." Later, when a congregation had been established in Antioch, where the name "Christians" appeared for the first time, they responded to a severe famine and provided help to its victims (Acts 11:27-30).

Care for the poor thus remained a central task, as Paul reports from his meeting in Jerusalem with the other apostles: "They asked only one thing, that we remember the poor, which was actually what I was eager to do" (Gal 2:10).

The New Testament documents show that the early church was engaged in what in our time would be described as ecumenical *diakonia*. Paul refers in his letters (Rom 15:31 and 2 Cor 8-9) to the *"diakonia"*, in the form of the joint action of collecting money, from the churches in the region to the church in Jerusalem that was passing through difficult times.. His appeal to the church in Corinth fills two full chapters (2 Cor. 8-9); it can be read as a theological exposé of ecumenical solidarity and *diakonia* (and even as a model for an ACT appeal in today's ecumenical context!).

Whilst *diakonia* in Greek thought meant philanthropic care and service to any one in need, in the Scripture philanthropy simply means service to people of the same race and faith. *Philanthropia* (charity) in ancient Greek literature carries several meanings, but its original means sacrificial love rather than simply kindness, and benevolence toward people of the same nation.

Charity in *diakonia, l*ove in practice, became a mark of distinction of the early Christian church. Christianity removed boundaries and broke down racial and ethnic fences, proclaiming that "there is neither Jew nor Greek, there is neither slave nor free, there is neither male or female" but all are one in Christ Jesus (Gal. 3:28). In its practical application, charity (philanthropy) went beyond Jews, Greeks and Romans. It stressed that "love is of God, and he who loves is born of God and knows God. He who does not love does not know God, for God is love" (1 John 4:7-8). God's love requires that humans love one another (1 John 4:11). There is no better account of the nature and the fruits of Christian charity than the thirteenth chapter of St. Paul's First Letter to the Corinthians. Agape is defined as the love of God expressed through the God-made-man event in Christ and as humanity's love of neighbour, the solvent of hatred of the enemy.

This philanthropic *diakonia* of the Church in history was greatly influenced by the sacrificial love of Christ (Jo. 3:16) but also by his teaching as we read it in the gospel of Matthew (Matt 25:31-46).

It is noteworthy that the Apostle Paul argues theologically when urging the Corinthians to share in what he calls the "ministry to the saints" (2 Cor 8:4). At no moment does he ask them to pity the poor and their suffering; instead, he reminds his readers of their identity and mission as part of the communion of believers in Christ. The example of their sister church in Macedonia should convince them: although being poor, they begged for "the privilege of sharing." Here Paul connects the two concepts communion *(koinonia)* and *diakonia*, indicating the organic connection between what they are and what they are called to do in Christ. Sharing thus has both an ontological and a practical dimension; for Christians, it expresses our belonging together and our care for each other.

In his further argument, Paul points to the example of "our Lord Jesus Christ that though he was rich, yet for your sake he became poor, so that by his poverty you might become rich" (8:9). This does not mean that they should give away everything, or take the role of always caring for the others. His point is "fair balance" (8:13-14) and mutual care, knowing that no person is without needs, as also no one is without gifts.

Interestingly, *diakonia*, according to Paul, refers both to the campaign of collecting money and to its good administration (8:19 Greek: *diakonoumene*). He presents his co-worker Titus as a responsible project administrator, who therefore enjoys the trust of all partners.

We have no information regarding this campaign beyond what Paul reports. The fact that this action and its interpretation by Paul are included in the apostolic witness points to its significance. It provides important impulses to the reflection on what it means to be church, even today.

Paul's sensitivity to the poor is consistent with the teaching of Jesus and of the early church. He understood that the word of Christ cut across sociological boundaries and that the church was made up of poor and rich alike (Gal 3:28; Col 3:11; cf. 1 Cor 1:27-29). His emphasis on the collection for the Jerusalem church exhibits this concern in a practical way (Rom 15:26; 1 Cor 16:3; 2 Cor. 8-9; Gal 2:10).

An important principle of the New Testament is the equality of persons before God, with the most powerful statement of the equality of rich and poor coming from James, who emphasizes God's sensitivity to the poor and their faith (2:5). He notes that discriminating between the rich and the poor is both a sin against God (2:9) and an insult to the poor (2:6).

There are many reports that the early church continued to serve the poor and suffering, however without using the term *diakonia* for this ministry. Its way of practicing hospitality and of visiting the sick, even in times of devastating plagues, caused public admiration and motivated many to join the church. In fact, many see what we today would call the diaconal work and outreach of the early church as the key to its rapid missionary attractiveness and success in the first three centuries. Under the leadership of St. Lawrence, known as "the defender of the poor," the deacons in Rome had developed an extensive charitable outreach by the middle of the third century. To relieve people from the famine, St Basil the Great (4th century) founded a very large philanthropic institution, which he placed in care of a monastic community. It provided people from neighbouring areas with medicine, good food, warm shelter, dry clothing and all the services of the church and communal living, making accessible to them God's love and the support of his church. It was a real hospital that his friend St. Gregory calls a veritable city of piety, "the New City." St Fabiola (ca. 399) founded a hospital in Rome. It "assembled all the sick from the streets and highways," and she "personally tended the unhappy and impoverished victims of hunger and disease and washed the pus from sores that others could not even behold."

According to the tradition of the early church, "deacon" literally means server. Deacons are the waiters (servants) at the table of the Lord (Cf. Luke 14:16-24; John 2:1-11). Therefore, they are usually found during liturgy around the altar helping the priest. Deacons are also the earthly equivalent of the angels who are intermediaries between God and people (Hebrews 1:14). So, they are often mediators uniting the laity with priests and bishops, or representing the Church's interests to the populous. Additionally, deacons are part of the ministerial structure of many churches, assisting pastors, priests, and bishops in certain moments of the worship and administering resources assigned to the care for the poor and the sick.

A comprehensive description of both the pastoral and diaconal work of early deacons, which were regarded an essential component in the ministry structure of any local church, was formulated in a Syrian church order from the 5th century, called "Testamentum Domini": "Let the Deacon do only those things which are commanded by the bishop as for proclamation, and let him be the counsellor of the whole clergy and the mystery of the church, who ministers to the sick, who ministers to the strangers, who helps the widows, who is the father of the orphans, who goes about all the houses of those who are in need, lest any be in affliction or sickness or misery. Let him go about the houses of the catechumens, so that he may confirm those who are doubting and teach those who are unlearned. Let him clothe these men who have departed, adorning them, burying the strangers, guiding those who pass from their dwelling, or go into captivity. For the help of those in need let him notify the church, let him not trouble the bishop, but only on the first day of the week let him make mention about everything, so that he may know."

This is a remarkable witness from the early orthodox church tradition that deacons were expected to engage in a broad-based spectrum of social services on behalf of the local church. This comprised visiting the sick, pastoral services to migrants, care for abandoned children, teaching the youth and younger catechumenates, providing burial liturgies as well as engaging in prison chaplaincy and public communication on the needs of the poor.

Remarkably, extensive patristic research shows that early church orders included clear reference to women serving and being blessed as deaconesses in some local churches, both in Greek-speaking churches, as well as in churches with Oriental Languages (except Egypt and Ethiopia).

Later, the monasteries became centres of hospitality and care. As Christianity spread, religious orders would expand their network and establish hospitals and other services in new parts of Europe and beyond. Through many centuries the religious orders have been the spiritual source, organizational stronghold and ecclesial backbone for the diaconal work of the Church.

2.3. The missionary era

Since the beginning, the church has been involved in mission work that would carry Christian faith across geographical, social and cultural boundaries. The missionary movement is the context in which the ecumenical movement, including ecumenical *diakonia,* has grown forth and developed.

The mission of the Eastern churches was mainly directed toward Eastern Europe and Asia; the Western churches sent missionaries to Western and Northern Europe, Africa and much of the rest of the world. Although the missionary enterprise would assume different expressions throughout the centuries, it would normally include care for the sick and suffering, in other words, what we today may describe as diaconal practice.

The modern missionary movement originated in Europe and North America and unfolded in various forms both in the pre-colonial as well as in the colonial period. Most missionaries went to Africa and Asia, a process that started already in the 18th century (such as David Livingstone in Southern Africa and the Herrnhuter Mission). In the colonial period in many cases, the establishment of mission fields went parallel with the expansion of Western colonial powers. To the evangelised and colonised, this created unfortunate imperialistic bonds; often the missionaries were perceived to be part of the colonial enterprise, lacked awareness of their own privilege and function as participants in the colonial enterprise, and served as representatives of Western values and life style that were in turn imposed on the evangelised. It should, however, be mentioned that, although there were missionaries that wholeheartedly supported colonial powers and exercised racial discrimination against the Africans, there were also many other cases during the colonial period where missionaries particularly served as pioneers in the first written script in dictionaries and Bible translations and severely criticised the misbehaviours of colonial powers. Through their services, people were educated and empowered to take the lead in the process toward independence and nation-building. Thus, despite the profound influence on education and social development and today even on development cooperation, mission work remains contentious terrain and a phenomenon with different faces, which have to be carefully analysed.

The ecumenical movement has affirmed the medical ministry as a main dimension of the church's mission. In 1964 and 1968, the World Council of Churches and the Lutheran World Federation together organized two consultations in Tübingen, Germany, focusing on medical mission in the global South and the role of the church in healing. As a follow-up, the WCC created the Christian Medical Commission (CMC) in 1968 with the aim of assisting member churches involved in health work. CMC also developed links with the World Health Organization and played an important role in promoting primary health care and a holistic approach to health and healing.

The history of the modern missionary movement must, however, place diaconal benefits to those evangelized in the greater confessional context of imperialism, historical harm, and colonialism; and in particular, acknowledge this harm when it comes to the situation of indigenous peoples in the West, and to minority groups. In 1993, the leadership of the Anglican Church in Canada addressed an *Apology to Native People* for the way it had treated indigenous children at residential schools. The policy of these schools, run by the church's mission in close cooperation with the Canadian government, was to remove children from the influence of the aboriginal culture and assimilate them into the dominant Canadian culture. Since the 1990s, the Anglican Church and other churches in Canada have committed themselves to overcoming the harms caused by this educational system, working toward healing and reconciliation. Similarly, in 2014 and 2016, the General Assembly of the Presbyterian Church (USA) issued an apology to indigenous peoples of the United States and, along with other historical denominations in the USA, repudiated the Doctrine of Discovery that had animated the cultural and theological basis of racist relationships and treatment of indigenous peoples, including church-run "Indian schools." Not all involved in similar work have taken a similarly brave position. The situation and the rights of indigenous peoples and minority groups continue to be an important issue on the agenda of ecumenical *diakonia*.

Since the 1960s, many mission agencies have been involved in development projects in cooperation with the partner churches in the global South. In cases where they have received public funding, they have had to follow the governmental requirements of not mixing evangelization and development work. This process has caused debate, especially among partners in the global South, which, in many cases, understand mission holistically, i.e. carrying out God's mission through development work and service, as acknowledged subsequently. In 1974 churches in Africa represented at the All Africa Conference of Churches' conference in Lusaka, Zambia, issued a call for missionary 'moratorium' so as to ensure African churches' self-determination, self-reliance and sense of identity within the growing tensions of the reality of Western dominance and African dependence within local and global church relationships.

The term *diakonia* did not become part of the missionary vernacular, due to the fact that it was not much used until the emergence of the diaconal movement in Germany in the 19th century, and was then mainly restricted to the work of deacons and deaconesses. Only recently have missionary organizations and ecumenical bodies started to apply it when presenting the holistic approach to which they subscribe. This is the case of the LWF document *Mission in Context* (2004); it presents holistic mission, encompassing proclamation, *diakonia* and advocacy. The WCC document *Together towards Life: Mission and Evangelism in Changing Landscapes,* presented by the Commission on World Mission and Evangelism (CWME) in preparing for the Busan assembly, points in the same direction. It affirms:

> an understanding of evangelism which is grounded in the life of the local church where worship (*leiturgia*) is inextricably linked to witness (*martyria*), service (*diakonia*), and fellowship (*koinonia*).

The document also states that:

> The church in every geo-political and socio-economic context is called to service (*diakonia*)—to live out the faith and hope of the community of God's people, witnessing to what God has done in Jesus Christ. Through service the church participates in God's mission, following the way of its Servant Lord. The church is called to be a diaconal community manifesting the power of service over the power of domination, enabling and nurturing possibilities for life, and witnessing to God's transforming grace through acts of service that hold forth the promise of God's reign.

There is a growing understanding, also among leaders of missionary organizations, that mission and *diakonia* are intimately connected, and that diaconal work in itself is an unfolding of the missional mandate. There is also growing recognition that mission and justice belong together. Some voices, for instance, of representatives of evangelical mission organizations, will continue to claim that proclamation is what really matters in mission work, with individual conversion as the basic objective. This view regards *diakonia* as a secondary activity, as facultative depending on the circumstances, and possibly supportive to the "real" matter of mission.

The history of ecumenical *diakonia* includes many actors and initiatives. It is not possible to list them all here or give an account of their valuable contributions.

The *DIAKONIA World Federation* is one of these, networking persons dedicated to the ministry of the diaconate, mostly women in all regions of the world. The work by members of the *DIAKONIA World Federation* ranges from work with women and youth living with AIDS to working for peace between Christian and Muslim communities.

Specialised diaconal agencies also include maritime chaplaincies offering pastoral care to seafarers, including members of the International Christian Maritime Association (ICMA).

It remains therefore a core task for world Christianity to reflect theologically on the true nature of mission, taking into consideration the experiences of the past and the challenges of today. Chapter 4 will bring further theological reflection on this matter from the perspective of ecumenical *diakonia*.

2.4. Interchurch aid

In the 19th century, problems of urbanization and industrialization mobilized churches to act together when addressing social issues, recognizing that their traditional structures would not suffice and that they needed to work together when dealing with such challenges. Urban Mission, the YMCA and similar organizations were set up with a clear interdenominational and diaconal profile, and their leaders largely contributed to the formation of the ecumenical movement. *Diakonia* has been a major impulse and dimension in the formation of ecumenism. The Life and Work Movement, from its first conference in Stockholm in 1925, expressed the vision that Christian unity and social issues are interrelated, and that the churches should act together.

The suffering in Europe after World War I convinced church leaders that this call required new initiatives and a firmer structure. In 1922, the European Central Bureau for Inter-Church Aid was established in Switzerland, under the auspices of the Federal Council of the Churches of Christ in America and the Federation of Swiss Protestant Churches, later joined by other European churches. Its purpose was to coordinate assistance to refugees and others in need of relief. This initiative modelled ecumenical *diakonia* as multilateral cooperation among churches in the decades that followed. In

1945, it merged with the World Council of Churches, which was in the process of formation, and was set up as the Department of Refugee and Inter-Church Aid.

The WCC Central Committee, meeting for the first time in Chichester, UK, in 1949, one year after the Amsterdam assembly, underscored that interchurch aid is a permanent obligation of the WCC, not a temporary task. Dr Visser 't Hooft, WCC general secretary from 1948 to 1966, strongly defended this position and called for a "system of mutual aid," holding the view that the practice of solidarity belongs to the essence of the new life, "a test of its reality," referring to 2 Cor. 8-9. Accordingly, he claimed, there would be no healthy ecumenical fellowship without practical solidarity.

Interchurch aid was perceived as cooperation between churches, within the understanding of mutuality and from the perspective that the historical context would decide whether a church should take the role of donor or recipient. The Division of Inter-Church Aid and Service to Refugees (DICASR), as the WCC department was renamed in 1949, would for many years have refugees as a special target group, not only in Europe but also in other parts of the world. In addition, it would support projects related to the situation of a local church, such as repairing buildings damaged during the war, or to programmes that would strengthen the internal capacities of the church, for instance education and social welfare. This would especially be the case of minority churches and of churches in Eastern Europe, then under Communist rule.

Several WCC member churches set up organizations with the purpose of financing interchurch aid. These organizations are often referred to as "related agencies" due to their close cooperation with the ecumenical movement and their mandate to finance the activities of the DICASR. Folkekirkens Nødhjælp (DanChurchAid) had started its work in Denmark already in 1922, while Christian Aid (UK and Ireland) came into being in 1945. After World War II, more organizations were founded, which was the case of Church World Service (USA) in 1946, and Norwegian Church Aid and Swedish Lutherhjälpen in 1947. Finn Church Aid was, at the time of its establishment in 1947, a recipient of assistance from abroad, serving the victims of war in Finland; it later became an agency that aided suffering people in other parts of the world.

The WCC leadership at that time mainly spoke of "interchurch aid". Church leaders using German and representing Northern Europe would prefer the term "*diakonia,*" which they were well acquainted with in their home churches, also from the view that the aid should not be restricted to churches and church members but should benefit those who suffered most. Since the 1830s, the so-called modern diaconal movement had promoted the establishment of diaconal institutions, first in Germany, later in other countries, also outside Europe. The majority of these institutions operate today in close cooperation with local or national governments that finance their activities. Most of them are not linked to nor represented in the global movement of ecumenical *diakonia*; they are sometimes regarded as a "different" kind of *diakonia*. It was, however, often church leaders from this background that would see interchurch aid and refugee service as a natural extension of the kind of work that diaconal actors had developed in their home churches.

Visser 't Hooft recognized the potential of applying the term *diakonia* ecumenically. At a consultation of DICASR in 1956, he presented the view that the mission of the church has three aspects of manifestation: *kerygma, koinonia* and *diakonia*. According to him, *diakonia* is "the ministry, the expression of faith in Christian love and compassion and in the service of the needs of men." This triad of *kerygma, koinonia* and *diakonia* has often been used since then as a way of expressing the link between the nature of the church and her holistic sending to the world.

The New Delhi assembly of the WCC in 1961 articulated a similar vision in proclaiming witness, unity and service (*diakonia*) as the three essential and indispensable core dimensions of the church, and called to engage in the "the ecumenical service of the churches." The integration of the International Missionary Council (IMC) with the World Council of Churches that occurred during this assembly certainly contributed to the manifestation of this vision.

2.5. Ecumenical *diakonia* and development aid

Assisting people in need always includes perspectives beyond the action there and then. For the churches involved in interchurch aid after World

War II, this action aimed at reconciliation and at establishing new bonds of solidarity among nations that had waged war against each other. Refugee work implies advocacy, defending the dignity and the social and political rights for people that have been forced to leave their homes. Humanitarian aid requires long-term assistance; it motivates aid agencies to engage in development work.

Until 1961, there were two major instruments for interchurch aid and ecumenical sharing: CICARWS (Division of Inter-Church Aid, Refugee and World Service, or in its earlier shape DICASR) and IMC (International Missionary Council, since 1921). The agenda of the first focused on reconstruction in Europe after the World War II with the main objective of interchurch aid, whereas missionary cooperation was the main agenda of the second focusing on the "selfhood of the younger churches" and "de-colonialization." A new sense of "'global responsibilities" of the churches and countries in the North heavily influenced the discourse in this period. The concept of "responsible society," which the WCC in Amsterdam in 1948 had adopted, was now projected into a global horizon.

The growing awareness of the mutual relationship between ecumenism and *diakonia* in the 1950s and 60s stimulated a process of gradual widening and merger of both agendas and their related instruments, and to the conceptualization of ecumenical *diakonia*. In 1957, an international consultation held in Berlin introduced the concept of ecumenical *diakonia*. It reflected a strong sense of post-war Christianity and its commitment to peace and struggle against hunger on global scale and to hold together the vision of a "responsible society" and the churches' commitment to "social *diakonia*," both to be understood in global perspective: therefore the new emphasis on "ecumenical *diakonia*."

DICASR and its ecumenical partners had started their work responding to the dramatic needs in Europe after World War II. However, in 1954 the WCC Evanston assembly recommended DICASR to provide support also to churches in Africa, Asia and Latin America. A secretary for non-European areas was appointed, later leading to the establishment of desks for Asia, Africa and Latin America in CICARWS. In 1956, DICASR for the first time presented a "project list," inviting funding partners in the North to support them. This indicated a shift from emergency work to long-term development work. At the same time, it opened up a new practice of organizing and implementing activities; development workers became key actors in the task of designing projects and ensuring professional standards when being implemented.

The widening of the agenda of DICASR led to the need of clarifying the relationship to the existing instrument of sharing resources within the IMC. In 1958, after intense talks between the WCC and the IMC, the Bad Herrenalb Agreement was worked out. It established regulations for how projects should be supported, ensuring that projects would receive funds by either DICASR or IMC. The integration of the IMC into the WCC in 1961 led to the establishment of DWME (Department for World Mission and Evangelism), and that same year for the first time a joint project list was worked out between DICARWS and DWME. The former separation between a reconstruction agenda in the North and a "development" or missionary cooperation agenda in the South had become obsolete.

In 1960, DICASR had been renamed DICARWS (Division of Inter-Church Aid, Refugee and World Service). Its emphasis was to strengthen a common "world service" of churches together, as stated in its mandate:

> The aim of the division shall be to express the ecumenical solidarity of the churches through mutual aid in order to strengthen them in their life and mission and especially in their service to the world around them (*diakonia*).

The key terms were still "aid," "*diakonia*" and "service"; soon, they would be more or less replaced by the concept of "development." In the discourse around DICARWS which became impacted by the development optimism of the 1960s, 'world service' tended to mainly mean development work and was oriented by the development theories of that era. Ecumenical *diakonia* thus reflected what happened in the secular world; on the other hand, it also contributed actively to the understanding of development, in particular by claiming it to be a matter of justice, and not of charity. The WCC conference on Church and Society in Geneva 1966 was an important event in this course of manifesting the concern of the ecumenical movement because of the presence and inputs from the global South. Another example of its public commitment was the cooperation with WHO, mainly through the WCC Christian Medical Commission, in formulating concepts of health and global health services.

The WCC's Fourth Assembly at Uppsala in 1968 represents a formal beginning of the intentional and organized engagement of the ecumenical movement for development cooperation. The years before 1968 had seen already strengthened cooperation between CICARWS and national or international agencies for interchurch aid. The implications of the transformation of interchurch aid into development aid were critically discussed before and during the Uppsala assembly. Whether or not to use government funds for church-related engagement in development cooperation had been an issue of internal critical discussion in DICARWS already in 1961.

The 1960s, according to the UN, "the first development decade," united public and humanitarian agents, including diaconal agencies, in their engagement for a better world. It led to the formulation of theories of development and to new awareness regarding objectives and working methods. This process of professionalizing development work also had consequences for ecumenical *diakonia*, and it brought many advantages. It raised the awareness of quality and competence when involved in development work, of considering the root causes of poverty and of addressing issues of justice and human rights. It caused a move away from benevolent charity models to more participatory and empowering practices. It addressed critical questions like the role of women in society and the situation of marginalized groups. It also fostered practices of responsible administration, of accountability when managing financial resources, and of honest and critical self-evaluation.

The consequence has been that diaconal agencies, together with most faith-based organizations (FBOs), enjoy a high degree of confidence among public donors, including governments. In general, they credit FBOs as responsible, professional, and effective. Governments in the global North have therefore increasingly funded projects operated by church-based actors, under the condition that they followed established requirements. The projects should be religiously "neutral" and not be used for promoting the church.

This indicates that the process of professionalization also brought some disadvantages. Project holders oriented by professional standards did not always see the professional value of working with local churches. DICARWS, from 1971 CICARWS (Commission of Inter-Church Aid, Refugee and World Service), defined its mandate as service to the world rather than solidarity between churches, "to help meet the needs on behalf of humanity and without distinction of creed, caste, race, nationality or politics."

From the 1960s, the related agencies had started to implement projects themselves in developing countries, bypassing the given ecclesial ecumenical structures. This meant a steady move from multilateralism to bilateralism, and consequently a move from interchurch cooperation to professional development work. Two important agencies came into being in this period, Bread for the World, in Germany 1959, and ICCO (originally an abbreviation for Interchurch Coordination Committee for Development Projects), in the Netherlands in 1964, both with a clear mandate to perform development-aid activities on behalf of their home churches.

The embracing of development theories implied also that church-related terms, such as *diakonia*, largely ceased to be used. Some would claim that from a professional point of view there should be no difference between church-based and secular agencies in implementing development projects. The main issue was to achieve established objectives. Others would question this position, asking why the agencies kept their church-related identity, if they in practice ignored the self-understanding of the churches they involved as partners when performing their work. In 1972, the Ethiopian Evangelical Church Mekane Yesus (EECMY) sent a letter to the LWF questioning the requirement of church-based development agencies to separate development work and evangelization when implementing projects funded by them. This letter became a symbol of African reaction to what was felt to be the imposition of a Western dichotomist anthropology in development work, that is, of viewing faith as a personal matter disconnected from social engagement.

Other voices questioned the very system of aid, claiming that it upheld the unjust division between North and South, between "donors" and "recipients." The WCC Church and Society conference in Geneva (1966) called churches to move away from direct aid, instead, they should support locally funded and local initiatives. The WCC Uppsala assembly (1968) affirmed this concern, claiming justice, not charity, and advocating for the transfer of power and mutual participation. In 1971, the WCC established the CCPD (Commission on the Churches' Participation in Development) with the aim of promoting popular movements all over the world, based on the conviction that their reflection and action would be more effective than aid when striving for a just and participatory society. A certain unavoidable tension marked the ideological and structural positions of CICARWS and CCPD. On the one hand, it contributed to a raised awareness regarding the complexity of international aid, and the necessity of addressing critical questions; on the other hand, this focus on overarching principles may have had as consequence that the WCC's position as coordinator and implementer of concrete projects was reduced.

2.6. A new paradigm emerging

Since the 1980s there was a growing understanding, both among secular and faith-based development actors, that the current development paradigm was not delivering, among other things, being too economic-centred. James P. Grant, the Executive Director of the United Nations Children's Fund (UNICEF), expressed this view at the International Conference on Population and Development in Cairo in 1994:

> Since the conference on population in Mexico City in 1984, it has become increasingly clear that development must be responsive to a new paradigm. If it is to be sustainable today, development must not only produce economic growth, sustainable in the environmental sense. It also must be sustainable in a human sense -- it must break the grip of poverty on the bottom half or third of society and slow population growth, while sustaining democracy, human rights, people's participation in the development process and peace.

The new paradigm of ecumenical *diakonia* that was now emerging drew learning from the secular discussion on development, as well as from theological reflection on the distinct nature of diaconal action. It is possible to point to three basic dimensions that gained more weight within this new understanding, each of them responding to critical questions raised in the previous period.

First, there is *the ecclesiological dimension of diakonia*. While ecumenical *diakonia* in the past often had been perceived as benevolent action, performed by specialists, emphasis was now given to its ecclesial nature. The WCC assembly in Vancouver in 1983 strongly expressed this understanding:

> *Diakonia* as the church's ministry of sharing, healing and reconciliation is of the very nature of the Church. It demands of individuals and churches a giving, which comes not out of what they have, but what they are. *Diakonia* constantly has to challenge the frozen, static, self-centred structures of the Church and transform them into living instruments of the sharing, healing ministry of the Church. *Diakonia* cannot be confined within the institutional framework. It should transcend the established structures and boundaries of the institutional church and become the sharing and healing action of the Holy Spirit through the community of God's people in and for the world.

The CICARWS consultation on "The Orthodox Approach to *Diakonia*," held in Chania, Crete, in 1978, paved the way for viewing *diakonia* as a "liturgy after the Liturgy," as "an integral part of a living Christian community's concern and pastoral care for all those within the community and for all those who come within range of its knowledge and loving care." Four years later, CIWARWS organized another consultation in Geneva, with the theme "Contemporary Understandings of *Diakonia*". It affirmed the ecclesial dimension, stating that

> *Diakonia* is essential for the life and well-being of the church... The heart of *diakonia* is in the eucharist; there is its origin where Christ is sharing his body with us and so heals us. In *diakonia* we become followers of the Lord.

The consultation added another perspective to this view, which underscores the role of the local church:

> *Diakonia* takes shape in the local church, for in their local contexts churches have to be servants of

the Lord, open to the needs of society in which they live.... In the local church we can discover that *diakonia* is never a subject-object relationship but a relationship of exchange in a healing and sharing community. Institutional forms of *diakonia*, useful though they may be, cannot take over the responsibility of the local Christian communities.

The ecclesial perspective on *diakonia* opened the concept for connecting it to "sharing," which had become a key theme in the WCC in the 1980s, and in particular in the quest for ecumenical sharing of resources. As Christ freely shares the gifts of belonging to his community, Christians are called to a life of sharing. Ecumenical *diakonia* thus becomes both a visible sign and an effective instrument of the church's vocation in the world.

Second, there is *the prophetic dimension of diakonia*. Questions related to justice and to the root causes of poverty influenced diaconal agents. If they in the past had presented their work as charity, and even as humble service, they now underscored the importance of responding to burning social and political issues. Diaconal action should aim at being rights-based; it should promote human dignity and work for justice, peace and the integrity of creation. The Crete consultation (1978), while affirming this understanding, linked it to the ecclesial dimension of *diakonia*:

> The object of Christian *diakonia* is to overcome evil. It offers deliverance from injustices and oppression. When the church fails to offer its witness and to be prophetic, the reaction of the world will be indifference and apathy. *Diakonia* is therefore an essential element in the life and growth of the church.

The Geneva consultation (1982) criticized diaconal services that were "ancillary to domestic capitalism and colonialism" and did not "contest the main social evils of these dominant socio-economic systems." It called for a *diakonia* that is liberating – "the prior concern needs to be the empowerment of people"—and asked churches to re-think their priorities, and "to engage in and support programmes for realizing justice . . .

The Larnaca consultation (1986) expanded this view. In many ways, it is the turning point in the process of conceptualizing ecumenical *diakonia*. The CICARWS director, Klaus Poser, described this as follows in the report from the consultation:

> There was relatively little discussion of development or projects; rather, discussion centred on the struggle for life and solidarity for justice. The consultation demonstrated that the manifestations of Christian love assume many diverse forms, and witness to the comprehensiveness of *diakonia* in the discipleship of Jesus Christ.

Diakonia is thus expected both to be political and prophetic. It is political in the sense that it recognizes the political context in which it is embedded and develops forms of action that denounce injustice and support processes toward a more just society. It is prophetic in the sense that it is inspired by the example of the Old Testament prophets and of Jesus, who defended the dignity and the rights of the excluded and announced the values of God's reign, among which are justice and peace.

Thirdly, there is *the new paradigm that underscored the holistic dimension of diakonia*. Already the Crete consultation (1978) had urged CICARWS to "give greater expression to the spiritual dimension of *diakonia*" and to pay attention "to the fact that specialized agency mandates as applied in current procedures may hinder a response to the real need of the churches."

In particular, those representing the churches in the global South questioned the way diaconal agencies performed their work, seeing little difference between them and secular organizations. They experienced the requirement of separating project work from other church-related activities as a manner of promoting a Western worldview. Instead, they advocated a holistic approach when working for a more just society, which would have to include the material, social and spiritual dimensions of human reality.

It should be emphasized that the three dimensions of this new paradigm are interrelated and justify each other mutually. The ecclesiological dimension affirms that *diakonia* is an integral part of the mission of the church as well as the holistic nature of mission; it encompasses proclamation, prophetic witness and diaconal action.

CICARWS had been instrumental in facilitating this new paradigm; at the same time its role as facilitator of joint diaconal action decreased. The

Canberra assembly (1991) decided to dissolve both CICARWS and CCPD. The new established Unit IV Sharing and Service was "less concerned with defending the word *diakonia*"; its main task was to network processes of reflection.

In 2002, *Diakonia* and Solidarity was established as a WCC programme. Its team produced some important texts that document the development of ecumenical *diakonia*. *From Inter-church Aid to Jubilee* presents its history, claiming that the concepts (interchurch aid, *diakonia*, sharing, solidarity) have changed over time, but the essence has been the same:

> The important constant is the understanding that the theological, spiritual and moral convictions of the ecumenical movement need to be translated into genuine acts of solidarity if the vision of ecumenism is to be credible, relevant and rooted in the lives of people.

Chris Ferguson and Ofelia Ortega, on behalf of the WCC Regional Relation Team, wrote another important text, *Ecumenical Diakonia*. They affirm the new paradigm of *diakonia*, presenting it as prophetic, transformative and justice-seeking, contributing to what is described as a "cycle of empowerment":

> This *diakonia* also involves participation in the continuing struggle for a just and equitable sharing of resources. Such sharing emphasizes the mutual responsibility and accountability of churches and ecumenical partners. Sharing must be married to justice, contributing to a "cycle of empowerment" so that "all may have life in all its fullness" (Jn.10:10) and shares in the Biblical vision that "each shall sit under their vine and fig tree and live in peace and unafraid" (Mic. 4:4).

This view is clearly inspired by the biblical vision of justice and peace and by an ethos of sharing and of mutuality. On the other hand, it implies guiding principles for diaconal action:

> True *diakonia* following Christ's example and rooted in the Eucharist involves immersion in the suffering and brokenness of the world. It will hear and respond to the signs of the times from the same faith in the God of Life but it will need to include new learning and new voices and respond to a different context. Our context forces us to overcome false dichotomies from the past. We cannot understand or practice *diakonia* apart from justice and peace. Service cannot be separated from prophetic witness or the ministry of reconciliation. Mission must include transformative *diakonia*.

2.7. The formation of the ACT Alliance

In the early 1990s, when CICARWS had ceased to exist, heads of agencies from the global North continued to meet regularly, with a growing concern for developing mechanisms of cooperation, especially when responding to emergencies. In 1995, Action by Churches Together (ACT International) was established, with its head office in Geneva. The WCC and the LWF both played a central role in this process, with the clear objective of creating a structure that would provide space for the diaconal engagement of their member churches and affirm the diaconal commitment of the ecumenical movement.

Another important initiative with the purpose of promoting joint action by ecumenical partners was the Ecumenical Advocacy Alliance (EAA), formed in 2000. One of its main objectives was to coordinate the global advocacy of churches and related agencies on particular issues, such as HIV/AIDS and food security.

The good experiences with these structures motivated the partners to expand the ACT structure. In 2007, ACT Development was formed as "a global alliance of churches and related organizations who are mandated to work ecumenically in development and who choose to work together," with the goal to "promote and facilitate cooperation between participants to improve their effectiveness in transformational development." The intention was to bring together ACT International and ACT Development, and in 2010, the governing bodies of the two organizations decided to merge their activities and create a unified ACT Alliance. Again, at that moment, the WCC and the LWF played an active role and affirmed ownership of the new structure.

As of 2016, ACT Alliance is a coalition of 140 churches and faith-based organizations working together in over 100 countries. It mobilizes about

$2.6 billion for its work each year in three targeted areas: humanitarian aid, development and advocacy "to create positive and sustainable change in the lives of poor and marginalized people regardless of their religion, politics, gender, sexual orientation, race or nationality in keeping with the highest international codes and standards." The founding document states the core values of the Alliance and its members, "grounded in our Christian faith and which guide our humanitarian, development and advocacy work":

> We believe that all persons are created in the image of God.
>
> We believe that God the Father as known through his Son Jesus Christ and revealed through the Holy Spirit and scriptures, is the God of love who stands beside the poor and oppressed.
>
> We believe the church is called to manifest God's gracious love for all people and work towards a reconciled human community. This witness is more clearly communicated to the world when we work together as members of one body of Christ.
>
> We believe that the earth and all it contains are God's gifts, given out of love and care for all created beings.
>
> We believe that the resources available to us are not our own, but are a gift from God, and our vocation to service calls us to be faithful to principles of good stewardship.

The term "*diakonia*" does not appear in this document. Nor does it in any other document of the Alliance, for instance, the policy paper titled *The Changing Development Paradigm*, approved by the ACT Executive Committee in January 2013. This document analyzes the global context in which ACT Alliance is working; it starts by affirming briefly the theological platform of the founding document, but it does not apply this theological language in the further analysis. This indicates that so far, ACT has not included the *diakonia*-terminology in its vernacular. Instead, it has opted for using a professional language that communicates with its external audience, the humanitarian sector, and with the network of back donors. The focus has been on the professional competence of the organization and its ability to respond to challenges from the structural and socio-political environment.

On the other hand, this language runs the risk of under-communicating the faith base of ACT Alliance, and in particular its relations to the church network. When this happens, local churches may perceive ACT as any international aid agent, without antennas for their role as local expressions of the constituency that has brought it into being. In September 2014, the WCC and the ACT Alliance jointly organized a consultation in Malawi on the relationship between churches and specialized ministries, addressing tensions as regards the operations of the international ACT members, claiming that they often have been bypassing the local churches and their diaconal engagement. The consultation acknowledged the need to strengthen relationships and proposed specific points of action that would contribute toward improving the relationship between churches and specialized ministries. Among these surfaced the idea to develop a document that clarifies "our joint understanding of ecumenical *diakonia*, and articulated who we are and what we do."

There is no contradiction between professional competence when performing diaconal services and affirming one's identity as a faith-based agent. It requires, however, an intentional effort to bridge the secular concept of development with the theological understanding of being a part of God's mission of healing and transformation. The ACT Alliance would gain from applying the *diakonia*-language when articulating its distinctive identity and mandate, and clarifying its role as a key agent within the field of ecumenical *diakonia*.

The second ACT Alliance Assembly, in Punta Cana, the Dominican Republic, in 2014, included a workshop on *diakonia*, as part of the discussion on how to contribute to more robust ecumenical relationships. The WCC general secretary, Olav Fykse Tveit, affirmed this concern when addressing the assembly:

> The biblical word for the service to which we are called is *diakonia*. This word, and the language we have connected to it, is a common basis for what we do as the WCC and ACT Alliance.

The formation of ACT Alliance has had a number of important consequences. It has provided their members a coordinated role within the global UN-related system, with more space for the professional expertise and interaction of specialized ministries within the global UN-related humanitarian and development sector. This has also strengthened the voice of the churches in the public space and has contributed to a wider recognition of the role of religion and of FBOs within the humanitarian and development work.

In addition, the ACT Alliance has given more visibility to the specialized ministries within the wider ecumenical movement and to their professional social role and engagement. Before the alliance was established, agencies had started to become more independent from WCC and LWF, carrying out bilateral relationships; they increasingly channelled their resources to non-church actors and NGOs, bypassing the churches. The agencies also felt that they did not have a major say in decision-making in the WCC, in spite of the fact that they were among the most important donors of WCC. The ACT Alliance has provided a new platform for addressing these issues and for building relationships that recognize both the distinct and the complementary role of diaconal agencies within the one ecumenical movement. It continues to be a challenge to do this in a way that affirms the shared mandate of agencies and churches, and that fosters mutuality and sharing of resources. Another important task is to improve the structures of cooperation in a manner that recognizes and strengthens the diaconal engagement of local churches, in particular on issues of social responsibility, advocacy and prophetic *diakonia*.

2.8. Summary

This chapter documented that, throughout history, *diakonia* has been an integral part of the church's mission. The diaconal practice has changed according to times and contexts. The needs of the marginalized and suffering have continuously challenged diaconal actors to be innovative and to cross borders – social, ethnic and geographical. As such, *diakonia* has given testimony to the mandate of participating in God's healing and liberating mission to the world.

For that reason, *diakonia* counts among the main forces that have formed ecumenism and its agenda. The architects of the ecumenical movement linked their vision of unity to the understanding of mission as joint action in service of people in need, and of promoting healing, justice and peace in a broken world.

The understanding of ecumenical *diakonia* has deepened over the last decades; in responding to challenges and critical questions, it has gained new insight and learned to articulate its role and mandate in new ways, and it has developed new organizational frameworks in order to be relevant and objective in today's socio-political reality.

As the document *From Inter-Church Aid to Jubilee* concludes:

> The history of ecumenical *diakonia* in the WCC has certainly not been without controversies, struggles and challenges. It has however always been the reflection, however limited, of the authentic desire of renewed discipleship on the part of Christians involved in the ecumenical movement, challenging and confronting the injustices, suffering and oppression of the world. In this way, the experience of ecumenical *diakonia* in WCC has been truly prophetic, and has served as spiritual and material resource for the broader ecumenical family.

CHAPTER 3

Diakonia in today's polycentric ecumenical movement

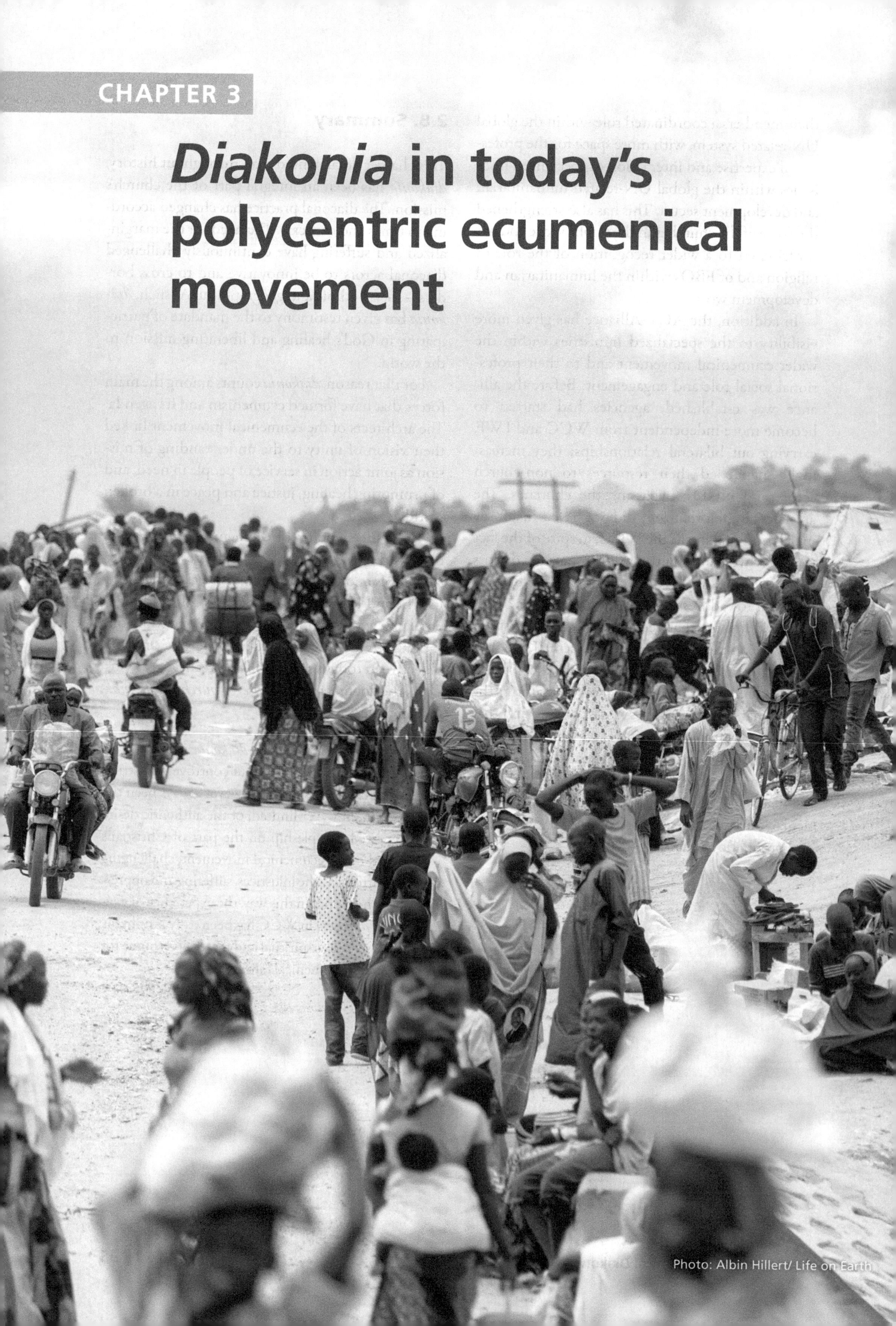

Photo: Albin Hillert/ Life on Earth

3.1. Introduction

The ecumenical movement today presents itself as polycentric. Nurtured by a rich variety of traditions and experiences in the life of member churches, it shares the vision of unity and sharing when called to be partners in God's mission of bringing hope and future to the world.

Polycentric means recognizing a changing ecclesial landscape as we have entered the 21st century. The centre of gravity of Christianity has shifted toward the global South. While the churches in the global North, in particular in Europe, experience declining membership, church life is vibrant in the global South and membership is growing. The shift also relates to the growth of charismatic and Pentecostal churches, mainly churches outside the traditional ecumenical family.

This new landscape challenged the World Council of Churches and other ecumenical bodies to reconsider their work and find new ways of relating to Christianity, acknowledging its polycentric nature. One important step in this regard has been connecting to the Christian world communities. The term "Christian World Communions" (CWCs) describes the globally organized churches or groupings (families) of churches with common theological and historical roots, confessions, or structure. Since 1997, the WCC has been engaged in establishing the Global Christian Forum (GCF), as an arena that affirms the distinctive and complementary roles of different ecclesial agents in the quest for Christian unity. In recent years, CWCs have also discussed among themselves and participated in processes related to the call for a reconfiguration of the ecumenical movement.

The process of approaching the wider ecumenical landscape has included rebuilding relations with the Lausanne movement, which in the past had been very critical of the WCC and especially its understanding of mission. When meeting in Cape Town, South Africa, for the third Congress of the Lausanne Movement in 2010, a delegation from the WCC was invited, led by General Secretary Olav Fykse Tveit. In his address, he spoke of Christians' "common vision of the holistic mission of God." He added, "Let us keep the road open, and the dialogue going, so that we learn from one another how we can participate in God's mission together with respect to others as one Body of Christ."

The concept of holistic mission is of pivotal importance in this re-approach. The Lausanne movement has strengthened its understanding of what is described as "integral mission":

> Integral mission is the proclamation and demonstration of the gospel. It is not simply that evangelism and social involvement are to be done alongside each other. Rather, in integral mission our proclamation has social consequences as we call people to love and repentance in all areas of life.

In many ways, this corresponds to the concept of holistic mission as developed within the ecumenical movement. It should be noted that the document from the Cape Town meeting does not apply the *diakonia*-terminology; it talks about "service" without qualifying this term theologically. However, this is also the case of the document *Together towards Life: Mission and Evangelism in Changing Landscapes* that the Commission on World Mission and Evangelism (CWME) prepared for the WCC Busan assembly. Admittedly, it mentions the term *diakonia* on two occasions, but only superficially and without reflecting on the theological significance of this term. It seems clear that a further dialogue would benefit from a more conscious application of the *diakonia*-terminology and the advantages it represents when addressing the social ministry of the church. Such reflection could also contribute to better communication and cooperation in the performance of ecumenical *diakonia*; the ecumenical movement, in particular the WCC and the LWF in cooperation with ACT Alliance could take a leading role in facilitating such a dialogue.

The term "changing landscapes" as introduced in chapter 1 refers to complex and intertwined global social and political processes. Chapter 5 will deal further with them and present some of the challenges they present to the ecumenical movement and in particular its diaconal commitment. The Continuation Committee on Ecumenism in the Twenty-First Century points in its report to the WCC assembly in Busan to some of the trends in today's world that challenge the ecumenical movement, and states:

> *Diakonia* is an immediate response to sufferings that are present in the world. *Diakonia* is a natural partner with mission in the 21st century. Justice is linked to *diakonia* in that it functions best when justice is at work. Justice wrestles with the underlying issues that make *diakonia* necessary. *Diakonia* without justice becomes anaemic. Justice without *diakonia* can be heartless and even destructive.

With this in mind, the report maintains a holistic understanding of the church's being and mission:

> Worship (*latreia*) and proclamation (*kerygma*) are essential for nurturing the fellowship in the ecumenical movement through love and prayer. Community (*koinonia*), witness (*martyria*) and service (*diakonia*) lend themselves to structure the interaction between the different sets of actors in the ecumenical movement. All these are important features intrinsic to the life of the church.

As will be presented in what follows, the Busan assembly responded to these challenges by inviting "Christians and people of good will everywhere to join in a pilgrimage of justice and peace." Thereby it called the ecumenical movement to embark on a transformative journey that would take it beyond traditional structures and positions, affirming that its aim is not only the wellbeing of churches but also the well-being of the world, with justice and peace as core issues.

3.2. *Diakonia* from the margins

As documented in Chapter 2, a significant change in diaconal reflection during the last fifty years has been a consistent emphasis on justice as the validating principle of *diakonia*. The complex realities of today's polarized and fragmented world reinforce more strongly the need to challenge diaconal actors to confront and transform structures that perpetuate injustice, suffering, oppression and exploitation of humanity and creation. *Diakonia* is faith-based due to its distinct identity, and in its performance *diakonia* is equally obliged to be rights-based.

This approach was marked at the Conference on Theology of *Diakonia* for the 21st Century that three WCC programmes (Justice and *Diakonia*, Just and Inclusive Communities, Mission and Evangelism) jointly organized in Colombo, Sri Lanka, in June 2012. The conference was part of preparations for the WCC 10th Assembly in Busan 2013, and its report was included in the *Resource Book* that was distributed to all delegates at the Busan Assembly.

The Colombo conference opted for a new approach when reflecting on *diakonia* in attempting "to re-imagine *diakonia* from the vantage point of those who are, in many cases, traditionally considered as recipients or objects of churches' *diakonia* – the vulnerable and marginalized communities." Recognizing that many of the current models of *diakonia* are designed and put in practice by agents located in the global North, it wanted to explore an alternative approach, asking, "what *diakonia* would be if seen from the vantage point of the global South where the dynamics of life are radically different."

Instead of presenting marginalized people as an object or target group for diaconal action, it spoke of "the *diakonia* of marginalized people." On the one hand, this refers to how marginalized people struggle for a better life; on the other, it points to the biblical accounts of "God's attention and caring love to people in situations of oppression and consequent deprivation. This is the *diakonia* of God: a *diakonia* of liberation as well as of restoring dignity, and ensuring justice and peace."

From this perspective, *diakonia* "is service that makes the celebration of life possible for all. It is faith effecting change, transforming people and situations so that God's reign may be real in the lives of all people, in every here and now."

The Colombo conference focused on *diakonia* as action "from below"; at the same time, it challenged the ecumenical organizations to accompany local churches, and to "facilitate dialogue with international diaconal agencies to encourage patterns of church cooperation and to foster mutual accountability." In addition, it opted for taking the experiences, perspectives and visions of the marginalized as the point of departure when pursuing new patterns of ecumenical diaconal practice, having in mind that the gravity of world Christianity has shifted its centre to the global South. The aim was not only to harvest the insight from what often is considered "the margins" – vulnerable and marginalized communities—but to acknowledge their faith and diaconal engagement, and thereby their strategic importance in the pursuit of transforming ecumenical *diakonia* "from patronizing interventions to catalytic accompaniment."

The conference highlighted several theological arguments for this approach. It referred to the biblical witness that "points towards God who is always present in the struggles of those unjustly pushed to the margins of society" and that locates Jesus among the marginalized of his time. "To that extent, the margins are the privileged spaces for God's compassion and justice and of God's presence in vulnerability and resistance."

Further, it rejected the tendency to see the margins only as places of disgrace and powerlessness; instead, it affirmed the necessity of recognizing the demands, legitimate rights and power of marginalized people to transform the world. "They resist injustice and oppression in their own ways and through their struggle for life, justice, dignity and rights for themselves and for all, unveil the presence and power of God in their lives."

The *diakonia* from the margins thus represents a unique opportunity for *diakonia* at all levels—local, national and international—for affirming its empowering and transformative potential, and for renewing the churches' engagement in realizing God's mission for the world. It recognizes that "every Christian community in every geo-political and socio-economic context is called to be a diaconal community, witnessing to God's transforming grace through acts of service that hold forth the promise of God's reign."

The report from the Colombo conference concludes by pointing to challenges and opportunities. It challenges local congregations to "become aware of the social, political and economic realities of life and people within which they exist as diaconal communities" and recommend that they "recognize and affirm the theological significance of *diakonia* through worship and proclamation."

It challenges larger church bodies to "encourage, support and accompany local churches as they respond to their own issues by developing and implementing diaconal work." Further, it points to the importance of the task to "recognize, strengthen and support prophetic voices and initiatives that strive to uphold the causes of human rights, justice and rights of the marginalized communities." In addressing theological institutions, it encourages them to "introduce *diakonia* as a discipline" and to "initiate advanced study and research on relevant diaconal practices."

Finally, the report addresses the WCC and similar international organizations and challenges them to "recognize *diakonia* as an essential ecclesial expression that their organizations' primary calling is not only to attempt certain diaconal actions on behalf of churches but necessarily to accompany the initiatives of the churches. This may also include capacity-building, fostering partnerships and mobilization of resources wherever necessary."

The agents of ecumenical *diakonia* are increasingly aware of these challenges and seek to place them high on their agenda. Since the quality and accountability "revolution" in relief and development work started, the WCC, the LWF and later ACT Alliance have been leading the work in the humanitarian and development sector to increased focus on affected populations. This has meant changes in internal practices of diaconal actors when communicating and engaging with the affected populations, acknowledging their voice in design and implementation of relief work. In 2015, the Core Humanitarian Standard (CHS) was launched to facilitate greater accountability to communities and the people affected by crisis. ACT Alliance has driven initiatives like CHS, Sphere standards and the rights-based diaconal practice seeking to enable the affected people to know what the actors have committed themselves to and to hold the organizations to account. In the context of reforming the multilateral humanitarian engagement and in designing the Sustainable Development

Goals and the Agenda 2030 it has, jointly with its members, echoed similar focus.

Diakonia from the margins also has another connotation and dimension for the ecumenical fellowship of churches, as it can refer to the wider contexts of the changing landscapes of Global Christianity.

The history of ecumenical *diakonia* does not stop with the missionary era, nor with the formation of institutionalized tools for ecumenical *diakonia* and the emergence of ACT Alliance as global umbrella body. This is mainly "our history", the history of organized professional *diakonia* within the ecumenical family of churches.

There is also the growing phenomenon of the emergence of some new types of churches in the changing landscapes of world Christianity, mainly the spreading of independent, charismatic and Pentecostal churches. While this development can by no means be idealized, as there are many questionable facets in the whole process, it can be observed, acknowledging that the learning process on Christian social services and *diakonia* does not stop with historical mainline Christianity. Many of the new churches from charismatic or independent backgrounds have their own distinct learning history on social *diakonia*. This is often not phrased in any of the classical terms of "development language", neither is this funded nor co-funded by state partners. A major part of this is the informal social support and basic social services systems performed by local churches (not by agencies). *Diakonia* and evangelism are not opposites in their understanding, but need to kept as an integral whole. The spiritual dimension of development is as important as the social or material dimension. Rather than speaking of development or ecumenical *diakonia,* they would use the terminology of integral mission, social service, community work and social ministries. In effect there is a renewal process at work in some of Pentecostal churches, which some would call a new "charismatic social gospel movement" which is rediscovering the social significance of the gospel and the need for training and professionalism in social services of the church. The learning opportunities and interests of these churches ought to be taken seriously. *Diakonia* from the margins has both new potential as well as critical challenges which need continued theological attention.

3.3. Busan 2013

At the 10th Assembly, held in Busan, Republic of Korea, Ecumenical Conversation 21 took up issues related to ecumenical *diakonia* under the theme "Compelled to Serve: *Diakonia* and Development in a Rapidly Changing World." Its purpose was to invite churches and ecumenical partners to

a deeper analysis of *diakonia* and development in a rapidly changing world and to identify its challenges; to reflect theologically on the implications of the changing development paradigm, in which the ecumenical movement is compelled to engage and to witness for and serve God.

In their report from this Ecumenical Conversation, the participants affirmed,

that churches, ecumenical partners, and the WCC must respond to the signs of the times by developing a common diaconal language. We are faith-based and rights-based and we need to identify what this means in practice, including defining our mandate and our core values and by mapping our diaconal assets.

The participants also affirmed the key role of local congregations and urged churches, ecumenical partners and the WCC to be in closer contact with them and support diaconal work at the grassroots level. In addition, they pointed at the need for responding:

to the social impact of gender, economic and climate injustice through networking, developing the capacity for policy analysis and transnational advocacy in order to promote equitable and sustainable development.

3.4. *Diakonia* and the Pilgrimage of Justice and Peace

The WCC assembly in Busan in 2013 concluded its work by unanimously inviting "Christians and people of good will everywhere to join in a pilgrimage of justice and peace." The word "pilgrimage" was chosen to convey that this is a journey with a deep spiritual meaning and with theological connotations. At the same time, it indicates a shift from a static to a more dynamic understanding of unity. The concern is not institutional structures, but rather the church's call to participate in God's own mission for the world following the example of Jesus, which means, "meeting him wherever people suffer injustice, violence and war."

This understanding of pilgrimage as "a transformative journey that God invites us to" clearly affirms *diakonia* as social practice responding to the signs of the times. It links to the WCC programmatic work on economic and ecological justice. The WCC Central Committee, when meeting in Crete in 2012, approved the documents *Economy of Life* and *An Ecumenical Call to Just Peace,* and recommended the launch of a pilgrimage of justice and peace based on the recommendations of these documents. As a seven-year programme emphasis, the Pilgrimage of Justice and Peace will combine community-based initiatives and national and international advocacy for Just Peace, focusing on

- life-affirming economies
- climate change
- nonviolent peace-building and reconciliation
- human dignity.

The invitation to the pilgrimage does not apply the term *diakonia*; it uses "service" three times, always in relation to mission. However, it clearly reflects the diaconal nature of being church and portrays God's promise of justice and peace in a way that affirms the importance of diaconal action. To make this link between *diakonia* and pilgrimage still remains a task. Ecumenical *diakonia* therefore benefits from participating in the process of mobilizing churches for the pilgrimage; equally, the pilgrimage will gain strength and relevance when connecting to diaconal concerns and activities, and thus avoiding an interpretation that limits it to mere spiritual exercises.

The local congregations, as diaconal communities with their unique charisms and strengths, are subjects of the Pilgrimage of Justice and Peace. The WCC, together with its ecumenical partners, is in a privileged position for facilitating a dynamic interplay of the global and the local, and of expanding the network of pilgrims through its recognition and support, encouragement and accompaniment of the local expressions of transformative and prophetic *diakonia*.

The Pilgrimage of Justice and Peace has enriched the ecumenical movement and the churches by providing new experiences of solidarity, sharing and reflecting together through mutual accompaniment. These are basic practices of *diakonia*. It is a way of moving together when committed to the cause of justice and peace.

3.5. Summary

This chapter has documented that *diakonia* belongs to the "table" that WCC has committed itself to "set" for the churches as well as other organizations and communities including the Christian world communions, specialized ministries, interfaith organizations and social movements. The 10th Assembly's *Statement on Unity* affirms the understanding that service (*diakonia*) is integral to the church's being and sending:

> As servant the Church is called to make present God's holy, loving and life affirming plan for the world revealed in Jesus Christ. By its very nature the Church is missionary, called and sent to witness to the gift of communion that God intends for all humanity and for all creation in the Kingdom of God. In its work of holistic mission – evangelism and *diakonia* done in Christ's way – the Church participates in offering God's life to the world. In the power of the Spirit, the Church is to proclaim the good news in ways that awaken a response in different contexts, languages and cultures, to pursue God's justice, and to work for God's peace. Christians are called to make common cause with people of other faiths or none wherever possible, for the well-being of all peoples and creation.

The call to be a diaconal community maintains that diaconal action cannot be limited to being remedial; it must also be preventive and creative. It must encompass service to the needy, advocacy by speaking to power, and service and advocacy about creation. As advocacy for justice and peace, it should listen to the voices of the marginalized, engage in transformative and prophetic action, and address the root causes of injustice embedded in oppressive systems and structures. As care and advocacy for creation, it should seek to build alliances, in particular with people of other faiths, when addressing climate justice both at global and local levels, promoting sustainability and mitigation.

The Pilgrimage of Justice and Peace, with its aim of holding together spirituality and practice, presents a unique opportunity for renewing ecumenical *diakonia* as shared mandate in the search for transformation for justice, peace and sustainability.

CHAPTER 4

Theological Reflection on *Diakonia*

Paul Jeffrey/Life on Earth

4.1. Introduction

There are two basic approaches when reflecting on *diakonia*: One focuses on diaconal practice, activities and projects run by agents that present themselves and/or their services as diaconal. Interchurch aid, refugee work, humanitarian aid, development work and advocacy are all important examples of ecumenical diaconal practice. Chapter 2 described the central position of such services in the life of the ecumenical movement; in addition, it has referred to some of the critical questions that diaconal practice has provoked, and claimed that diaconal action must be prophetic, promoting justice and peace.

The other approach starts with the biblical and theological setting of *diakonia*. The New Testament uses the three so-called *diak-* words (*diakonia*, *diakonein* – the verb: to do *diakonia*, and *diakonos* – the person who performs *diakonia*) around 100 times. They are key words in central passages that take up the nature of the ministry of Jesus and how his example models the life and service of his followers. As such, they bring important impulses to our reflection on the nature and mission of the church today. They may help us to overcome patterns of understanding of *diakonia* shaped in a North-Atlantic context in the past and stimulate a new understanding of the church's mandate and role in times like ours, in particular connected to the challenge of viewing *diakonia* from the perspective of the margins, strengthening its prophetic and transformative commitment.

These two approaches are complementary. Chapter 2 documented that diaconal practice requires theological reflection; in a similar manner, theological deliberations on *diakonia* only become relevant when related to practice. This will be a guiding principle when we look closer at some of the biblical and theological insights that inform the understanding of *diakonia* in this chapter.

Reflecting on the essential relevance and biblical meaning of *diakonia* as the most ancient and binding heritage on Christian social service rooted in Biblical tradition, does not minimize the importance of other language traditions. It also does not prevent us from applying intercultural and interdenominational sensitivity in terms of different language traditions that describe similar phenomena of social commitment in Christian churches. There are many different terminologies used. In some parts of Christianity, the terminology of "*diakonia*" is new and not much used at all. Churches in Asia often speak of Christian social service, or social ministries. In other traditions, including some Orthodox contexts, Christians speak of "Christian *Philanthropia*" or "Social Commitment and Outreach". In other environments the language of "holistic or integral mission" is used. *Diakonia* is not only a known term for Christian social services, but even a brand name in the commercial field, as a Christian service provider like *Diakonia* in Protestant Churches, competing with other religious or secular social service providers. We have to realise that Christians use different terminologies in their current contexts to describe similar phenomena, dependent on their cultural, political and mission-related histories. However, all Christian traditions have one common Biblical tradition and can be inspired to deepen their common understanding and theological vision of Christian social practice relating the Christian heritage and vision of the mandate and vocation of *diakonia* to contemporary challenges and learning processes.

4.2. Biblical reference: the diak- words

The Greek word *diakonia* is often translated as "service," as care for the sick and poor. This understanding reflects the view of the diaconal movement that emerged in Germany in the 19th century and the kind of charitable services it developed. It emphasized personal obedience to the example of Jesus; it idealized humility and self-giving when serving people in need.

Recent research has radically questioned this understanding. The Australian scholar John N. Collins has documented that the *diak-* words themselves originally have no connotation of charity, or of self-effacing service of the poor. In ancient Greek, *diakonia* rather means an assignment, or a task, as messenger or as go-between. The term itself does not indicate what kind of activities the task entails, its focus is the relation to the one in whose service the *diakonos* stands and who authorizes and instructs for action.

The New Testament's use of the *diak-* words should be interpreted in light of this insight. In the Gospel of Mark, Jesus affirms that he "did not come to be served (*diakonethenai*), but to serve (*diakonesai*), and to give his life as a ransom for many" (Mark 10:45). This is said when he and his disciples are on their way to Jerusalem, and two of them, filled with expectations of what might now happen, approach him asking for privileged positions (10:37). Jesus strongly rejects this view of his messianic ministry; his mission is to walk the way of the cross, not to take the easy way of glory, the one that the devil had tempted him to follow (Matthew 4:1-11).

Jesus interprets his ministry with reference to the Son of Man, the messenger that God will send in the final age (Daniel 7:13), thus affirming that he is coming from above. However, he links this expectation to another messianic figure in the Old Testament, that of the suffering Servant of the Lord (Isaiah 53). Unlike the rulers of this world, he will not establish his kingdom by exercising power from above. His mission, or *diakonia*, is to be incarnated in the midst of human reality, walking around, teaching, "proclaiming the good news of the kingdom and curing every disease and every sickness among the people" (Matthew 4:23). It was indeed a ministry of transformation and empowerment. The religious and political authorities, however, considered it subversive, endangering the established order, and therefore decided to kill him. The first Christians interpreted his way of the cross, of denouncing injustice and announcing in words and deed the dignity of the excluded, as integral to his messianic ministry. It implied that he "poured out himself to death, and was numbered with the transgressors; yet he bore the sin of many, and made intercession for the transgressors" (Isaiah 53:12).

Jesus calls his disciples to follow him on the way of the cross (Luke 9:23). "As the Father has sent me, so I send you" (John 20:21), he said when meeting with them after the resurrection. The apostle Paul reiterates this vocation, admonishing his readers to "have the same mindset as Christ Jesus" in their relationships with one another. Jesus "made himself nothing by taking the very nature of a servant, being made in human likeness. And being found in appearance as a man, he humbled himself by becoming obedient to death—even death on a cross!" (Philippians 2:5-8).

These passages emphasize both the relational dimension of the disciples' mission and the model Jesus himself has given them in words and deeds. It encompasses proclamation and action, the announcement of God's reign and the practice of restoring broken relationships and affirming the dignity of the marginalized. In today's language, we describe this as holistic mission. The ecumenical tradition uses the term *diakonia* to uphold the social and prophetic dimension of the church's mission, affirming it as an intrinsic part of the good news that Jesus brought to the world (Luke 4:16-21), as messianic authority (*exousia*) with power to lift up, forgive, include and empower (Mark 1:27; Luke 5:24).

John 1:12 affirms that the messianic authority of Jesus gives all who receive him, those who believed in his name, "the right (*exousia*) to become children of God" (NIV, many other translators read "power to become"). The narrative in Acts 6:1-6, interpreted in the context of this document, underscores the diaconal dimension of the message, pointing to the gift of belonging to the community. It tells of a vulnerable group who was being neglected in the "daily *diakonia*." This is often translated as "the daily distribution of food" (e.g., NRSV), but there is no indication that this refers to such an activity. KJV reads "the daily ministration," which probably is more accurate. "*Diakonia*" here most likely refers to how the community practiced their mission as followers of Jesus, especially related to the table fellowship, its inclusiveness and routines of sharing. The fact that widows of Hellenist background experienced being excluded, contradicted the very mission of the church. The apostles therefore called the whole community together to discuss the matter, they maintained their responsibility to "serve the word" (*te diakonia tou logou*), and proposed a new leadership group of seven for the task of ministering at the table (*diakonein trapezais*), for the sake of securing a more inclusive and participatory praxis.

This story highlights several important issues. In the first place, it points to inclusiveness and sharing as hallmarks of being church. The community runs the risk of losing its Christian and diaconal identity if it allows mechanisms of exclusion to be established; as today, issues of ethnicity, social status, gender and age counted among the issues that would cause discrimination against some groups. As such, the story establishes an important fundament for conceiving diaconal practice as rights-based. Second, it holds together the "*diakonia* of the word" and "*diakonia* at the table" as two fundamental dimensions of the church's mission, organically bound together as expressions of its identity, with the purpose of mutual affirmation and strengthening. Third, the diaconal identity requires structure and administration. The group of seven, who according to the tradition were the first deacons, was authorized (ordained) in front of the whole community when they assumed their task (6:6). Fourth, church leadership includes attention in relation to "the daily *diakonia*."

It is noteworthy that precisely *diakonia* (Latin: *ministerium*) was chosen as the key term for leadership in the church. Paul uses the term *diakonia* when affirming his relationship to the triune God who has called him (Acts 20:24; 2 Cor. 3:8; 5:18-20), and to Christ who has authorized him to be his *diakonos* (1 Cor. 3:5; Eph. 3:7; Col. 1:25). For Paul the decisive matter is who has given him his *diakonia*; it is not a ministry that he himself has invented, based on his own will or ambitions. When performing this task, the model will always be the *diakonia* of Jesus, as Paul reminds his readers when motivating them to participate in his campaign of collecting money in favour of the poor in Jerusalem. This campaign is simply called the *diakonia* (2 Cor. 8:4; 9:1.12-13); the willingness to share with the poor is presented as a way of testing the sincerity of their love, oriented by the example of Jesus.

In a few cases, *diakonos* refers to the specific diaconal ministry. The instructions in 1 Timothy 3:8-13 give no indications as to what the deacon is expected to do. Rather they focus on spiritual and moral qualities, similar to those in the parallel instructions regarding the bishop (3:1-7). It seems that bishops and deacons paired the leadership functions in the early congregations (Phil. 1:1). The mention of the deacon Phoebe seems to affirm this: she clearly has a leadership role; but she has the reputation of being "a benefactor of many" (Rom. 16:1-2). There are no indications in the biblical material that the deacons only served the needy; they had their share in the whole ministry of the church encompassing worship and proclamation of the gospel. If we are to think that Stephen and the group of seven mentioned in Acts 6 were deacons, Luke presents both him and Philip as evangelists.

This reading of the New Testament makes us arrive at understanding *diakonia* as a commission to fulfil an important task or mission, more specifically, God's mission in the world. According to the biblical view, God's love and sending to the world are the beginning of the church's *diakonia*. This brings us to the next topic, relating the Christian concept of the Triune God to *diakonia* as task and ministry of the church.

4.3. Trinitarian perspectives on *diakonia*

Luke tells that when Jesus had been baptized, the heavens were opened, and the Holy Spirit descended upon him. A voice came from heaven, "You are my Son, the Beloved; with you I am well pleased" (Luke 3:21-22). At this crucial moment of initiating his mission, his heavenly Father affirms the messianic sending of Jesus, and the Holy Spirit empowers him to walk the way of the cross. This indicates that the triune God is at work in the sending of Jesus into the world.

This opens up an understanding that sees *diakonia* in a trinitarian perspective, in the sense that roots it in the Christian faith in God the Father, the Creator, in Jesus Christ, the Saviour and Liberator, and in the Holy Spirit, the Giver and Upholder of Life.

The biblical narratives of creation announce God's good will for everything and everyone whom God has called into being. Creation not only refers to what God did in the beginning, it is a continuous process (*creatio continua*) of upholding and renewing life. In the stories of creation, the creation of humankind is unique; only the man and the woman are created in God's image, enabled to assume the vocation to be God's co-workers in caring for creation. The wording in Genesis 1:28 of "subduing" the earth and "rule over" every living creature has often been interpreted as a divine authorization to exploit nature, in a way that places human beings in the centre and reduces the rest of creation to mere objects. This is clearly a misreading. Within the concept of creation, humans are not autonomous beings left to make their own destiny and to exploit the gifts of creation for their own satisfaction alone; every person is destined to have a role as steward and caretaker of God's creation (Gen 2:15). The order to "subdue" and to "rule over" cannot be disconnected from the responsibility of reporting to the Creator on how creation is taken care of; the concept of being created in God's image includes thus a relationship of communication, as mandate and responsibility.

A key Hebrew term for this role is *'abodah,* which means work or service; which is used in Genesis 2:15. The word *'ebed,* servant, the person who performs *'abodah,* occurs 870 times in the Old Testament. The purpose of Israel's calling was to serve God (Ex 7:16); the covenant is established so that the people can serve God and do what is right. The *'ebed-Yahweh,* or Servant of the Lord, is prophesized as the fulfilment of this vocation, as the one who brings justice and peace to all nations (Is. 42:1-9). It makes sense to draw a line from *'abodah* to *diakonia,* and from the expectation connected to the figure of *'ebed-Yahweh* to the ministry of Jesus, as Jesus himself is reported to have done according to Mark 10:45.

Diaconal action thus includes care for creation and commitment to promote human dignity and justice, in solidarity with the poor and excluded, working with all people of good will. In light of the dramatic consequences of climate change and of the threat to the eco-system through pollution and irresponsible exploitation, *diakonia* must give priority to ecological stewardship and be engaged in action for climate justice and a fair and sustainable use of natural resources. Interfaith cooperation is a central strategy in this endeavour, affirming the biblical message that the Creator has called and empowered every human being, irrespective of religious affiliation or social status, to be a steward and caretaker of creation.

From a theological perspective, such action confesses, "The earth is the Lord's and all that is in it, the world, and those who live in it" (Ps. 24:1). On the other hand, diaconal action also recognizes the reality of evil forces, injustice and death that are at work to destroy God's creation and enslave men and women. The diaconal vocation is a call to resist evil, denounce its forces, and to promote justice, and act boldly as a sign of hope – hope based on faith in the God of Life who gives future and hope (Jer. 29:11). This hope includes the suffering creation as a whole, as affirmed in Romans 8:20-21, "the creation itself will be liberated from its bondage to decay and brought into the freedom and glory of the children of God."

Jesus Christ is the true incarnation of *'ebed-Yahweh.* According to the testimony of the apostle Peter, "God anointed Jesus of Nazareth with the Holy Spirit and with power; how he went about doing good and healing all who were oppressed by the devil, for God was with him" (Acts 10:38). Jesus affirms this prophetic dimension when initiating his ministry, when speaking to the faith community that he belongs to in Nazareth:

> The Spirit of the Lord is on me, because he has anointed me to proclaim good news to the poor. He has sent me to proclaim freedom for the prisoners and recovery of sight for the blind, to set the oppressed free, to proclaim the year of the Lord's favour (Luke 4:18-19).

The ministry of Jesus entails different elements that all affect the theological understanding of *diakonia.* First, it expressed God's will and powerful presence. Thus, when Peter told a crippled beggar to stand up and walk, he did this "in the name of Jesus Christ of Nazareth" (Acts 3:6). Second, it was presence in the midst of human reality, with a particular sensitivity for suffering and marginalized persons (Mark 5:25-34; 10:46-52). As such, it challenges the church to be sensitive to similar situations, and in its diaconal practice to be attentive to voices that often are silenced. Third, its action was holistic in the sense that it responded to the many dimensions of suffering and injustice; this asks *diakonia* to be aware of and interrelate with the physical, mental, social and spiritual side of being human in its work. Fourth, the ministry of

Jesus was performed in the public space (John 18:20). On the one hand, this meant that everybody, in particular the poor and excluded, had access to him and his caring love; on the other hand, it implied public critique of the ruling ideology as established by the religious and political authorities. In a similar manner, the church's *diakonia* cannot be limited to the comfort zone of ecclesial or institutional structures, but must be public and include advocacy and bold action in favour of the excluded. Fifth, it was performed in light of the message of the coming of God's kingdom and its gifts of "righteousness and peace and joy in the Holy Spirit" (Romans 14:17). *Diakonia* witnesses to that same promise, its actions are signs of what Christians hope for and long to anticipate already in the present world.

According to the Gospel of Luke, the Spirit was upon Jesus and anointed him for his ministry. In the passage of Luke 4, proclaiming good news to the poor is connected to the story of the widow of Zarephath (Luke 4:25-26; 1 Kings 17:7-24), living in a deep humanitarian crisis. Luke several times returns to the theme of Jesus serving the widows and advocating for their rights (Luke 7:11-17; 18:1-8; 20:45-47; 21:1-4). Likewise, freedom of the prisoners is connected to the story about Naaman, who was infected with leprosy (Luke 4:27; 2 Kings 5:1-19). Although not locked in a prison, society had excluded him and condemned him to isolation. On several occasions, Luke announces the healing action of Jesus in relation to lepers; he approaches and touches them, and cleanses them from the stigma that had caused so much suffering (Luke 5:12-14; 17:11-19).

In Acts, Luke demonstrates how the same Spirit that led Jesus to the vulnerable of his time led the church to the widows and the marginalized (Acts 6:1-6; 9:36-42). Instead of people with leprosy, the Spirit is guiding Peter and Paul to another untouchable group, the gentiles. Luke's motivation for writing is "so that you may know the certainty of the things you have been taught" (Luke 1:4). He reminds his readers that the Spirit has guided the church in surprising ways in order to bring joy, liberation, and reconciliation to a broken world. They are thereby encouraged to be open for the unexpected calling of the Spirit to serve people they previously have ignored or despised.

On the day of Pentecost, the coming of the Holy Spirit empowered the apostles to witness publicly about "God's deeds of power" (Acts 2:11). On that occasion, Peter quoted the prophet Joel, interpreting what they now were experiencing as a fulfilment of God's promise: "Even upon my slaves, both men and women, in those days I will pour out my Spirit; and they shall prophesy" (2:18). The special mention of slaves, both men and women, makes apparent the liberating and empowering nature of the work of the Holy Spirit; it brings into life the principle of letting the last be the first, and the first be last (Matt. 20:16).

From this perspective, *diakonia* is committed to affirming the dignity and power of those involved in its work, and especially of those judged as poor and helpless. Empowering *diakonia* means opting for practices that allow people to be subjects in the process of working for a better future; this can be perceived as a diaconal application of the Pentecostal gift of experiencing "God's deeds of power" in one's own language, or in other words, rooted in local contexts of life and gifts.

The New Testament portrays the Holy Spirit as advocate and guide into all the truth (John 16:7-13), as God's careful presence and intercessor in the midst of human struggle and weakness (Rom. 8:26-27). These images are fundamental to the spirituality of *diakonia*, which finds its strength in God's care and power, even when this is experienced from the perspective of the cross (2 Cor. 12:9-10), and they are in line with the longing prayer that was the theme for the WCC 7th Assembly in Canberra 1991: "Come Holy Spirit, renew the whole creation."

4.4. *Diakonia* as an integral part of the church's being and mission

The trinitarian understanding has laid the foundation for understanding the diaconal nature of the church. Through God's sending of Jesus and the Holy Spirit, the church is called into being and mandated to participate in God's mission to the world.

Within the ecumenical movement, Orthodox theologians have contributed substantially to developing this understanding. The report from the consultation "The Orthodox Approach to *Diakonia*" (1978) states:

Christian *diakonia* is rooted in the gospel teaching according to which the love of God and the neighbour are a direct consequence of faith. The diaconal mission of the Church and duty of each of its members to serve are intimately bound with the very notion of the Church and stem from the example of the sacrifice of our Lord himself, our High Priest, who, in accordance with the Father's will "did not come to be served but to serve and give up his life as a ransom for many" (Matthew 20:28).

This view not only maintains an intimate relation between the diaconal mission of Jesus and the *diakonia* of the church. It amplifies it – pointing to the organic link between the liturgy and *diakonia*, or as this is formulated in the report, Christian *diakonia* "flows from the divine liturgy," it is a "liturgy after the Liturgy." The Vancouver assembly (1983) was strongly inspired by this "eucharistic vision" and affirmed that *diakonia* as "the church's ministry of sharing, healing and reconciliation is of the very nature of the church." As Christians experience the gracious gifts of sharing, healing and reconciliation at the Lord's table, they are commissioned to a lifestyle and to practices that bring these gifts to the world. In other words, *diakonia* in the world is "rooted in faith and nourished by the eucharist."

In many ways this corresponds to the expression "ministering at the table" in Acts 6:2. *Diakonia* is a visible manifestation of the relation between the being and the doing of the church.

One of the consequences of this understanding is that *diakonia* cannot be an optional activity in the life of the church; it is an intrinsic part of its being. The report refers to the narrative of the final judgment (Matthew 25:31-46) and describes "in this sense" *diakonia* "as a judgement upon our history."

Another important insight from the 1978 Orthodox consultation is that *diakonia* is "an expression of the unity of the church as the body of Christ." As each local congregation is church in its full sense when celebrating its faith, it is also fully gifted to realize the diaconal mandate of the church. Ecumenical work is based on the recognition of the local congregation as a fundamental church body; in a similar manner, ecumenical *diakonia* must acknowledge the diaconal gifts and capacity of the local church and foster the unity of the church.

This understanding is embedded in a sacramental understanding of the church, seeing it as a sign and servant of God's design for the world. It opposes views that limit the church to its own social and religious confinements, and is thus in line with the notion of "missional church." The risk is that the image of an ideal church can block critical discernment of how churches in fact appear as social bodies and perform their diaconal mandate. The very meaning of *sacramentum* (Greek: *mysterion*) suggests the simultaneity of divine and human action and must include awareness of human weakness and the need of prophetic voices that question inappropriate attitudes and practices within the church.

With this in mind, it makes sense to limit the use of the term *diakonia* to the caring ministry of the church and of Christians; the term expresses the distinctiveness of its faith-based action. At the same time, it is important to acknowledge that it is not only Christians who are doing good works; all humans are created in God's image and empowered for loving care and for promoting justice. Many of them are more committed than many Christians, some of them are people of other faiths, and others have no faith. In concrete diaconal action, it therefore makes sense to cooperate with all people of good will, and promote networks of solidarity and joint action.

4.5. *Diakonia* as discipleship

The ecclesial dimension of *diakonia* includes the understanding that every Christian shares the mandate to serve. This corresponds to the great commandment to love God and "your neighbour as yourself" (Matt. 22:37-39) and is in line with the call of Jesus to follow him. It implies a life style of caring for others, as expressed in the commissioning of the disciples (Matt. 28:20): to make disciples includes "teaching them to obey everything that I have commanded you."

According to John 12:26, Jesus connects *diakonia* and discipleship: "Whoever serves (*diakone*) me must follow me, and where I am, there will my servant (*diakonos*) be also." The expression "where I am" refers to his sending to the world and his healing ministry. The relation to Jesus is both a gift and a task; his sending is also their sending into the world, with the promise of God's care and blessing: "Whoever serves (*diakone*) me, the Father will honour" (12:26b).

The story about Jesus washing the disciples' feet (John 13) affirms the duality of gift and task in diaconal discipleship, although the *diak-* terminology is not used here. Jesus' words, "Unless I wash you, you have no share with me" (13:8), state that only by allowing Jesus to serve him, is Peter included in the community of followers. Once this is made clear, the imperative follows, "So if I, your Lord and Teacher, have washed your feet, you also ought to wash one another's feet. For I have set you an example, that you also should do as I have done to you" (13:14-15).

There are good reasons for reading this story as referring to the eucharist, due to the fact that John places it where the other gospels tell about the last supper. That would be in line with the way of seeing *diakonia* as "liturgy after the Liturgy," as presented above. It also corresponds to Luke's narrative of the last supper; when the disciples started to discuss which of them was to be regarded as the greatest, Jesus reacts, saying: "The kings of the Gentiles lord it over them; and those in authority over them are called benefactors. But not so with you; rather the greatest among you must become like the youngest, and the leader like one who serves (*hos o diakonon*). For who is greater, the one who is at the table or the one who serves? Is it not the one at the table? But I am among you as one who serves" (Luke 22:25-27). The expression "the one who serves" occurs three times here, referring to the ministry that Jesus in a unique way fulfils, and then to the example his disciples are called to follow.

The story of Jesus washing the disciples' feet also points in the direction of baptism, the sacrament that incorporates the believer into the body of Christ and thereby embodies relations of love and care within the community of believers. It makes sense to view baptism as an ordination to the "diaconate of all believers"; according to an old tradition in the church, the deacon gives a candle to the newly baptized, as a reminder of the vocation to be a light in the world (Matt. 5:14-16). Baptism is not to be regarded as an isolated act, or just a *rite de passage*. Rather baptism is an act of renewal, it announces the newness of life into which the baptized is included and empowered to serve. The *Baptism, Eucharist and Ministry* document underscores this, stating: "God bestows upon all baptized persons the anointing and the promise of the Holy Spirit, marks them with a seal and implants in their hearts the first instalment of their inheritance as sons and daughters of God. The Holy Spirit nurtures the life of faith in their hearts until the final deliverance when they will enter into its full possession, to the praise of the glory of God (2 Cor. 1:21-22; Eph. 1:13-14)".

At the time of the Lutheran reformation, Martin Luther emphasized that God called Christians to realize their vocation in ordinary life, in their family, neighbourhood and workplace, rejecting the idea that discipleship requires joining a religious order or performing religious services. The relation to Christ grants full freedom as God's child; at the same time, it implies the vocation to be Christ-like in relation to one's neighbour. This corresponds to the Orthodox tradition of viewing discipleship as the vocation to be a "Christ-bearer" (Greek: *Christóforos*), incarnated in the world as Christ was incarnated.

Christian discipleship experiences God's grace in both relationships – to God and to one's neighbour – both of them expressing the newness of life in Christ. John Wesley, the founder of Methodism, used the term "holiness" when maintaining that salvation entails renewal of both individuals and the world. Conversion and repentance should be accompanied by "fruits meet for repentance" (Matt. 3:8), he claimed. For Methodism and other churches within this tradition "holiness of heart and life" remains a vocation to "works of piety" and "works of mercy." "Our love of God is always linked with love of our neighbour, a passion for justice and renewal in the life of the world."

In the history of the church, *diakonia* has always linked love for one's neighbours with the passion for justice and sustainability. It has become common understanding in world Christianity that this takes different forms which are complementary and cannot be played off against each other. These different dimensions of the mandate for a diaconal church and for diaconal discipleship are not expressed in equal manner in all circumstances, but depends on the cultural, political and institutional contexts of different churches. The following dimensions and different forms of diaconal ministries can however be found and affirmed by the majority of churches around the world – though with different degrees of professionalization and institutionalization:

- Social *diakonia* as individual acts of care, healing and reconciliation in a local church or community
- *Diakonia* as institutionalized assistance for marginalized groups and those suffering, by churches or specialized diaconal agencies
- *Diakonia* as community work and empowerment for strengthening conviviality
- Political or transformative *diakonia* comprising of efforts to transform living conditions and political frameworks contributing to injustice and conflicts, addressing the whole of society in advocacy and lobbying work on behalf of those suffering
- Prophetical *diakonia* addressing misbalances of power, access and participation in societies, speaking truth to power, denouncing structural injustices
- Ecological *diakonia* addressing fundamental issues of the protection of the environment and of climate justice.

The main intention of ecumenical dialogue on *diakonia* is to enable churches to learn from each other and their different emphases and shapes of diaconal ministries, in order to engage in a comprehensive understanding and broad concept of *diakonia,* while keeping in mind their local contexts and living conditions.

4.6. *Diakonia* and proclamation

As an integral part of the church's mission, *diakonia* is meaningful in itself; diaconal action aims to serve the neighbour in need and should not be perceived as a means for achieving other goals, as for instance recruiting new members for the church. The ecumenical movement has clearly renounced proselytism and called for responsible relations in mission. It mentions the practice of offering humanitarian aid or educational opportunities as an inducement to join another church as an example of irresponsible action.

ACT Alliance, which in its founding document clearly expresses its faith-based mission and commitment to "give priority to the role of local churches and their ministries in responding to the humanitarian and development needs of their local community," has included in its Code of Good Practice a non-proselytism statement. It affirms that:

ACT Alliance does not use humanitarian or development assistance or advocacy programmes to further a particular religious or partisan political standpoint. This means that ACT Alliance and its members

- Reject the use of any aid, either to an individual or to a community, to advance religious or partisan political standpoints
- Reject the use of their programmes to advance religious or partisan political standpoints
- Reject the use of manipulation, coercive techniques, force or exploitation of people's vulnerability to advance religious or partisan political standpoints
- Are truthful and transparent about their identities and motivation when asked and offer information about the goals of their organisations and programmes if requested
- Advance through their engagement and programmes, where necessary, with tolerance of differences in belief and protection of those whose human rights are not respected.

There are many external reasons for taking this clear position. Faith-based organizations will often be met with suspicion if they operate in areas where the population is of another faith; in particular, this is the case of Christian agencies working in Muslim countries. The issue is not just popular trust and accessibility; it also concerns the security of the aid workers.

Equally important, however, are the internal arguments. The New Testament is clear in reporting that Jesus assisted people in need unconditionally. He did not require that they should become disciples. His acts of healing and care are gracious gifts; they express God's unconditional love and freedom to restore human dignity; as Jesus confirmed when commissioning his disciples for the healing ministry: "Freely you have received; freely give" (Matthew 10:8). In a similar manner, diaconal action must be unconditional and not be reduced to an agenda, neither open nor hidden, for obtaining other goals, neither religious nor political.

Diaconal action normally implies the exercise of power, structural and personal, and very often within asymmetric relationships. When meeting with people in vulnerable life situations, there is always a risk of abusing power, in particular religious power. Diaconal agents must be sensitive to this risk and protect the dignity and integrity of the persons with whom they work.

On the other hand, it is a fact that all social intervention, including secular development work, implies exercise of power and promotion of opinions and value systems. One question is rather how to raise awareness of this undeniable fact; another is to develop religious literacy among development workers, as an integral part of their professional competence. For diaconal workers this implies activating one's own identity in a way that strengthens the ability to be responsible when engaged in activities that envisage a better future for all involved. Chapter 6 will discuss this matter further.

Therefore, *diakonia* cannot keep silent when it comes to religious or ideological issues. The ACT Alliance principle referred to above – to be "truthful and transparent about their identities and motivation when asked" – intends a pro-active reading; it does not imply a wish that nobody ever will ask such questions. It is normal that diaconal action provokes questions regarding motivation and objectives; the dialogue that follows action should therefore seek to be truthful and transparent. Diaconal actors must be prepared to deal with the consequences their service may have: in some cases, people will answer diaconal action with sympathy and wish to know better the faith that has motivated it; in other cases, people will become suspicious, in extreme cases, they may react with violence wishing to stop it. This is how it has been since the times of the early church: the *diakonia* of the church caused both admiration and rejection, it convinced some to become followers of the Christian faith while others remained sceptics or adversaries.

In a theological perspective, *diakonia* adds its voice to the cosmic proclamation of God's reign and good will for the whole of creation: "The heavens declare the glory of God; the skies proclaim the work of his hands" (Ps. 19:1). *Diakonia* is *martyria*-centred in the sense that it witnesses to its faith in the God of Life and answers to the vocation to serve the Lord, knowing that this witness may provoke resistance and lead to martyrdom. Even so, it always aims at lifting up signs of hope that announce God's reign (kingdom) to come, with its promise of justice and peace. How people will interpret these signs is a matter of freedom. It is not a part of the diaconal mandate to proclaim with the purpose of convincing people to change their faith.

For that reason, *diakonia* must on the other hand always be ready to offer an account of its faith, its vision and value system. Acknowledging that faith-based action may be misinterpreted, it must be able to clarify the true nature of its distinct identity and the code of conduct to which it is committed.

It is notable that, as of 2019, the German agency *Diakonie Deutschland* is involved in a national conversation about strengthening its diaconal profile, emphasising the Christian nature of its service provision.

4.7. Summary

This chapter has analyzed the understanding of *diakonia* from a theological perspective. It has given an account as to the use of the *diak-* words in the New Testament, and the question of how to translate and interpret these words today, in particular, in relation to the way churches today apply the term *diakonia* as Christian social practice. It has emphasized the prophetic dimension of *diakonia* as embedded in the ministry of Jesus and in his vocation to his followers.

The biblical material underscores that *diakonia* has a strong Christological connotation. In addition, it informs the understanding of the nature and the mission of the church. *Diakonia* thus relates Christian faith to the triune God, and to the vocation to participate in God's mission to the world. God the Creator calls all human beings, Christians and all people of good will, to be stewards of creation and to promote human dignity, justice and peace. Jesus Christ, the Saviour and Liberator, gives his disciples a share in his sending to the world with the mandate to heal, include and empower (John 20:21). The Holy Spirit, the Giver of life, empowers for this mission, equipping God's people so that they have the needed energy and wisdom to serve as agents of transformation.

Diakonia thus proves to be a key biblical and theological term, giving expression to fundamental insights shared by the ecumenical family, as stated by former WCC moderator, His Holiness Aram Keshishian, Catholicos of the Great House of Cilicia:

> *Diakonia* belongs to the very nature of the church. Being in communion with Christ is loving one's neighbour, being with the sick and afflicted. These are not just the "moral obligations" of the church but rather its constitutive element. The church does not "have" a *diakonia*; it is *diakonia*, namely a continuous and committed discipleship to Christ for the rebuilding of world community and re-creating the fallen world according to the plans of God. Through *diakonia* the church becomes one with Christ and at the same time brings Christ to the world. *Diakonia* is both the expression of the unity of the church and the implementation of the gospel message.

As a theological concept, *diakonia* offers the potential of adding new perspectives to ongoing processes of reflection and renewal within the ecumenical movement, in particular the understanding of what the churches are called to be and to do together in today's world.

CHAPTER 5

The Changing Landscape of Diaconal Action

Photo: Albin Hillert/WCC

5.1. Introduction

In January 2013, the ACT Executive Committee adopted a paper titled *The Changing Development Paradigm*. It points to some fundamental changes in the global development context. Many of them relate to the process of globalization, described as "the widening scope, deepening impact and speeding up of interregional flows and interaction within all realms of social life, from the economic to the ecological, from the cultural to the criminal." It also acknowledges fundamental changes regarding the understanding of development, and a growing scepticism about traditional concepts of aid. It reflects a world with more global problems and at the same time fewer global tools to solve them.

This chapter seeks to present some of the main elements that justify the description of this "landscape" as a changing paradigm. It will start by giving account of some of the consequences of globalization and the new patterns of poverty that it is causing. Next, we present the Sustainable Development Goals (SDGs) as a new platform for international cooperation, based on the conviction that they provide a relevant agenda for ecumenical *diakonia* to renew its commitment and identify new forms and areas of action.

For ecumenical *diakonia,* the new paradigm implies a conscious shift from aid to justice, both when it comes to approaching the challenges of today's world and when implementing action. The second part of this chapter will present some of the main concerns in this process of moving from development aid to transformative practices toward justice, focusing on economic justice, eco-justice, gender justice, and health justice.

5.2. New faces of poverty in today's world

Globalization brings the world together, a process that obviously has many positive effects; at the same time, it causes new divisions, mainly between those who are rich and those living in poverty. One of the serious effects of globalization is the way economic and political power now is being exercised, emptying the role of local, national and international authorities and undermining their democratic legitimacy. Instead, transnational structures that do not have to give account of how they are acting are expanding their power.

For agents involved in development work, including actors in ecumenical *diakonia,* this means a shift from traditional aid to a struggle for justice. The face of poverty has changed; what is new is that large areas of poverty exist within middle-income countries. In many cases, growing poverty is a result of political mismanagement, corruption, warfare and climate change, and not because of lack of development.

More than a billion men, women and children continue to be imprisoned by poverty. In the past two decades, the world has achieved remarkable progress in reducing the number of people living in extreme poverty. International actors foresee that extreme poverty can be eradicated by 2030. The task of ending extreme poverty requires, however, a committed engagement by the international community and the will to deal with the underlying causes of poverty. It also includes a change in habits that cause poverty: greed and waste, numbness to the pain of others, and exploitation of people and the natural world. This is strongly affirmed by the World Bank initiative "Ending Extreme Poverty: A Moral and Spiritual Imperative," in which the

WCC is involved, together with leaders of diverse religious traditions.

A strong civil society sector will have an important role in this endeavour. It will mobilize and organize people to engage in matters that are important for them, promoting justice for all. They represent horizontal structures of power in a society, counterbalancing the vertical power of the ruling elite. In many places, faith communities and diaconal agents have consciously assumed roles as agents within civil society, seeking to build active citizenship, and engaging in networks that work for a just, inclusive, participatory and sustainable society. The UN system and many governments acknowledge the importance of civil society organizations (CSOs) and human rights defenders (HRDs), in particular their role in promoting transparency and accountability.

This is, however, not always the case. In a number of countries, the space for citizen and civil society actions is being restricted and threatened. Reports tell of arbitrary detention, torture and killings of civil society actors; governments introduce laws that make the work of international NGOs more difficult. This also affects faith-based actors. In one country where several ACT Alliance members are working, 17 organizations had to change their focus and exclude human rights issues from their programmes due to a restrictive NGO law.

In a time when reports about terrorism and warfare often dominate the news, issues related to development and the wellbeing of the poorest in the world gain less attention. Many governments are diverting ODA (official development assistance) money from development aid to humanitarian assistance in regions that are in conflict. In some cases, this appears more to be an issue of securing their own political and economic interests than of promoting change and common good.

In preparing for the World Humanitarian Summit (WHS) in 2016, the ACT Alliance presented its vision for a humanitarian system in a world that "is experiencing greater disaster risks and a growing number of conflicts due to factors like climate change, rapid urbanisation, poverty, ecosystem decline and diminishing respect for humanitarian principles and International Humanitarian Law." With a strong overall emphasis on placing people at the centre, it envisages "a bottom-up approach, where resilient communities define their own needs and where local actors (including people at risk themselves) lead the response."

This vision recognizes the distinct role of faith communities and religious leaders in the work for a better world. Based on experiences from the field, ACT Alliance suggests that faith-based organizations (FBOs) that work closely within local communities can use their unique strength – the unifying and ameliorative power of shared faith – to facilitate disaster resilience. At the same time, it admits that religious traditions can be misused to create hatred and suspicion, and that they in some contexts resist change and suppress expressions of basic rights and freedom.

Providing safe spaces for people from different religious traditions to meet and work together for the well-being of all can contribute to reducing mutual suspicions and be a tool for overcoming conflicts. For this reason, international *diakonia* has included *diapraxis* in its agenda (cf. chapter 7.6); it remains a priority task to develop further strategies and methods in order to improve its capacity within this area.

5.3. The Sustainable Development Goals as socio-political environment for *diakonia*

The Sustainable Development Goals (SDGs), officially known as *Transforming Our World: The 2030 Agenda for Sustainable Development,* is a set of 17 global goals and 169 targets, adopted by the United Nations in 2015. The SDGs intend to give continuity to the eight Millennium Development Goals (MDGs) that were established in 2000. It followed the adoption of the United Nations Millennium Declaration, which affirmed a "collective responsibility to uphold the principles of human dignity, equality and equity at the global level" and the duty of the global political leadership to "all the world's people, especially the most vulnerable and, in particular, the children of the world, to whom the future belongs."

There are some key differences between the MDGs and the SDGs. The first counted only eight, and they mainly focused on development issues located in the global South. the SDGs number 17, with their related 169 targets they seek to address global challenges the world is facing. In addition, they are presented as global, with relevance both for the global North and the global South. The MDGs came into being at a time marked by the enthusiasm of entering a new millennium; as such they expressed the hope of initiating a new era. The context in which the SDGs were adopted was different, more characterized by political crises and pessimism. The MDGs were formulated by a few experts, whereas the SDGs were a result of a consultative process with a broad range of actors, including civil society and faith communities.

From a critical point of view, it may be claimed that the focus of the SDG agenda is too broad, containing too many goals and targets. When addressing issues such as poverty, it lacks an approach that analyzes root causes and questions ruling political and economic models. There is a glaring weakness in the SDGs, in that there is no reference to the United Nations Declaration on the Right of Indigenous Peoples (UNDRIP). UNDRIP is essential understanding for all parts of the world. Diaconal ministry, economic development, missionary work and colonialism have had and continue to have enormous impact on indigenous communities worldwide. Resource extraction, land ownership and usage, and sustainable development are inextricably tied to Indigenous peoples' rights.

The SDG agenda – as a document resulting from a political compromise between governments – also has inbuilt tensions and unsolved contradictions with regard to a reconciled understanding of sustainability and economic growth. The SDG agenda does not satisfactorily answer the question what kind of growth is appropriate, ethically responsible for the future of the whole of humanity and reconcilable with the planetary boundaries, which have become more obvious than ever before. Therefore, there is a contradiction between the economic goals of the SDG agenda (No 1-11) and the ecological goals of the agenda (No 13-15). If the economic goals were to be achieved with an unaltered pattern of economic growth, the ecological goals could no longer be achieved at all. A proper recognition of the urgent need to reconcile economy, ecology and human civilization in a comprehensive effort towards both social and ecological *diakonia* is still at stake. Thus, the mandate and horizon of churches' public theological and social engagement reach much beyond the current SDG agenda. This engagement asks questions of the understanding of human dignity according to the gospel and of an alternative concept of growth which are not yet answered by this document of political compromise (which even now is questioned by several national governments). We should be reminded, and not lose the focus, that the ecumenical movement has provided an alternative to economic growth-oriented development. This alternative is based on justice, focusing on sustainable communities in which the prospering of human dignity – that protects human rights and the sustainability of the people – and the planet are the foci. It is this critical engagement with the SDG agenda which is part and parcel of prophetic *diakonia*, as has been also spelled out in the Religion and Development Strategy of ACT and WCC in the document produced for the Uppsala Assembly of ACT Alliance (October 2018).

The UN's SDGs are, for the most part, commendable goals for ecumenical *diakonia*. Some, in particular SDGs 8, 9, and 12, require careful scrutiny and are in danger of being used to continue the imposition of powerful economic interests in industrialised countries at the expense of our planet and many people who are already exploited. Nevertheless, the goals manifest the will of the global community to move in the direction of a sustainable world order and of fostering processes that will strengthen human rights and wellbeing.

Sustainable development is as much a process as a goal, leading to a life of dignity for people in relationship to the overall context of their community and the environment that sustains them. Development that isolates persons from part of themselves, from the community, or from the ecosystem which supports life, is not sustainable. As well, development of a local area that is not linked to the sustainability of the social, economic and environmental wellbeing of the human family is likewise not sustainable.

Development is not a new concept for the ecumenical family. Churches and diaconal agencies have decades of experience on which to build. The WCC and other FBOs have been engaged in the areas that the SDGs address, long before the SDGs were formulated. The shift in discourse toward greater recognition of religion's role in development processes coincides with the shift from technical, limited United Nations Millennium Development Goals (MDGs) to the holistic, integrated and universal agenda of the Sustainable Development Goals (SDGs). The convergence of these two trends holds great potential, yet they also challenge churches, faith communities and diaconal organizations to find proper means and methods of engagement with this framework.

People of faith represent a key community for change, as has been shown throughout Christian history (such as the leading role played by Christians in campaigns to abolish slavery in the 19th century). Faith has led to Christians exercising diaconal care throughout Christian history; faith continues to motivate billions of people around the world to justice and peace. According to Mr. David Nabarro, in 2016 serving as UN Special Adviser on Sustainable Development, he counts on faith communities to do the following in relation to the new agenda:

- They promote inclusion, not exclusion, of different groups that could be engaged in this kind of activity
- They provide peaceful channels for resolution of conflict, so reducing the threat of violence when there are communal differences
- They uphold human rights, especially of the most vulnerable, making sure that no one is left behind
- They remind political leaders of their duty to enable all people to realize their rights
- They can help to make sure that investments take place in communities, with people at local levels making those investments with their own resources
- They can mobilize people everywhere, especially young people, so they use the elements of the 2030 agenda within their own activism for a better world
- They can share their expertise on how to deliver services to those who are harder to reach.

From the perspective of ecumenical *diakonia*, the SDGs provide an important platform for action. The SDG agenda deserves all kinds of support, both political and practical. It is a universal agenda that applies to all countries, it is integrated, it is indivisible, and it is based on a clear set of borrowed principles. They were established with the purpose of engaging civil society and voluntary organizations, including faith communities, and of promoting active citizenship.

The ACT Alliance, together with other ecumenical and faith communities, have been engaged in the discourse on sustainable development and participated actively in the process of formulating the SDGs, and have joined in initiatives to lobby governments to address inequalities, governance, climate change, and conflict and fragility. Advocacy, mass mobilization and communication are the key part of any strategy for implementing the 2030 sustainable development agenda. Faith communities can help to localize development objectives, to empower people for their direct and continuous participation in the places where they live.

Recognizing the importance of this new discourse, ACT Alliance members came together to form a Community of Practice on Religion and Development in 2015. Both the WCC and ACT have been involved in some of the most important faith-based partnership initiatives related to the SDGs – including the Moral Imperative to End Poverty convened by the World Bank (MI), the International Partnership on Religion and Development which convenes UN agencies, bilateral donors and faith actors. It has agreed to focus on three major working streams, related to reproductive health (SDG 3), to peace (SDG 16) and to gender and empowerment (SDG 5).

An important task now is to equip churches and diaconal agents at national and local levels to engage in the SDG process. All of the ACT priorities are featured within the 17 proposed goals, including stand-alone goals on gender equality, inequality, climate change, peace, accountable government, and rule of law, as well as targets in areas such as disaster risk reduction, social protection, and anti-corruption. ACT National Forums will learn to use SDG indicators in their work, and look for ways of coordinating better with civil society and governmental authorities. There will also be the need for revising theological curricula to include a better understanding of the diaconal mandate of the church, of what this means in the social-political context of today's world.

5.4. Migration and refugees

As long as humanity existed, people have migrated from one place to another. In historical perspective, migration is normal. The ACT Alliance document, *The Changing Development Paradigm*, states that:

> Human mobility is a distinct feature of globalization. Today, approximately one billion people are migrating internally or across borders to improve their income situation, to flee from poverty or conflict, to improve health and the educational status of their families or to adapt to environmental change, climate change impacts and economic shocks.

The document continues to affirm that migration is a global phenomenon and that it can contribute to sustainable development. However, for millions it is the cruel reality of fleeing from poverty and violence, and encountering new situations of insecurity, hostility and discrimination. It is especially alarming that the number of refugees has increased dramatically over the last years, and that they experience less protection when arriving in countries where they had hoped to be safe. Not only conflicts force people to leave their homes; climate change and the environment forcibly uproot millions around the world. According to estimates reported by the UNHCR, an average of 26.4 million people per year has been displaced from their homes by disasters brought on by natural hazards since 2008. This is equivalent to one person being displaced every second. Unless strong climate mitigation and adaptation measures are implemented worldwide, alongside disaster-preparedness and disaster risk reduction measures, this trend is expected to increase. It should be remembered that migration also has negative consequences for the countries that see many of their gifted citizens move out. Brain drain implies that rich countries receive competent workers whose education has been paid for by poor countries.

As documented in chapter 2, ecumenical *diakonia* has a long record of engaging in refugee work, and it continues to be a major challenge in many parts of the world. Many congregations are actively involved in this work, they welcome refugees in their homes and worship places; they volunteer in organized activities and support them with their money.

The ACT Alliance has formed a Community of Practice group (CoP) on Migration and Development. Its purpose is to share experiences and develop useful interventions for the protection of migrants' rights. The group's common working issues include migrants' rights, statelessness, migration and livelihoods, migration and climate change, and trafficked persons on the move. It also aims to strengthen and increase the visibility of ecumenical structures related to migration and development.

The WCC has continuously advocated for the rights of migrants and refugees, claiming that human trafficking and migrant smuggling constitute modern-day slavery. In September 2016 it organized an event at the UN General Assembly on "Bearing Witness: Combating Human Trafficking and Forced Migration," pointing to the fact that during 2015 more than 65 million people had been forced to flee their homes in fear of their lives. Responding to the fact that too many encounter rejection and exclusion, the WCC urged states "to refrain from measures that undermine and do not respect the relevant obligations under international refugee and human rights law" and called for "much greater and more effective international solidarity in responding collectively to this global crisis."

The SDGs do not address migration and the social challenges they represent, although it is possible to establish several links to this issue. Nor do they refer to the situation of refugees and the lack of international mechanisms to deal with this crisis. This lack of attention can be interpreted as a downgrading of the international responsibility to assist refugees and of the duty of national governments to provide security to people who seek shelter and a new future in their country.

In times when the basic rights of migrants and refugees are threatened, churches and diaconal agents must engage in advocacy and public action, as part of their calling to defend human dignity. Their action must include practices of welcoming and accompanying, of sharing and celebrating the multiplicity of gifts that migrants and refugees bring with them. These are ways of professing "the right to hope" to which WCC General Secretary Olav Fykse Tveit has referred on various occasions, as an integral part of human rights, as well as an affirmation of the churches' Pilgrimage of Justice and Peace.

5.5. Economic justice

Economy may be defined as "the process or system by which goods and services are produced, sold, and bought in a country or region." Today's globalized economy has developed systems that accumulate resources in the hands of a small elite. Oxfam's annual report on poverty from 2016 revealed that 62 rich individuals own as much as the poorest half of the world's population. One year later, Oxfam updated the number of rich to eight, all of them being men. The report, titled *An Economy for the 99%,* documents that growth in the present economic system benefits the richest, while the rest of society – especially the poorest – suffers. It concludes: "The very design of our economies and the principles of our economics have taken us to this extreme, unsustainable and unjust point." This trend of increased difference between the richest and the poorest is not only seen at a global level, but also in most countries.

Today's globalized and financialized economy promotes an unfair distribution of wealth, goods and services. Its institutions and policies reflect power structures that protect the rich and sacrifice the poor when striving for more profit. Among the consequences of rising inequalities are unemployment, low wages, unsafe jobs, tax evasion, corruption, abuse of power, breakdown of social cohesion, violence, crime and growing insecurity.

Though the underlying causes of rising inequality are multidimensional, economic justice is an important response to many of these issues. It recognizes that social justice and transformative development will not be possible unless political decision makers take measures, at national and international levels, to reform and transform the economic system, securing a fairer distribution of resources (to include financial flow), and of power structures. This view is clearly affirmed in the Accra Confession, adopted by the delegates of the 24th General Council of the World Alliance of Reformed Churches in Accra, Ghana (2004) stating (# 19-20):

> Therefore, we reject the current world economic order imposed by global neoliberal capitalism and any other economic system, including absolute planned economies, which defy God's covenant by excluding the poor, the vulnerable and the whole of creation from the fullness of life. We reject any claim of economic, political and military empire which subverts God's sovereignty over life and acts contrary to God's just rule.
>
> We believe that God has made a covenant with all of creation (Gen 9.8-12). God has brought into being an earth community based on the vision of justice and peace. The covenant is a gift of grace that is not for sale in the market place (Is 55.1). It is an economy of grace for the household of all of creation. Jesus shows that this is an inclusive covenant in which the poor and marginalized are preferential partners and calls us to put justice for the "least of these" (Mt 25.40) at the centre of the community of life. All creation is blessed and included in this covenant (Hos 2.18ff).

The ecumenical movement is committed to the cause of economic justice. In the 1990s, the WCC's Advisory Group on Economic Matters (AGEM) worked on Christianity and the world economy. It was followed up by the Alternative Globalisation Addressing People and Earth or AGAPE process, a seven-year global study process with contributions from all regions of the world and involvement of a number of Christian world communions, leading to the WCC Assembly in Porto Alegre, Brazil, in 2006. Its concern for holding together issues of economy and ecology was maintained by the WCC Poverty, Wealth and Ecology process. In 2012, the WCC together with other ecumenical partners invited economists, church leaders, activists, politicians and theologians to a global conference in São Paulo, Brazil, with the purpose of developing a plan of action toward constructing just, caring and sustainable global financial and economic structures. The meeting concluded by calling for an *International Financial Transformation for the Economy of Life.* It proposed a financial and economic architecture that:

- is based on the principles of economic, social and climate justice
- serves the real economy
- accounts for social and environmental tasks
- sets clear limits to greed and instead promotes common good.

Since then, a Global Ecumenical Panel has been convened with the purpose of giving continuity to the São Paulo Statement. In 2014, it submitted a report titled *Economy of Life for All Now: An Ecumenical Action Plan for a New International Financial and Economic Architecture,* calling on the ecumenical partners to implement it.

Economy for Life challenges agents of ecumenical *diakonia* to strengthen their commitment to economic justice. The following statement of ACT Alliance is representative of how their membership views poverty and the importance of addressing its root causes:

> Eradicating poverty is not just about addressing symptoms like the lack of income or material assets held by individuals. It is also about addressing the systemic and structural factors essential for overcoming poverty, factors that deprive women and men of their dignity, rights and entitlements. Policies that hope to eradicate poverty also need to focus on the processes that contribute to the social exclusion and exploitation, discrimination in access to productive resources, and exclusion from participation in decision-making bodies that bars certain women and men from the full enjoyment of their rights. In addition, eradicating poverty also requires growing opportunities for decent and fairly compensated work for all in dynamic and sustainable economies.

Rights-based *diakonia* therefore seeks forms of action that promote economic justice. It aims to empower rights-holders to engage as active citizens, claiming economic and social rights. The SDGs serve as a relevant point of reference, in particular when engaging in advocacy and public debate.

Several of the SDGs affirm economic justice as a precondition for achieving the goals.

SDG 1, *End poverty in all its forms everywhere,* points to the importance of social protection for the poor and vulnerable, of increasing access to basic services and of supporting people harmed by climate-related extreme events and other economic, social and environmental shocks and disasters.

SDG 8, *Promote sustained, inclusive and sustainable economic growth, full and productive employment and decent work for all,* encourages governments "to take immediate and effective measures to eradicate forced labour, end modern slavery and human trafficking and secure the prohibition and elimination of the worst forms of child labour. . . .

SDG 10, *Reduce inequality within and among countries,* calls for reducing inequalities in income within a country. It also addresses inequalities among countries, and argues for building effective accountable and inclusive institutions to achieve sustainable development.

Economy is vital for people's life and wellbeing; it cannot be limited to the responsibility of economists alone. Politicians must take their share. So must people of faith, churches and diaconal actors.

From a faith perspective, economy is a means of securing fullness of life, as intended in God's care of all of creation. Economy is never an objective in itself; it should be regarded as an autonomous reality, free to establish its own norms and objective. The Economy of Life rejects as heresy absolute faith in the market and its mechanism, and condemns trust in Mammon as idolatry. It confesses that the earth and all that is in it belong to God (Psalms 24:1), and there is enough for all our needs if we share God's resources.

5.6. Climate justice

The WCC, together with its members and ecumenical partners, has long since had care for creation and the development of sustainable communities on its agenda. In the 1970s, the WCC began to recognize the connections between justice, peace, and ecological sustainability. At the Vancouver Assembly in 1983, the WCC encouraged member churches to publicly commit to addressing environmental concerns as part of a common effort to promote Justice, Peace, and the Integrity of Creation, which became known as the JPIC process. In 1988, the WCC launched its Climate Change Program to promote the transformation of socioeconomic structures and personal lifestyle choices that contribute to global warming. In the 1990s, a study process on "theology of life" invited local churches and groups to reflect on what this meant in their context, and how they could strengthen their engagement in justice, peace and creation issues. There continues to be good evidence in member communions that there is emerging what we might call an "ecological *diakonia*," in which it is becoming central to churches' witness and mission in the world to care for creation and all in it. The UN deliberations about how to develop a new system to Earth Jurisprudence (UN Global

Dialogue process on Harmony with Nature from 2016) and mechanisms of protecting and defining the rights of nature over human civilization needs special attention by all Christian churches and a widened concept of ecological *diakonia*.[1]

Access to safe drinking water is an issue that in particular has engaged the ecumenical movement and its diaconal commitment. Knowing that one in four people drink contaminated water, and one in every three do not have adequate access to sanitation facilities – and also knowing that coastal erosion, sea level rise, drought, flooding, storms and other impacts of climate change affect the life and livelihoods of vulnerable populations first and hardest, – water justice is a key issue of climate justice that crosses economic and health disparities. All indications are that climate change will make the situation more serious for even more people in the years to come, and that by 2025, two-thirds of the world will be water-stressed. The struggle for access to clean water, and the intensifying of other hardships by climate change, is likely to increase violent conflicts around the world. So, there are many reasons why churches engage in diaconal work with creation care as a major emphasis that intersects and works alongside other emphases.

The advocacy working group of the Moral Imperative Group on SDGs has zeroed in on water and land rights as pilot projects for faith communities' engagement on SDGs. Several member churches and organizations of the WCC, the LWF and ACT Alliance are engaged in water issues, either through humanitarian aid, or through advocacy for the human right to water and sanitation.

Engagement for climate justice has always been connected to the public agenda on environment and development, especially after the Earth Summit that the United Nations organized in Rio de Janeiro in 1992. The ecumenical movement has actively participated in the COP-meetings (COP = The Conference of the Parties) that the UNFCCC (UN Framework Convention on Climate Change) has organized since 1995, and has advocated for implementing measures that will safeguard the ecological integrity of the biosphere and defend the rights of the poorest and most vulnerable in times of ecological change.

For the COP 17 meeting in Durban, South Africa, in 2011, WCC together with other faith groups organized an interfaith rally that gathered thousands under the theme: "We have faith! Act now for climate justice!" On this occasion, Archbishop Desmond Tutu delivered a petition with 200,000 signatures to the COP leadership.

The concept of "climate justice" has been gaining space since 2000, when an Alternative Summit was organized parallel to the COP 6 meeting in The Hague, the Netherlands. Here speakers called for solutions to the climate change problem that promote human rights, equity, labour rights and environmental justice. Climate justice thus maintains global warming and climate change as an ethical and political issue; it acknowledges that those who are least responsible for this development suffer its gravest consequences.

The ecumenical movement has subscribed to this understanding of climate justice, and it has sought to ground it by theological arguments. The God of the Bible is a God of justice who protects, loves and cares for the most vulnerable among his creatures; the Bible teaches the wholeness of creation and calls human beings to take care of the garden of Eden (Gen 2:15).

Consequently, climate justice has become a key concern for ecumenical *diakonia*, affirming that churches and Christians are called to speak out and act when creation is threatened, as an expression of their commitment to life, justice and love. The engagement became very visible during the COP 21 in Paris in 2015 and may have contributed to the positive outcome of this meeting. Before the meeting, over 150 religious leaders signed a statement encouraging the participant to take bold decisions, showing "real and visionary leadership," reiterating what the Interfaith Summit in New York had said:

> As representatives from different faith and religious traditions, we stand together to express deep concern for the consequences of climate change on the earth and its people, all entrusted, as our faiths reveal, to our common care. Climate change is indeed a threat to life, a precious gift we have received and that we need to care for.

During the Paris meeting, "climate pilgrims" and church leaders were strongly engaged in different

1. See: https://www.un.org/en/ga/search/view_doc.asp?symbol=A/71/266.

arenas in order to influence the outcome. WCC general secretary Olav Fykse Tveit could address the high-level segment of the conference, urging them to "serve the world by showing the best of human creativity and capacity." He concluded by saying, "We believe you must, you can and you will. We have hope. We have reasons to hope. We have the right to hope."

The ACT Alliance is heavily involved in climate change advocacy. It has monitored and engaged in the COP meetings, and conducted several capacity building initiatives for its membership. It has launched an Act Now for Climate Justice Campaign together with its members, to create positive and sustainable change in the lives of poor and marginalized people. It has organized trainings on international climate politics for its members, building on their initiatives, also with the purpose of supporting members with practical and technical knowledge.

Another important area of action for the ACT Alliance has been to encourage members to build disaster risk-reduction and climate change adaptation into their work. This is an integral part of the plan to provide adequate support for building resilient societies and to promote sustainable solutions for a better development, eradicating poverty in the long term.

SDG 13, *Take urgent action to combat climate change and its impacts*, does not apply the term "climate justice" but affirms its agenda:

- Strengthen resilience and adaptive capacity to climate-related hazards and natural disasters in all countries
- Integrate climate change measures into national policies, strategies and planning
- Improve education, awareness-raising and human and institutional capacity on climate change mitigation, adaptation, impact reduction and early warning

Ecumenical *diakonia,* understood in this special dimension as ecological *diakonia*, has an important role within this agenda, both as advocate and as agent. Its distinctness as faith- and rights-based actor gives it a privileged position in mobilizing churches and other people of faith, promoting engagement for climate justice. This necessitates a theological response through the emerging discipline of *ecodiakonia*.

5.7. Gender justice

Every human being holds the right to live in dignity and in freedom, and to be subjects in their own lives. Ecumenical *diakonia* affirms the fundamental importance of gender justice, recognizing that it is indispensable for development and poverty reduction, and thus an integral component in all struggle for justice and peace. Working for gender justice presupposes critical analysis of social, cultural and religious power structures, envisaging equity in the way women and men share power and responsibilities, at home, in the workplace, and in the wider community.

Still women are deprived of their economic, political, social and cultural rights. More women than men are hungry, and they more often experience exploitation, discrimination and violence. Women continue to be under-represented in decision-making processes, both locally and in institutions that claim to be democratic. In situations of conflict and social insecurity, women suffer most.

SDG 5 refers explicitly to gender justice: *Achieve gender equality and empower all women and girls.* Among the targets are:

- End all forms of discrimination against all women and girls everywhere
- Eliminate all forms of violence against all women and girls in the public and private spheres, including trafficking and sexual and other types of exploitation
- Eliminate all harmful practices, such as child, early and forced marriage and female genital mutilation
- Recognize and value unpaid care and domestic work through the provision of public services
- Ensure women's full and effective participation and equal opportunities for leadership at all levels of decision-making in political, economic and public life
- Ensure universal access to sexual and reproductive health and reproductive right
- Undertake reforms to give women equal rights to economic resources.

Assuring women's rights through legal frameworks is a first step in addressing discrimination against them. Violence against women and girls violates their human rights and hinders development. Surveys indicate that 21 percent of girls and women aged between 15 and 49 have experienced physical and/or sexual violence at the hands of an intimate partner in the previous 12 months. Human trafficking affects mainly women and girls; 70 percent of all victims detected worldwide are female.

Early child and forced marriage is most common in Southern Asia and sub-Saharan Africa, with respectively 44 and 37 per cent of women married before their eighteenth birthday. The harmful practice of female genital mutilation is another human rights violation that affects girls and women worldwide. Fortunately, the overall rates of female genital mutilation have been declining over the past decades.

Sexual misconduct at church is a very serious matter. It is a sin, an abuse of spiritual power and a betrayal of sacred trust. Its effects are devastating, especially when children are involved as victims. Sexual harassment is a wider form of sexual misconduct; it includes any unwanted sexual comment, advance or demand, either verbal or physical, that is reasonably perceived by the recipient as demeaning, intimidating, or coercive. Many churches are now addressing this issue openly and have established practices that seek to end and prevent misconduct, and to defend the dignity and the rights of the victims. This continues to be a serious diaconal task, which requires the transformation of deep and enduring patriarchal traditions, teachings and practices, and is an important area of action for international *diakonia*. In 2006, the WCC published a pastoral and educational response to sexual harassment, *When Christian Solidarity Is Broken*. LWF established a Code of Conduct concerning sexual harassment and exploitation for participants in its events in 2010.

The WCC has a long tradition of, and strong commitment to, gender justice and advocacy for a just community of women and men in church and society. Already in 1953, it began the Programme of Women in Church and Society, stating that the renewal of a dignified life after World War II was only possible if women were an active part of every initiative of justice and peace by the churches in society. It had a leading role in organizing the WCC Ecumenical Decade of Churches in Solidarity with Women (1988-1998) and in focusing on violence against women as a key to the WCC Decade for Overcoming Violence (2000-2010). It has collaborated with churches, women's networks, civil society, raising awareness and offering on-the-ground training on gender analysis, gender-based violence awareness, women's rights and HIV-competence in health and pastoral care.

This commitment includes public witness and advocacy. In 2014, the WCC established a gender advisory group and a Human Sexuality Reference Group representing member churches, with the aim of developing procedures and policies to help the WCC in accomplishing gender justice in institutions, communities and societies – an objective at the core of its vision of a "Pilgrimage of Gender Justice."

The LWF has also long since been committed to gender justice. It instituted a women's desk in 1970, later established a programme named Women in Church and Society (WICAS). The two main pillars of its work have been women's empowerment and gender justice, with a strong accent on women's leadership. In 1984, the LWF established the principle of at least 40 percent women's participation in assemblies, a position reaffirmed in 2010 when the 11th Assembly adopted principles of inclusivity and gender policy. In 2013, the LWF launched a Gender Justice Policy with the aim of encouraging member churches to take concrete steps to implement gender justice.

In June 2010, the ACT Alliance Governing Board approved a Humanitarian Protection Policy; several of the principles that it contains refer to gender justice. It commits all ACT members to "Prioritise the safety, dignity and empowerment of women, girls, boys and men at all times without discrimination" (Principle 1), and to "Make a 'core commitment' to mainstreaming gender and protection into all humanitarian assistance programmes" (Principle 2). Humanitarian work must include protection work, which requires gender analysis and gender mainstreaming. The policy document urges ACT members to "Ensure mechanisms are in place to prevent and respond to the occurrence of sexual exploitation and abuse and other forms of gender-based violence" (Principle 5). This implies being proactive in addressing violations of human rights, and to establishing safe referral and reporting processes to competent organizations where members lack the required skills, experience or resources.

As a follow up, ACT Alliance produced a *Gender Inclusive Rights Based Manual* for its members and partners in 2015. It aims to facilitate the integration of rights-based and gender equality development programming. It contains training materials that explore key concepts, introduce practical analytical tools, and facilitate reflection on strategies for integrating gender equality and human rights principles and standards.

In response to a call from the 10th Assembly of the World Council of Churches (2013), the WCC has created a Reference Group on Human Sexuality. The work of the Reference Group is separate from this document on ecumenical *diakonia*. Accordingly, this document does not seek to preempt the detailed work done by the Reference Group on Human Sexuality.

Christians affirm the basic conviction that every human being is created in the image of God. To promote gender justice is therefore, in a faith perspective, to affirm the dignity and gifts that the Creator has bestowed on every human being, women and men.

5.8. Health justice

As affirmed in chapter 2, health and healing have always been on the agenda of the church's caring ministry and sending to the world. In many countries, churches and missions, through their diaconal services, have pioneered the establishment of modern health care. The ecumenical movement has equally been committed to health ministry; its Christian Medical Commission (CMC) played an important role when the World Health Organization (WHO) was in the process of formulating universal principles for primary health, and established the well-known definition of health at the Alma-Ata conference in 1978, affirming that

> health, which is a state of complete physical, mental and social wellbeing, and not merely the absence of disease or infirmity, is a fundamental human right and that the attainment of the highest possible level of health is a most important world-wide social goal whose realization requires the action of many other social and economic sectors in addition to the health sector.

The CMC had argued for including a reference to the spiritual dimension of well-being, and formulated later an alternative definition, often referred to as the WCC-definition of health:

> Health is a dynamic state of well-being of the individual and society, of physical, mental, spiritual, economic, political, and social well-being – of being in harmony with each other, with the material environment and with God.

Both definitions underscore a holistic understanding of health, corresponding to the multi-dimensional nature of being human. The CMC-definition emphasizes that health is something dynamic, a state that requires care and relations of harmony; it points to the relation with God as a distinct resource for well-being and hope. The WHO-definition underlines that health is a fundament human right; political authorities have the duty to provide relevant health services to all citizens; this is not a matter of charity or being able to pay for the services.

In today's globalized world, health justice has become an urgent matter. It has convinced the WCC and other ecumenical organs to engage in public discussions on global health. One important task has been to facilitate networking and advocacy on behalf of church-related health networks, enabling them to participate in official WHO meetings and similar events, with the aim of providing ways for civil society to influence the global governance of resources for health for all.

Another important issue has been to assist churches and related networks to deal with urgent health challenges. In some countries, for instance in Malawi, Christian Health Associations have been established with the goal of promoting the development and sustainability of church-based health services. The task of building awareness and competence when working on HIV has been a major task for the ecumenical movement. It has included theological studies on HIV, and compiling, publishing and disseminating information on church action and lessons learned. Ecumenical *diakonia* has challenged churches to include persons living with HIV in their lives and encouraged them to engage in advocacy securing them adequate health services. The African Network of Religious Leaders living with or personally affected by HIV and AIDS (ANERELA+) (now INERELA+) has empowered many to break the silence and advocate for human dignity. The Ecumenical HIV and AIDS Initiative in Africa (EHAIA) has played a significant role in this work. In recent years, the experiences and diaconal practice on HIV and AIDS have created pioneering spaces to discuss stigma and sexuality within the churches, and thereby a context that compels the churches and diaconal actors to address sensitive issues on human sexuality.

Mental health is another issue that challenges ecumenical *diakonia*. At least 10 percent of the world's population, including 20 percent of children and adolescents, suffer from some sort of mental disorder. In many parts of the world, people with mental illnesses have no access to health services; in addition, they continue to be victims of prejudices and discrimination, often due to religious understandings. This fact obliges churches and other faith communities to engage in activities that seek to provide relevant medical care for this group of patients, and to provide space for care and accompaniment.

Mental health disorders are critical in conflict settings and in areas where people have suffered because of war. The task of working on healing and reconciliation is increasing. It challenges ecumenical *diakonia* to be involved in psychosocial healing and post-conflict social reconstruction, and to support and equip churches and faith communities to become safe spaces where people can seek and grant forgiveness, thus promoting a culture of healing and reconciliation.

SDG 3, *Ensure healthy lives and promote well-being for all at all ages*, seeks to give continuity to the good results achieved in relation to the health goals of the MDGs. The final report reveals that the global under-five mortality rate has declined by more than half, dropping from 90 to 43 deaths per 1,000 live births between 1990 and 2015. New HIV infections fell by approximately 40 percent between 2000 and 2013, from an estimated 3.5 million cases to 2.1 million. This shows that change is possible, and that universal health coverage, one of the targets of SDG 3, is a realistic aim. It requires, however, commitment by the political leadership and solidarity action by the international community; it is a matter that calls civil society and ecumenical *diakonia* to be involved and engage in advocacy.

The MDGs targeted very specific issues, while other fields were neglected to some degree. They were implemented in a top-down manner without including people at local levels in a significant way. In the area of health, for example, it has been said that HIV and AIDS attracted huge amounts of funds and distracted health professionals from other areas, especially from church institutions, so that the health systems were weakened instead of being strengthened. Therefore, one of the lessons learned during the MDG era is that sustainable development needs a system- and a bottom-up approach. This is a window of opportunity for the churches to become vital partners of the governments in implementing the SDGs. While the MDGs were developed and implemented with minimal contribution from churches, governments now see that FBOs are partners for change.

SDG 3 aims to "ensure universal access to sexual and reproductive health-care services, including for family planning, information and education, and the integration of reproductive health into national strategies and programmes." Ecumenical *diakonia* shares this concern, acknowledging that there exist religious traditions that hinder girls and women from holding their rights within this area. Churches and diaconal actors have therefore engaged in campaigns to end dehumanizing practices such as female genital mutilation (FGM), early and forced marriage, and other forms of sexual violation of women and girls.

Health is not just a matter of making diagnosis and providing medical treatment. It is also an issue of wellbeing and of enjoying the gift of being. Health justice therefore also includes advocacy for persons and groups that are discriminated against because of their physical or mental health. EHAIA has addressed the issue of adolescents who were born HIV-positive and are now facing the challenge of dating, marriage and the desire to have children born HIV-negative. The Ecumenical Disability Advocates Network (EDAN) is a WCC programme mandated to advocate for the inclusion, participation and active involvement of persons with disabilities in the spiritual, social, economic and structural life of the church in particular and society in general. In 2016 it presented the document *Gift of Being: A Church of All and for All*, which was adopted by the central committee of the WCC and commended to member churches for further study.

These examples show the relevance of health justice and the importance of ecumenical *diakonia* to be engaged as faith- and rights-based agent.

5.9. Summary

This chapter has presented some of the elements of the changing landscape in which ecumenical *diakonia* operates; they are complex issues and more facts and perspectives could have been added to each of them. Other important topics could have been included in this presentation; some of them, for instance the situation of indigenous peoples and minority groups, racism and the use of hate language, are high on the agenda of the ecumenical movement and also a challenge that engages ecumenical *diakonia*. Limited space does not give justice to all nuances of the changing landscape of diaconal action. It must therefore be emphasized that most of these issues are intertwined; climate change affects poor people first; marginalized groups are more likely to be victims of injustices and targets of violence.

This reality challenges diaconal actors to evaluate critically their approaches, objectives and working methods. Ecumenical *diakonia* must be well informed about the mechanisms in today's world that marginalize people and cause new forms of poverty, and be able to respond to challenges of justice and human dignity.

The SDGs represent a unique opportunity for upholding public and political engagement for just global causes of justice. The commitment to "leave no one behind" is a compelling vision that corresponds to what Christians hope and pray for and seek to achieve through diaconal action. In the years to come, it will therefore be a key task to engage in activities that support the SDG agenda. This includes advocacy and building capacities to hold governments accountable for their commitments, and building awareness and capacities among diaconal actors in order to engage with SDGs.

SDG 16, *Peace, justice and strong institutions*, aims to "promote peaceful and inclusive societies for sustainable development, provide access to justice for all and build effective, accountable and inclusive institutions at all levels." It reminds everyone that is committed to the cause of overcoming poverty, of defending the rights and dignity of migrants and refugees, and of promoting justice in relation to economy, climate, gender and health, of the basic importance of just peace. Without peace, stability, human rights, space for civil action and accountable governance, based on the rule of law – we cannot hope for sustainable development.

It also reminds ecumenical *diakonia* of the vocation to be agents of reconciliation and peace, in particular in contexts where the "politicization" of religion and the "religionization" of politics nurture mistrust among people and cause open conflicts. Churches and diaconal agents should take a leading role in establishing safe spaces for interfaith dialogue and interreligious platforms for promoting social justice and development.

The increasing recognition of the role of religion in development, represents an opportunity for ecumenical *diakonia*. Of the world's population, 85 percent belong to a faith community; faith does matter in their everyday lives; it forms their motivation and commitment when engaged in the struggle for a better future. For agents of ecumenical *diakonia* this represents a unique possibility of building alliances with people of faith and with religious communities, affirming their hopes and distinct assets. In addition, it affirms the distinct identity and competence of the faith-based actor, and adds energy to the commitment to save lives and struggle for justice.

CHAPTER 6

The Distinctiveness of Diaconal Practice

Photo: Sean Hawkey/Life on Earth

6.1. Introduction

This chapter discusses what characterizes *diakonia* and diaconal practice. On the one hand, this refers to the distinct identity of *diakonia*, its rootedness in the being and the mission of the church. On the other hand, it also presupposes that this identity marks the way in which diaconal actors perform their service, in developing working methods and setting aims. Together the two perspectives express the statement that *diakonia* is both faith-based and rights-based, and the connection between the two.

In chapter 4, we presented the basic elements of the theological nature of *diakonia* with the claim that *diakonia* expresses an intimate connection between what churches are and do. Here the focus is rather on how the diaconal identity takes shape in concrete action. In what way can people recognize their actions as diaconal?

To clarify the distinctiveness of diaconal action does not imply a claim of superiority, that diaconal agents are better and more trustworthy than other social agents. It simply means recognizing what has motivated Christians to take initiatives and establish institutions and organizations, and asking how their traditions and values, their bonds of social belonging and partnership, can be activated and become valuable assets in the daily performance of diaconal service.

6.2. The aim of diaconal action

The immediate objective of diaconal action is to assist people in need, to defend their human dignity and the rights they hold as citizens, regardless of their formal citizenship or nationality, and to support processes that promote justice, peace and the integrity of creation. *Diakonia*, whether performed by local churches, diaconal institutions or international agencies, aims to promote the common good; its action addresses all humans and not only Christians. To serve humanity, promoting life, is meaningful in itself; it should never be reduced to be a tool for obtaining other purposes, be they ideological, socio-political or religious.

Diakonia has no hidden agenda. Christian faith affirms the commandment to love your neighbour without conditions, as the parable of the Good Samaritan illustrates well. In his practice, Jesus responded to human need. He never required adherence to his teaching or that those that he helped would have to follow him.

This fundamental understanding requires some further reflection. This first relates to the fact that all social action, including development work and ecumenical *diakonia*, inevitably embeds worldviews and value systems. They influence the formulation of objectives, the motive for and how action is justified. No social agent is "neutral," but is always moved by ideals and concerns, that reflect either ideological, religious or secular convictions. There is no reason to deplore the role of visions and values; on the contrary, they are fundamental in the formation of active citizenship and the construction of civil society. The issue here is rather to question their impact on power relations. History has proved that ideas and concepts may lead to practices where people become tools when striving for "higher" purposes.

What is distinct for diaconal actors is that they refer to religious concepts, in addition to secular, when explaining their action and its objective. This is an expression of the interdisciplinary nature of *diakonia*; it is social action rooted in socio-political knowledge and analysis, and, at the same time, it is faith-based and rights-based action. Its practice is guided by the norms and values of this basis. *Diakonia* thus requires the ability to express itself accordingly, using the kind of secular terminology that is required of disciplined social action as well as the language of faith in the form of disciplined theological language. Only then is it possible to communicate the distinctive nature of diaconal work properly, internally as well as externally, and, in addition, to carry out a broad and critical reflection on diaconal praxis.

This ability to hold together its identity as faith- and rights-based actor is critical in the understanding of the relation between *diakonia* and development. Is it correct to say that development is the goal of ecumenical *diakonia*? The term itself is value-laden; some critics consider it too economy-centred and dependent on Western ideology. Faith-based organizations, and most of the ACT Alliance membership, have nevertheless opted for using it, in the first place because of its wide use, especially in the public arena. Others, in particular radical voices from the global South, hold the view that the term "development" does not address the unjust structures in the world, many of which have roots back to colonial times. They prefer concepts like liberation, and state the need for a terminology that affirms the importance of radically changing the global system of power and dominion.

ACT Alliance has expressed uneasiness when applying the term "development," and has added "transformational" to it, indicating that development cannot be limited to economic matters. It includes political, social and cultural components, all of which must be considered. In addition, transformation challenges all involved partners critically to examine their attitudes, life style and patterns of action. In that regard, transformation has a clear theological connotation as it reflects the admonition in Romans 12:2 not to "conform to the pattern of this world, but be transformed by the renewing of your mind," listening to God's "good, pleasing and perfect will."

It is questionable if one single term can fully express the goal of diaconal action, be it development, transformation, change or renewal. All of them express the need for responding to burning humanitarian, social, economic and ecological issues, for defending human dignity and promoting a vision of a more just and peaceful world. As stated in an input from the Africa and Middle East Regional Consultation when responding to the ACT consultative process on the changing development paradigm:

> In a context where people have suffered exclusion, conflicts and persecution, the ACT Alliance is challenged to work for restoration, transformation and renewed hope.

Instead of constructing one overarching goal, it is more meaningful to indicate sets of goals, as is the case of the Sustainable Development Goals (SDGs) adopted by the UN. They point to the complex reality in which ecumenical *diakonia* operates, as do all agents of development. In this context, nobody has the authority to define for others what their goal and aims should be. Ecumenical *diakonia* will strongly claim people's right to formulate their own vision for a better future, and to be the principal agents in working for it.

Beyond aid and development, ecumenical *diakonia* also promotes the building of sustainable communities in the long term. Any harmonious community is dependent on healthy and respectful relationships rather than exploitation, sectarianism or discrimination. The ecumenical dimension to *diakonia* is thus of critical importance to promoting such stability.

From a faith perspective, the future ultimately belongs to God. *Diakonia* is inspired by God's promise of hope and future (Jeremiah 29:11). The kingdom that Jesus brought near, announces "righteousness, peace and joy in the Holy Spirit" (Romans 14:17). That kingdom is still to come in its fullest sense. As an integral part of the church's mission, *diakonia* shares the mandate to announce its coming, in the first place by promoting and anticipating its values. From this perspective, faith will always remain a fundamental resource for diaconal action, providing a spirituality of resistance against all evil forces – hope against hope, and confidence in the God of Life. From that same perspective, *diakonia* will always be committed to justice as an integral part of the hope God has given creation. The theme of the WCC's 10th Assembly in Busan, "God of Life – lead us to justice and peace," articulates well what *diakonia* strives for, as faith-based and rights-based action.

6.3. The connection between what churches are and what churches do

Diakonia belongs to the very essence of being church and is an integral part of its mission. According to former LWF General Secretary Ishmael Noko, *diakonia* belongs to the DNA-structure of being church; the church can therefore not outsource *diakonia* to specialized ministries and organizations. They play an important role, not least in ecumenical *diakonia*, and as such, they are the work of the churches. Nevertheless, if the churches would leave the diaconal mandate to them alone, they would lose a fundamental dimension of their very being.

The church is both local and global; every Christian congregation is church in its full meaning, and at the same time intimately connected to the worldwide Christian community. In a theological understanding, both dimensions express the nature of belonging to the body of Christ. *Diakonia* unites the church, both locally and globally. Mutual sharing of resources and actions of solidarity and assistance affirm our belonging to each other.

This does not mean that diaconal work targets only church members or the worldwide communion of churches. As Christians, we share a common vocation to serve and to care for all people in need and to promote causes of justice and peace wherever human dignity is threatened and to be responsible stewards of God's creation.

The understanding of belonging together as churches goes beyond our action together. We recognize each other as members of the same family and its bonds of faith, hope, prayers and faithful discipleship, before we engage in concrete diaconal work together. These bonds have the potential of adding quality to diaconal action; they may foster mutual respect, participatory practices and sustainability.

Partnership in ecumenical *diakonia* is therefore in the first place a gift; it is more than establishing relations for practical purposes. Partnership opens for mutual enrichment and learning; it requires mutual respect and sensitivity for the concerns of each partner. Differences among partners should be a strength, not in the first place a limitation. Jesus taught his disciples to invert the ruling value systems and acknowledge the gifts and skills of the poor (Mark 12:41-44; Luke 18:1-8). This corresponds to the findings of the Colombo consultation, which attempted to re-imagine *diakonia* from the vantage point of the vulnerable and marginalized communities.

The intimate relation between being and doing works in both directions; diaconal practice challenges our self-understanding as a faith community, and calls us to repentance and renewal. Ecumenical *diakonia*, together with other expressions of international solidarity, has nurtured the life of the churches, its worship life, its understanding of ethical questions and the formation of church members as active citizens.

6.4. *Diakonia* as faith-based and rights-based action

Faith is biblical, and its interpretation or application in terms of protection of human rights is defined by *agape*. Faith gives both depth and passion to human rights. The depth and the passion find its expression in theological integrity, in spiritual depth, and in moral force, that purely secular approaches may lack. Faith communities believe that all people are created in the image of God. Faith communities will never stop affirming the dignity of all people.

Human rights sharpen the eyes of faith, so that the structural scope of the needs of the world are seen. Human rights help to frame diaconal work that achieves lasting change for the better. It draws our attention to the universal scale; beyond our own borders to the regional and global scale. It prevents us from falling prey to particularism or sectarianism. Therefore, faith-based and rights-based actions affirm each other.

Affirming the dignity of all people means acknowledging that every single person is a rights-holder. Refugees can lose almost everything but never their right to justice.

Advocacy is an integral part of *diakonia*. In practice, it seeks ways of empowering people to stand up for their rights and engage in processes that promote good governance, social protection and welfare for all as active citizens. As rights-based action, *diakonia* also adheres to the principle that universal and indivisible human rights are the cornerstone of international human rights legislation, as emphasized in the Universal Declaration on Human Rights in 1948, and reiterated in numerous international human rights conventions, declarations, and resolutions. It is not a coincidence that the founding churches of the World Council of Churches played an active role in the formation of this Universal Declaration of Human Rights. Diaconal actors are ready to work with all who are committed to human rights and seek to build networks and strategic platforms in order to implement and practice human rights.

Central constituents of Christian faith give depth and passion to rights-based action: the image of God as a loving and caring God; the image of human beings as created in God's image and created to live in community with each other; the memory of Jesus and his prophetic ministry; the promise of God's Spirit that brings life and energy for liberating action. These elements motivate diaconal action. They affect the formation of its ethos and working style. In addition, the faith base of diaconal agents connects to a worldwide network of churches and Christians, with the potential of establishing partnerships and a commitment for just causes. One significant asset of ecumenical *diakonia* is that it belongs to the global network of churches, which on the one hand actively links churches at the local level with their diaconal engagement, and on the other hand organizes initiatives of advocacy at the international level.

Diakonia's rights base refers to justice as a central theme in the biblical tradition. In a biblical perspective, justice is a gift of God, not a human achievement or an external phenomenon. Justice is God's commitment to his people; it "emerges from the faithful relationship between God and humanity, and manifests itself as love, righteousness and liberation in the life of God's people." God's justice is salvific; its intention is to liberate humans from the bondage of sin, injustice and suffering. The prophets in the Old Testament strongly criticized systemic injustice and the way the mighty abused their power. Jesus affirmed this prophetic tradition and announced justice as a way of action that goes beyond merely keeping the law (Luke 10:42). Promoting justice is a core dimension of active discipleship, as a mandate to build right relationships among human beings, in relation to the whole of God's creation, and thereby also to God.

This tradition mandates *diakonia* to be prophetic, to denounce injustice in all its forms, and to promote the biblical vision of justice and peace. The Hebrew term for justice, *sedaqah*, announces a living together where righteousness reigns, that recognizes every individual as neighbour and citizen, with fair access to common goods. Justice and peace belong together; the Hebrew term *shalom* has a much wider meaning than peace as the opposite of war. It means well-being and the harmonious living together. From this perspective, there is no justice without peace, and no peace without justice. Ecumenical *diakonia* as rights-based action is therefore committed to both.

How does the performance of ecumenical *diakonia* reflect its faith and rights base? It will affect the way of formulating the vision and objectives for the work. In addition, it will influence the choice of areas of action, of partnerships, and of working methods. This reflection should be "disciplined," both in the sense that it is based on an interdisciplinary understanding of the distinct nature and role of ecumenical *diakonia*, and that it is praxis-oriented in the sense that is can strengthen the professional competence of its actors.

6.5. The distinctiveness of faith-based organizations

Faith-based organization (FBO) first appeared as a term in the USA in the 1970s. Today it is widely used for organizations that base their mission and values on religious faith when assuming roles as social agents. The World Bank has largely contributed to the recognition of FBOs since it in 1998 invited religious leaders to engage in a dialogue on the role of religious actors in development.

FBOs, among them diaconal agencies, are important actors in civil society, in particular in development work. Both the UN-system and national governments include them in their working plans and are ready to finance their activities. There are many reasons for this. One is their reputation as professional and efficient actors on the frontlines of combating extreme poverty, protecting the vulnerable, delivering essential services and alleviating suffering; another is a growing recognition of the role of religion in development. In what follows, this will be reflected in relation to FBOs in general, but also with reference to diaconal agencies.

Governmental donors recognize FBOs for representing "added value," related to both how they work and how they are organized. They are grassroots-oriented, they reach the poorest and mobilize civil society. In addition, they employ committed people, have low administrative costs, are mobile, and able to handle small projects. People trust them and their moral authority. Their presence is not limited to the period of implementing programs and projects – relations of belonging together are in place before, during and after being engaged in such activities.

This reputation does not, however, always correspond to the reality, and in some cases, it may be a result of mistrust in governmental development work and public policy. FBOs should therefore be self-critical when affirming their own strengths and distinctive values. At the same time, they should affirm the importance of governmental responsibility and the need of public welfare systems.

From the perspective of the FBOs, it makes sense to talk about "core values" rather than "added values." The points referred to above express what many of them would state in their vision and describe as the heart of what motivates them for action. The point here is not to claim that FBOs are more effective and abler to put their values into practice, for instance, with other NGOs. It is rather to emphasize the particular potential of these organizations when relating to religious communities, and their insider understanding of faith as a motivator for social change.

While religion was for decades a non-issue in development, this has changed since the turn of the millennium. There are many reasons for this growing awareness of the importance of religion in development. Here we shall focus on only two: the role of religious leaders as moral authorities, and the importance of faith as motivation and energy in the life of ordinary people.

The campaign to mitigate HIV and AIDS revealed the crucial role of religious leaders in development, both for better and for worse. As long as they silenced the reality of the pandemic, and even contributed to moral condemnations of its victims, the campaign met with severe hindrances. This changed when religious leaders began to break the silence and invested their authority in convincing people to test for HIV and themselves to lead by example, as well as in advocacy for the access to medical treatment. In campaigns against FGM, and in efforts to prevent the spread of Ebola, religious leaders have assumed similar roles.

The same is the case when FBOs are engaged in humanitarian work. This was strongly affirmed at a gathering organized by UNCHR in Geneva in 2012 with the theme "Faith and Protection," where the High Commissioner highlighted the important role that faith-based organizations and local religious communities play in protecting asylum-seekers, refugees, the internally displaced and stateless people. During this meeting, a consensus emerged regarding the key principles of humanitarian work, including humanity, impartiality, non-discrimination and respect for the beliefs of others, diversity, empowerment, equality, and protection against any form of conditionality.

Faith matters in the lives of ordinary people. Faith orients people's worldview and value system, their hope and struggle for a better life. Therefore, development workers, and in particular diaconal agents, cannot ignore faith and its energy in people's lives. One important element is its potential for creating active citizenship. Faith will form a person's identity. When asking, "Who am I, what am I for?" it will create relations and nurture a sense of belonging. Faith will offer arenas of action, training places for active citizenship and leadership skills.

Because FBOs are rooted in faith communities, they have easy access to religious leaders and can involve them in their work, respecting their integrity. Many FBOs will also be able to engage leaders of different faiths, which may contribute to reducing local social and political tensions.

Development agents need competence in matters of faith and religion. In the past, this has not always been the case, even for people employed by FBOs. The important point is to acknowledge familiarity with matters of religion and faith as an integral element of professional competence. For diaconal agents, it is the other way around: they should be aware of, and able to articulate in secular language the distinctiveness and core values of diaconal work when (critically) partnering with development agents. In other words, in order to establish fruitful partnerships with governmental and other secular organisations, diaconal workers need to be 'bilingual', speaking both faith and secular language.

6.6. Diaconal assets

Within development work, there has been a shift of focus from a needs-based to an assets-based approach, which means emphasizing local resources and competence rather than what is lacking.

When referring to assets, we are talking about kinds of social capital that a community, a group, or even an organization may possess. It may link to their collective experiences and insight, their social practices, their faith and to the richness of individual talents and skills. Research related to health has revealed the complex reality of health assets that people will activate when falling ill. They do not only include tangible assets such as hospitals and medical doctors, but also intangible ones, many of them related to their faith, such as prayer and blessing. Health workers who ignore these intangible assets will have a limited understanding of their patients' "health world," and its ability to empower people to cope with health challenges.

How can we apply this insight in relation to diaconal practice? As joint action, ecumenical *diakonia* becomes an arena where different partners cooperate in order to achieve shared objectives. Local churches, diaconal institutions and departments as well as international agencies contribute with resources of different kinds, both tangible and intangible. These diaconal assets, as we may name them, affirm the distinctiveness of diaconal action, its core values and the basis of its professional strength.

Many of the diaconal assets are tangible. In the first place, the longstanding *practice of caring for sick and needy people,* which always has been integral to the church's pastoral ministry. In recent times, such service has taken the form of programmes and projects, of service delivery, of educational programs, of advocacy and promoting human rights. It includes the large number of institutions and structures, the wide variety of diaconal installations such as hospitals, training centres, offices, etc., established with the purpose of delivering services. Diaconal organizations and specialized ministries – local, national and international – also represent such assets, as well as local congregations, national churches and ecumenical bodies.

Diaconal practice has often been *pioneering*; this is another asset. It introduced new health and social services. In the 19th century, diaconal institutions were among the first to establish services for persons with physical and mental disabilities, which meant a significant change in the life situation for those involved, and for their recognition as members of society. Diaconal work has also promoted the role of women and thereby given a witness to gender equity. In many contexts, diaconal initiatives are responding to situations of discrimination, neglect of human rights and social marginalization due to irresponsible political leadership.

The primary asset of diaconal service is the individual Christian. Christian women and men, motivated by faith to a Christian calling of love in action, whether acting individually or collectively, are indispensable to diaconal care. Much individual *diakonia* is unheralded (and often unpaid – even with the individual paying expenses out of their own pocket), yet is vital to social care. A visit to a lonely elderly neighbour or a person in hospital is in direct obedience to the teachings of Jesus: "I was sick and you visited me . . . (Matt. 25:36). Such human interactive care cannot be replaced by machinery or technology.

Reflecting the contribution of individual Christians, *human resources* constitute a large group of tangible assets. Diaconal action counts on skilled personnel. Many of them combine professional competence with a strong personal motivation founded in their faith. Some will call this an ethos of service.

Further, *diakonia* counts on *economic resources.* Diaconal action is possible thanks to funds and foundations, properties, but also to donors and financial supporters, private and public. Churches in the global South are increasingly recognizing the importance of raising local funds as an expression of building self-reliance and dignity.

Lastly, there are *communication resources.* Publications, educational material and other forms of communication are assets used to promote attitudes, responsibilities, opportunities, and the relevant competence in order to work for change.

This presentation of tangible assets may give the impression that they very much depend on Western patterns of organizing diaconal work, with its dependency on financial resources and professional performance. In this perspective, diaconal action may appear as implemented "from above." A focus on intangible assets presents a different angle and opens space for seeing *diakonia* "from below," with prime attention given to the role and resources of ordinary people.

The intangible assets are more difficult to group. What follows are some indications:

The collective memory of the past. This includes a variety of narratives, in the first place the biblical stories about Jesus, who set an example when caring for the sick, the hungry and the poor. There are also other stories, including ordinary women and men known from people's own history and community. They may be founding mothers and fathers, persons who have pioneered diaconal action. This "cloud of witnesses" encourages and inspires others to follow their example and nurture the conviction that it is possible to make a difference. Stories of healing, of transformation, reconciliation and empowerment in the past will make people confident that something similar is possible today.

Then there are *rites and rituals.* People share sacred moments that foster and strengthen their faith, hope and love. This is experienced in church services, when singing and dancing together, even in funerals. Sacraments and rites of intercession, blessing and consecration will often nurture the vocation to serve one's neighbour, even in times of suffering and struggle.

Connected to this, *the diaconal ethos*, based on the concept of human dignity, of life being sacred and the vocation to protect and defend human life. Communities of faith will propagate value systems and attitudes that promote the practice of justice, fairness, inclusiveness, mercy and care. The distinctiveness of Christian *diakonia* often materializes in attitudes which can be described only spiritually (or as invisible assets), such as an attitude of loving care, of patience, of humility, of utmost dignity expressed to victims of violence, to sick people, to the dying, an attitude of persistent hope in situations of despair. These attitudes are not measurable like economic figures or professional medical standards on social services, but it is them to add decisively to the quality and distinct flavour and profile of Christian *diakonia*.

In addition, *the sense of belonging together and of being part of an extended family.* These relationships are able to foster the notion of being a subject with tasks to fulfil. They motivate practices of hospitality and visitation as expressions of mutual care and they empower persons for active citizenship.

All these elements form people's worldview, and their basic understanding of what is real, what makes sense, and what gives meaning. They are diaconal assets because they have the ability to mobilize ordinary people to do something for the common good, and to empower them to engage in processes that promise a better future for themselves and their community.

This presentation of assets may appear as too idealistic, not corresponding to real life. Christians are not necessarily as committed as the description above may indicate, nor are congregations always wholeheartedly engaged in diaconal work. Nor do agencies always give importance to cooperation with local churches, recognizing their assets. Such critical observations are important, but they should however not lead to an underestimation of diaconal assets, or to their disregard. Rather, they should motivate all involved partners to engage in a dialogue on how to mobilize the diaconal assets there and strengthen their role in concrete activities.

Diaconal agents are *trusted as social agents*, and as interpreters of international solidarity, by people in general and by popular movements, local authorities and international agencies, including governmental bodies. Such trust is another asset, and it is a result of longstanding commitment to people's wellbeing. *Moral authority* is another asset, to be used when dealing with sensitive issues, and when promoting ethical behaviour, as for instance addressing corruption and abuse of public power. Admittedly, churches and diaconal agents have not always adopted this prophetic role and in some cases, they have used their moral authority for other purposes. As long as such assets are there, the opportunity of prophetic presence and witness remains.

It is of paramount importance that professional diaconal actors understand the potential of diaconal assets and know how to relate to them when performing their work. Diaconal assets are often under-communicated or even neglected, especially the intangible ones. The consequence is a missed opportunity of articulating the distinctiveness of professional diaconal action and its core values. An asset-based approach that recognizes the variety of diaconal assets has the potential of adding quality to diaconal work, to secure a higher level of local participation and a sense of ownership when implementing projects and programmes. After all, sustainability and lasting effect depend on the degree to which activities are embedded in the worldview and value system of those involved.

6.7. Diaconal language

Language matters; language has the power to assign names to persons. There is a great difference between naming a person as recipient or as right-holder. Naming activities includes a similar power of definition. It makes a difference whether it is called *diakonia* or development work.

In the past, many church-based diaconal agencies have been hesitant in using the term *diakonia* and in employing a "diaconal" language when describing their activities. A main reason has been the view that the *diakonia* terminology does not communicate well, in particular with outsiders, such as governmental back donors. In many contexts, the term *diakonia* remains unknown. They have therefore opted for using ordinary development language when writing applications and reports related to their work. On the other hand, it is notable that this secular language does not fully satisfy the need of expressing the identity of diaconal action. This becomes clear when governmental back donors ask faith-based agencies to give account of their added value and distinctiveness as development agents. The same question is asked by local churches, who ask what distinguishes the work of diaconal agencies from that of secular NGOs.

The report from Ecumenical Conversation 21 during the WCC Busan assembly in 2013 addresses this issue:

> The participants affirm that churches, ecumenical partners and the WCC must respond to the signs of the times by developing a common diaconal language. We are faith-based and rights-based and we need to identify what this means in practice including defining our mandate and our core values and by mapping our diaconal assets.

This statement points to the gains of developing a diaconal language; it provides all partners involved in ecumenical *diakonia* with a shared platform that expresses what we are, what we do, and what we aim at together. It represents an opportunity to articulate the distinct nature of diaconal work, which includes both its theological fundamentals and a disciplined reflection on its action from the perspective of social sciences.

Diaconal language, in other words, implies the ability to use both religious and secular terminology, not as separate languages, but in an interdisciplinary way. Its approach is dialectic in the sense that it recognizes both the religious and the secular "dialects" as legitimate and necessary in the process of building diaconal professionalism, which means to be competent in its doing, its ability to analyse, to plan, to perform, to evaluate and to report.

Being able to use more than one language strengthens the capacity to communicate with different audiences. It should, however, not be understood as speaking with two tongues, in the sense that the message will differ according to its secular or religious context. An interdisciplinary and dialectic approach implies critical communication between the two. The secular language will question the validity and range of the religious terms, and vice versa. This links to the fact that words are not able to capture reality in its fullness, as different words give a broader insight to understand the complexity both of human life and of social processes.

Summing up, there are many reasons for developing a diaconal language. It will strengthen the ability to articulate the distinctiveness of *diakonia*, and help to give a fuller account of its assets, its strengths and weakness. It will provide a terminology that will facilitate communication, both internally among churches and diaconal agencies and in their relation to external partners. Last, but not least, it will strengthen the professional competence of diaconal agents, providing tools for mapping and mobilizing diaconal assets and for developing innovative practices.

6.8. Diaconal professionalism

In some churches, in particular the churches of the Reformation, there is a long tradition of diaconal training. The modern diaconal movement that emerged in Germany in the 1830s had training of deaconesses and deacons as a fundamental element; the diaconal institutions offered education as nurses and social workers, however always accompanied by theological studies. Diaconal training has since had this mark of "double qualification", and has developed a professionalism that has sought to integrate knowledge from different disciplines.

The principal reason for this approach is that human life, and in particular human suffering, is multi-dimensional. This is evident when it comes to illness, which often encompasses the physical, the mental, the social and the spiritual side of being human, often intertwined, which may add suffering to suffering. Diaconal professionalism therefore enhances interdisciplinary knowledge and the development of skills that regard the human being as a whole person. Not only health workers recognize the importance of a holistic approach when intervening for the sake of healing and empowering an ill person. In a similar manner, when working for social change and for eradicating poverty, this holistic approach makes a difference, as poverty has many sides, not only an economic and a political, but also a mental and a spiritual. For this same reason, diaconal professionalism should learn how to mobilize the rich variety of all diaconal assets, and not overemphasize some of them.

Diaconal training is connecting theory and practice. Deaconesses and deacons always spent a substantial part of their training in hospitals and similar working places where they could develop practical skills parallel to acquiring theoretical knowledge. The professional gifts used in these diaconal ministries range from experience and training as educators, community organisers, nurses, farmers, community economic development, chaplains, parish ministers, social workers, counsellors, managers and administrators. Affirming the professional gifts of these people and the organisations they work for would show credibility of this truly being a priority for ecumenical *diakonia*. The diaconate, as represented by the *DIAKONIA World Federation*, has had an evolving understanding and a wide variety of expressions and programmes of *diakonia* for over a hundred years. Its insight represents a valuable asset for theological and other educational institutions involved in diaconal training. This expresses the view that diaconal professionalism in the first place is practical. In addition, it claims that praxis is a prime source for new and innovative insight. Within the framework of diaconal knowledge, theory is primarily critical reflection on practice, with the aim of improving its quality.

Critical reflection in particular concerns questions of methodology and working style. Like all professional intervention, diaconal work may take paternalistic forms that cause passivity and dependency. Today ecumenical *diakonia* is committed to a rights-based practice that regards people as rights-holders and addresses those in power as duty-bearers. This means a preference for working methods that secure participation and empowerment. At the same time, it includes advocacy and awareness as an integral part of its prophetic vocation. Gender awareness and gender analysis are key components in the formation of diaconal professionalism.

Diaconal competence requires attention and training. Church leaders in general would benefit from basic knowledge of the nature and the practice of *diakonia*, however, most theological seminaries have not included *diakonia* in their study programmes. Equally, few leaders of diaconal activities have had a chance to study *diakonia* and to build their professional competence from its interdisciplinary way of reflecting on praxis. It remains a shared responsibility for all actors within ecumenical *diakonia* to establish plans for building diaconal competence, and in particular encouraging training institutions to offer study programmes within this field.

6.9. Summary

This chapter has presented different perspectives on the distinctiveness of ecumenical *diakonia*. It has affirmed *diakonia* as an expression of the church's nature and mission, as a concept that holds together what the church is called to be and to do, at local, national and ecumenical/global levels. This understanding of diaconal identity implies conceptualizing diaconal action as faith- and rights-based. Both are inseparable and non-negotiable dimensions of its being and doing, both are normative in processes of identifying objectives for its work and for developing value systems and working methods. As faith-based and rights-based action, *diakonia* is obliged to defend human dignity and to promote justice, peace and the integrity of creation.

Two thousand years of diaconal practice in many different contexts have brought a richness of experiences and insight; together they represent resources that this chapter has presented as diaconal assets. It has further argued that diaconal actors, at all levels, have access to such assets, both tangible and intangible, and recommended an asset-based approach that seeks to mobilize them when engaging in activities.

Diaconal agencies are recommended to raise their awareness of the multiplicity of diaconal assets and acknowledge the role they may have, in professional diaconal work also. This chapter has argued for developing a diaconal language that is able to communicate the distinct identity of diaconal work, using both a theological and a secular discourse in an interdisciplinary manner, with the purpose of building diaconal competence, in the first place for diaconal practitioners. References have been given to examples of formal diaconal training, with indications of components to be included.

The purpose of focusing on the distinctiveness of diaconal identity and practice is not to claim superiority compared to other social agents. Nor is it to envisage a society where church-based actors have gained for themselves dominant political or social roles. Such a view can bring with it a taste of clericalism and theocracy that has nothing to do with the spirit of *diakonia*. In its shortest term, the aim of *diakonia* is to assist persons in immediate need; in a longer term, the aim is to contribute to the common good, as one among many agents within civil society. *Diakonia* therefore recognizes the rights and the duties of public authorities, in no way can it seek to replace them or to weaken them. At the same time, *diakonia* recognizes its public role as a social actor. A clear understanding of its distinct identity and assets is intended to empower diaconal actors to assume their role in the best possible way.

CHAPTER 7

Contemporary Challenges

Photo: László Lehel/HIA

7.1. Introduction

This chapter presents some of the challenges that ecumenical *diakonia* faces today. Some of them relate to external factors, such as the changing landscape described in chapter 5. These factors require the agents of international *diakonia* to review their goals and strategies. In particular, the SDG agenda represents an opportunity for reorientation and for building networks of cooperation. When dealing with these challenges, ecumenical *diakonia* will have to strategize according to its distinctive role as faith- and rights-based agents, described in chapter 6.

In what follows, three focus areas are presented. The first relates to resources, acknowledging that they are limited. How can diaconal actors be responsible stewards of resources and cooperate better in order to use them in the best possible way? The second addresses this issue from the perspective of working together with others; it points at the strategic importance of networking within and outside the family of Christians. The third focus area, advocacy, affirms the prophetic dimension of ecumenical *diakonia* as a key strategy when answering challenges in today's changing landscape.

7.2. Limited resources – resource sharing

The interchurch aid, organized in response to the refugee crisis in the aftermath of the world wars, depended mainly on campaigns addressing congregations and individuals, urging them to support the work financially. National agencies were established with the purpose of coordinating this work, and of transferring the money to ecumenical agencies in Geneva. One of the donations the LWF received in support of their refugee programme, which started in 1947, came from congregations in today's Namibia, thus revealing the ecumenical nature of this work.

Throughout the history of the church, diaconal activities have depended on the generosity of faithful Christians, following the example of the Apostle Paul and the collection he organized in favour of the poor in Jerusalem.

In Europe, many diaconal institutions are funded by government money, in particular health and social work. Since the 1960s, with a growing focus on development work, many diaconal agencies based in the global North have sought funding from public donors, in the first place national governments. The UN system has also been an important funding partner, in particular the UNHCR (the United Nations High Commissioner for Refugees). The LWF World Service is among their largest partners globally and in 2012, they could support 1.4 million refugees, thanks to this funding. In 2014, the UNHCR signed a Memorandum of Understanding with the LWF, on which occasion Janet Lim, UNHCR's Assistant High Commissioner, commenting on the record levels of forced displacement globally, described the LWF as "a long-standing close partner, and we're delighted to see the scope for our joint work expand."

While diaconal agencies can still count on public support for refugee work and humanitarian aid, this is not the case for long-term development work and advocacy activities. The Dutch agency ICCO (Inter-Church Organisation for Development Cooperation) has experienced dramatic cuts in governmental funds over the last years, consequently, it has had to reduce staff and activities. Many other agencies experience the same trend of draining public funds. This has made some look for alternative funding partners, for instance companies committed to corporate social responsibility (CSR).

Still a substantial part of the funding for ecumenical *diakonia* comes from congregations and individuals. While governmental funding obliges the agencies to follow strict public requirements, collected money is normally not earmarked, which gives the agencies more freedom when allocating it, for instance in partnership with churches and ecumenical bodies.

However, church donations are also going down. Many churches experience membership decline. This is the case in Germany, where the volume of church taxes has been significantly reduced over the last decades. Other churches, for instance in the Nordic countries, are facing new challenges as their relation to the state is changing, with increased responsibility for maintaining the economy of the church.

It is likely that this trend will continue and that less money will be available for ecumenical *diakonia* in the future. This is influencing the agencies and their ability to engage. Many have initiated a process of reducing the number of countries where they are working, while there is also a trend to downscale the number of activities, and to move from large projects to smaller and more targeted activities.

This situation challenges all partners involved in ecumenical *diakonia* to strive for better coordination. ACT Alliance has already established well-functioning routines of cooperating aid in emergencies. It is also engaged in processes of cooperation in long-term development work and in public witness and advocacy. This effort envisages an ecumenical sharing of resources. It is evident that new strategies have to be worked out in order to envisage the best possible way of using available resources, and to establish adequate structures of sharing and cooperation. In a context where donors question the role of intermediaries in development work, it becomes an urgent task to explain the advantages of multilateral actors and of coordinating mechanisms.

Another important task is to develop coordinated strategies and mechanisms for fundraising. Agencies are becoming international also in the sense that they are fundraising globally, even in the South. This may create situations of tension between them. Agencies involved in ecumenical *diakonia* should avoid competing for the same funds and surrendering to market language. Strategies for fundraising must include commercial companies and their social responsibility. Diaconal actors should also address local governments arguing that diaconal work is for the public good, and therefore entitled support by public funding.

It also remains an important task to teach people and in particular church members to give and share their resources in solidarity with others. Stewardship continues to be a relevant theme, especially in a time that promotes individualism and consumerism. Offering and caring for the neighbour are dimensions of Christian discipleship requiring theological foundation, teaching and preaching, in all churches and in all social contexts.

Stewardship is not only about money. Churches are capable of mobilizing significant human resources through the engagement of volunteers, and this is an asset that requires recognition by professional actors. Although financial resources are fundamental for many of the activities of ecumenical *diakonia*, it may be misleading to point at money as the only resource that matters. In the past decades, ecumenical *diakonia* may have had a too easy access to public funds, with the consequence that diaconal agents did not pay sufficient attention to non-pecuniary resources that condition the success of diaconal work, such as local participation and ownership.

Ecumenical *diakonia* can learn from the Good Samaritan, who used available resources when assisting the victim of violence. The Apostle Peter did not let the lack of silver and gold disempower him when meeting with a beggar, in the name of Jesus Christ he helped him to stand on his own feet (Acts 3:1-10). Also, today diaconal action can draw wisdom from the statement of St Lawrence, the deacon in Rome, when challenged by the Emperor who claimed the riches of the church. He declared that the poor and their faith are "the true treasures of the Church."

7.3. Bilateral or multilateral diaconal work?

Interchurch aid was established by churches that were convinced that joint action would be more effective when addressing human need in the aftermath of wars. In addition, they wanted to testify to the unity of the church. Especially in times when warfare had caused hatred among peoples, they hoped that cooperation in offering aid would promote reconciliation and relationships of mutual trust.

Ecumenical *diakonia* in its modern form thus started as multilateral action. Ecumenical agencies, located in Geneva, were responsible for coordinating the work that was supported by resources brought together from different countries and churches, and for implementing it in cooperation with local churches in the areas where people in need were assisted.

Later, as church-based agencies began to build their professional capacities and were more involved in long-term development work, ecumenical *diakonia* changed its operational form from multilateral to bilateral action.

According to a survey undertaken by the WCC and ecumenical partners in 2003, church-related development agencies raise and spend USD 740 million every year. This does not include activities of individual mission societies, partnerships between congregations, etc. More than 50 percent of the sum was used for long-term development projects, 14 percent for disaster and emergency relief, and only 6 percent for advocacy. The WCC received only 3 percent of the funds raised; 4 percent went to ACT, and 6 percent to the LWF. The establishment of ACT Alliance has partly changed this picture in the sense that activities, especially related to emergency response, now are better coordinated. A survey from 2016 indicates that more funds now are spent on emergency response – reports from ACT members show that 18 percent of their total expenditure (USD 486 million) was used for this area of work. They spent USD 215.7 million (77 percent) on development work, and USD 144 million (5 percent) on advocacy. Expenditures on advocacy have apparently gone down, but the situation is rather that this concern is now being integrated in most forms of ecumenical *diakonia*.

The WCC introduced the practice of round tables as a mechanism to promote cooperation and communication and to mitigate the negative consequences of growing bilateralism. Some of these round tables continue to exist today. The formation of ACT Alliance has provided its members, churches and agencies both in the South and in the North, a structured framework for working together. Compared with former interchurch aid, when funds were channelled via Geneva, ACT Alliance plays the role of coordination and communication, while members continue to have the responsibility of fundraising and of implementing the work.

At the same time, a number of ecumenical entities expressing multilateral diaconal cooperation continue to play an important role. What follows are some examples: The Ecumenical Advocacy Alliance (WCC-EAA) is a global network of churches and related organizations committed to campaigning together on HIV and AIDS, food security and sustainable agriculture. EHAIA (Ecumenical HIV and AIDS Initiatives and Advocacy) promotes HIV competence among churches and work with theological institutions to integrate and mainstream HIV into theological curricula as well as addressing the root causes of the pandemic. EDAN (the Ecumenical Disability Advocates Network) supports the work of individuals, churches and church organizations concerned with issues affecting disabled people globally.

Advocates of a multilateral approach to ecumenical *diakonia* will point to the following strengths:

- Such an approach connects more actors. Joint action affirms the unity of churches engaged in ecumenical *diakonia*, envisaging equal space for all partners, not regarding their size or economic strength
- Its processes have a broader effect, shared learning reaches more people
- It seeks coordination and cooperation in the implementation of diaconal activities
- It promotes mutuality in relationships and enhances more balanced power relations
- It represents a wider horizon for action, which makes it easier to include public witness and advocacy.

Experience has shown that this multilateral approach also includes disadvantages:

- It may bring into being intermediate structures that makes the work less efficient, with time-consuming procedures
- Such structures will imply more costs for administration
- They may also lead to centralization and to concentration of power, thereby hampering efforts to promote downward accountability and transparency.

The advocates of bilateralism list the following advantages when applying this approach:

- Direct contact expedites efficient communication, which in turn facilitates active fundraising
- Institutional and personal relations are developed, and they may be strengthened by mutual visits and exchanging visions and experiences
- It provides closer and faster monitoring of project management
- It is easier to facilitate procedures that secure transparency and mutual accountability when implementing projects.

On the other hand, bilateralism also bring with it disadvantages:

- Asymmetry in power relations may contribute to maintaining the traditional division between "donors" and "recipients", which in the past often developed structures of dependency and attitudes of submission to goals, objectives and methods as defined by the donor agencies
- Dependency on one single partner may have dramatic consequences if this partner suddenly withdraws its support or presents new requirements for partnership
- In cases where a local church or a diaconal agency in the global South has established working relations with many partners in the North, this may require complex administrative competence, due to different regimes and different requirements established by their partners.

Some advantages may become disadvantages, it seems, and vice versa. Ecumenical *diakonia* should therefore seek to establish structures that take into account the advantages of both multi- and bilateral cooperation in a way that honours the concerns of the partners, both in the global South and North.

7.4. Cooperation and partnership in ecumenical *diakonia*

The invitation to the "International Consultation on the Relationship between Churches and Specialized Ministries," in Malawi, September 2014, referred to "rising tensions within the ecumenical movement between the specialized ministries and churches in different parts of the world." It expressed concern regarding "friction within the ecumenical family borne out of misunderstandings and a breakdown of meaningful communication."

There may be different causes behind these tensions. Some church leaders, especially in Africa, have expressed their perception of ACT Alliance in the first place as an alliance of agencies based in the global North, and that in their activities they would rather work with secular NGOs than with local churches. This gave churches and their leaders a feeling of being bypassed, and of having their diaconal competence and work ignored. They therefore raised the question if ACT Alliance in its practice was an expression of the ecumenical movement and of all churches belonging to it.

The specialized agencies on their side claim that their mandate is wider than the churches; their target group is the poor and marginalized, independent of religious affiliation. They also refer to the professional standards that they are obliged to follow when implementing projects, responding to requirements of governmental back-donors. Local churches will often lack the needed institutional capacity, they claim. For such reasons, agencies often prefer professional local NGOs as partners.

The Malawi consultation aimed to provide a safe space for constructive dialogue on these issues. It proposed actions points related to three areas: relations, values and foundations, and areas of cooperation. Regarding relationships, and in order to strengthen them, it recognized the need to:

- Be clear about our common calling, identities, mandates and the distinct roles of each. This is important in order appropriately to address misconceptions
- Develop and clearly communicate a joint understanding of the history and traditions of multilateralism and the sharing of resources in various contexts
- Acknowledge, value and uplift each other's gifts and resources (tangible and intangible assets)
- Clearly communicate the distinct ways in which each of our organizations functions, including their respective contexts and constraints, and provide clarity about expectations and relevance to our relationship as we engage in ecumenical *diakonia*.

Communicating and acknowledging the complementarity of roles and of resources stands out a key strategy for achieving better cooperation between churches and specialized ministries. All implied partners should recognize the rich mosaic of actors in *diakonia*, in which each part represents a unique quality and beauty, and where they together form a picture that none of them alone is able to present.

Among the strengths of local churches is their rootedness in the context and ability to read what happens according to local expectations, value systems and experiences. Chapter 6.6 gives an account of some of the diaconal assets that local churches can activate when cooperating with specialized agencies. One important asset is the ability to mobilize volunteers, which may contribute decisively to securing local participation and a sense of ownership when implementing projects. Another is the moral authority of church leaders, which allows them to address critical social and political issues and engage people to struggle for a better, future integrating public witness and advocacy in diaconal work.

Equally, churches should recognize the strengths and distinct assets of the specialized agencies. They bring insight from a broad field of practice and they have developed various kinds of competence, both related to theory and practice. Their knowledge includes ability to do social analysis, to elaborate clear plans of action, to identify appropriate methods of intervention, to monitor ongoing work, and to report and evaluate. In addition, they often belong to networks of professional agencies with their potential for sharing best practices and of engaging in joint action.

Ecumenical *diakonia* will clearly benefit from connecting the competence of local churches and specialized agencies. The message from the LWF "Global Consultation on *Diakonia*," held in 2008 in Addis Ababa, Ethiopia, claims that "new synergies and connectivity" will make churches, agencies and mission societies more effective in their work. It therefore called for "an attitude that embraces a 'culture of listening' to what is on the ground and builds on it in all forms of diaconal praxis," stating that this "is especially valid for actors within international *diakonia*."

Agencies should be encouraged to develop strategies for working more closely with churches. Professor Christoph Stückelberger, the founder of Globethics.net, claims that churches can often play a broader reaching role than single NGOs in transformation processes. He therefore recommends that agencies support processes that envisage strengthening democratic practices in the churches, developing responsible leadership, building competence, and creating corruption-free churches.

Equally, local churches should be encouraged to have patience with specialized agencies and contribute actively to processes of fostering new synergies and connectivity. That includes recognizing their distinct role and potential as diaconal agents, and looking for opportunities for connection and uniting efforts. In addition, churches should claim ownership of ecumenical *diakonia*, in particular of the ACT Alliance, which in its Founding Document states that its vision is to be "a global alliance" of WCC and LWF member churches and related organizations "committed to working ecumenically." Local churches have their share in the task of making this vision true and of strengthening ACT Alliance, so that it becomes what it is intended to be: an expression of the worldwide communion of churches and their diaconal mandate.

This requires continued reflection on the true nature of partnership within ecumenical *diakonia*, acknowledging that it builds on mutual relationships that exist before and after partners act together. It further requires recognition of the variety of gifts and assets that local churches and specialized agencies bring with them when working together, and the strength of complementarity this richness represents for diaconal work. Not least, it requires transparency and mutuality throughout the process of working together, from planning to implementation. Transparency includes sharing of information at all levels, as often as possible, not leaving to one of the partners to decide when and what to inform. Mutuality means balanced power relations, in the sense that it does not reduce one partner to being an instrument of others.

7.5. Working with secular organizations

The WCC Pilgrimage of Justice and Peace invites "all people of good will" to join. This corresponds to a long tradition within *diakonia*, of seeking support from and cooperation with individuals and organizations outside the church's own constituency, and with governments. Based on the view that all humans carry the image of God, *diakonia* is convinced that all are enabled to be God's co-workers promoting the common good and a dignified life for all. The notion of "people of good will" should not be interpreted as if it refers to morally superior individuals. All are called to be "people of good will." Unfortunately, not all opt to follow this calling, which should not stop the church from inviting them to join in.

Civil society provides new arenas for cooperation, and also for diaconal agents to build strategic alliances with others, including secular organizations. This is of paramount importance in times when many civil social organizations and NGOs face shrinking political and operational space in their daily work on the ground. Diaconal actors are challenged to identify strategic platforms and networks in order to influence social processes that secure human rights and welfare for all.

Can diaconal agents work with any secular organization? This depends on the context and on the nature of cooperation. In principle, diaconal actors should be ready to work with every person and organization "of good will". In practice, however, it will be necessary to establish some criteria in order to discern the understanding of "good will" that an organization stands for. One such criterion would be its attitude and practice regarding human rights, another could be its way of promoting values and ideals, a third its structure and ways of exercising power.

Most often, diaconal agencies prefer to work together with like-minded organizations, whether they are faith-based or secular. It is possible that this practice has been too cautious, with the consequence that *diakonia* does not assume a sufficiently bold role as an agent of change in civil society. Popular movements, human rights groups, workers' unions, organizations representing minorities or marginalized groups – these are some examples of strategic partners when diaconal agents engage in public witness and advocacy,

Diaconal agents do not work with secular organizations with the aim of evangelizing them. Their secular identity requires recognition in the same way that faith-based organizations expect their distinctive identity to be respected. Nor is the aim to Christianize public space. Our aim as Christians is "to make all areas within the public space freely accessible to everyone, without distinction of any kind, such as colour, caste, religion and gender." This view is based on the theological understanding that God's action in relation to creation cannot be limited to the church nor the action of Christians. God's care for human beings manifests itself through the establishment of social, political and juridical orders, and of responsible leadership that defends human dignity and promotes justice and peace. Christians are called to active citizenship, and to engage in activities that enhance equal access to common goods, safety for all, especially for the vulnerable, and meaningful participation by and interaction among all groups in society. These are all key issues on the agenda of ecumenical *diakonia*, and they challenge diaconal agents to work with "all people of good will," which includes looking for opportunities for working together with secular organizations.

7.6. Diapraxis – working with people of other faiths

Today religion is increasingly recognized as an important social and political factor, and in matters related to development work. Some scholars describe "the return of religion" as a process of de-privatization in which religious leaders commit themselves to contribute to the common welfare, others point to the necessity of including religious actors in civil society and in processes of building democracy in "post-secular society."

The role of religion and religious leaders in development is disputed. Some regard them as reactionary forces that resist social change and that in certain situations provide fuel for social and political conflicts. Others point to their importance for mobilizing people for responsible social action, and for promoting ethical discernment, with the consequence that religious actors may play a key role in working for reconciliation, justice and peace.

It is evident that development agents cannot ignore religion in their work. Religious literacy must be a part of their professional competence. This is especially important for FBOs and ecumenical *diakonia*, which should take a leading role in engaging people of faith in their work, and in working with religious leaders in processes of promoting the common good. In contexts of religious mistrust and tension, diaconal agents can provide safe space for joint action and reflection and thus initiate processes of reconciliation and transformation.

Diapraxis is a method of providing such safe space for people of different faiths, of meeting and doing things together, with the purpose of overcoming prejudices and constructing mutual trust. The term "*diapraxis*" was proposed by the Danish theologian Lissi Rasmussen, who had observed that Christians and Muslims developed new relations of co-existence when engaged in activities of common interest. As a method, it envisages involving ordinary people at local level, in practice, it is a form of citizenship training, of empowering people to work with people across religious and social boundaries.

The ecumenical movement, and in particular the WCC, has a long history of interreligious dialogue. *Diapraxis* adds qualities to this tradition by focusing on social issues that equally challenge people of different faiths and by claiming the advantage of joint action.

Agents of ecumenical *diakonia* are already involved in *diapraxis*, and many ACT Alliance members work in partnership with Muslim aid organizations, in particular in the Middle East. In 2014, the United Nations High Commissioner for Refugees (UNHCR), the Lutheran World Federation (LWF) and Islamic Relief Worldwide (IRW) signed a memorandum of understanding to cooperate in humanitarian work. This was the first official cooperation between a global Christian and a global Islamic humanitarian organization, and it gives a clear message of the how people of different faiths can join forces based on shared visions and values. This view is clearly expressed in the ACT Alliance document *The Changing Development Paradigm*, stating that "the changing development paradigm presents new opportunities for working in concrete ways, including in advocacy, between and across faith lines. ACT recognizes the importance of interreligious challenges and opportunities related to humanitarian and development work."

Ecumenical and diaconal actors have taken several initiatives in order to follow through on this. They have participated in discussions in the UNCHR on the role of faith in protection of refugees, asylum seekers, and displaced and uprooted persons. The WCC has played an active role in the faith-based framework "Ending Extreme Poverty: A Spiritual and Moral Imperative" that was launched in 2015 by over 40 global religious and FBO leaders. Its main objective is to end extreme poverty by 2030, relating to the SDGs as a shared platform and commitment.

It remains a challenge to connect these initiatives at the international level to concrete diaconal action at the local level. The commitment to generate and be guided by evidence, to advocate by engaging the moral authority of religious leaders and their constituencies, and to foster more effective collaboration between religious and other development actors will then make a difference and contribute to achieving the goal of ending extreme poverty.

7.7. Advocacy – prophetic *diakonia*

Advocacy is an integral part of diaconal work. It cannot be limited to a possible extra concern depending on given circumstances. The distinct identity of *diakonia*, its biblical roots and Christian vocation, compels ecumenical *diakonia* to be prophetic, to side with the poor and marginalized, to unmask systemic injustice and promote human dignity, justice and peace. The ecumenical movement, together with churches and diaconal agents, has increasingly committed itself to this task; what follows is one example of formulating this mandate:

> Advocacy is a prophetic activity of the churches, in which we accompany and support our sisters and brothers who struggle mightily for justice and peace in the context of injustice and violence against fellow human beings and the rest of creation. Advocacy involves speaking up for those who are silenced in their efforts to rectify injustice. It demands our engagement with the issues and initiatives of those who struggle for life, justice, equity, rights, and peace. Advocacy is a mission activity of the church in the world. It is one way in which the church participates in the ongoing *missio dei.*

The pursuit of justice and peace has been essential part of the life and calling of the WCC since its foundation in 1948, as it has been for member churches and ecumenical partners, which has been expressed in many programmes and engagements throughout its history, as described in chapter 5. The Ecumenical Advocacy Alliance (EAA), established in 2000 and now an ecumenical initiative within the WCC, has continued to support churches and partners in their advocacy work, focusing on campaigns related to HIV and AIDS, food security and sustainable agriculture.

Advocacy for just peace has been another important area of ecumenical action. The WCC Decade to Overcome Violence (2001–2010) addressed the need to replace violence with a culture of peace. It concluded with an "Ecumenical Call for Just Peace," which motivated the Busan assembly in 2013 to adopt a statement on "The Way of Just Peace," affirming the WCC as convener and facilitator for global ecumenical peace and advocacy work, based on the conviction that:

> Churches can help build cultures of peace by learning to prevent and transform conflicts. In this way they may empower people on the margins of society, enable both women and men to be peacemakers, support non-violent movements for justice and human rights, support those who are persecuted for their refusal to bear arms for reasons of conscience, as well as offer support to those who have suffered in armed conflicts, and give peace education its rightful place in churches and schools.

The concept of just peace is rooted in the self-understanding of the churches, the hope of spiritual transformation and the call to seek justice and peace for all. It builds on the concept of social justice, which confronts privilege; economic justice, which confronts wealth; ecological justice, which confronts irresponsible consumption; and political justice, which confronts abuse of power.

Peacebuilding, conflict transformation and advocacy for a just peace continue to be priority tasks that challenge prophetic *diakonia* to engage in social issues. Key themes for advocacy are human rights and human security, in particular for women and children in contexts of social and political conflicts, accountability in peacebuilding and the rule of law.

7.8 Abuse within diaconal institutions

Physical (including sexual) and emotional abuse of both adults and children is entirely contrary to the standards of the gospel. High profile court cases have shown both clergy and diaconal workers being prosecuted and convicted. Above all, the harm caused to the victims is utterly reprehensible.

Cases of abuse severely affected confidence in diaconal institutions, development agencies and other organisations. Much good diaconal work can be undermined or even destroyed by the actions of a malevolent individual or undermined by inadequate safeguards at an institutional level. Payment of compensation to victims can never make up for the harm caused, while such payments can also be financial ruinous to a diaconal organisation.

Jesus' call for "life in all its fullness" (John 10:10) challenges all diaconal institutions to prevent abuse, irrespective of reputational harm (which is often exacerbated once discovered and reported on by the media). Ecumenical *diakonia* must involve learning from different contexts globally. The sharing of good practices internationally, such as effective child protection safeguarding measures and professional training to spot signs of inappropriate conduct, may be of critical importance in helping to prevent abuse.

7.9. Summary

This chapter has given an account of some of the challenges that face ecumenical *diakonia* in today's world. Some challenges relate to the changing landscape of development aid, of cuts in public funding due to growing scepticism about the effectiveness of aid, which obliges agencies of ecumenical *diakonia* to develop new innovative practices for funding their work. It also urges them to develop new strategies for coordination and cooperation, renewing the vision of ecumenical sharing of resources.

The analysis of the changing landscape underscores the social and political dimension when engaged in work for the common welfare, justice and peace. In many places such engagement is hindered due to shrinking public space and political measures that are intended to limit the role of civil society, in particular rights-based actors. This challenges ecumenical *diakonia* to engage in building networks and in establishing strategic alliances, partnering with local churches, with secular organizations, and with people of other faiths. In all cases, whether through aid work or diaconal institutions, physical or emotional abuse is always unacceptable and effective safeguarding measures must be put in place to prevent this.

These challenges urge ecumenical *diakonia* to affirm its nature as a rights-based actor, and to develop strategies that strengthen its prophetic role in public witness and advocacy as integral dimensions of diaconal action.

CHAPTER 8

Ecumenical *Diakonia* in a confessional context

Photo: Paul Jeffrey/Life on Earth

8.1. Introduction

This chapter attempts to discern ecumenical *diakonia* through different confessional contexts, showing similarities and dissimilarities in the approach to *diakonia* throughout Christianity. In attempting to show diversity, Christians of differing traditions may be able to discern and develop areas of communality. Through humility, a quest for mutual enrichment and a dependence of the grace of God, Christians of different traditions, cultures and backgrounds can mutually contribute to a building of a truly ecumenical *diakonia.*

8.2. An Orthodox understanding of Ecumenical *Diakonia*

Christian "*diakonia*" is rooted in the gospel teaching according to which the love of God and the neighbour are a direct consequence of faith. The diaconal mission of the church and the duty of each of its members to serve are intimately bound up with the very notion of the church, and stem from the example of the sacrifice of our Lord Himself, our High Priest, who, in accordance with the Father's will "did not come to be served but to serve and to give up his life as a ransom for many" (Matt. 20:28). The church inherited the main body of its teachings on assisting the poor from the Old Testament, preserving these doctrines and giving them a new context in the light of the example of its founder, Jesus Christ, who "came into the world not to be served but to serve" (Mark 10:45). The apostles continued to live in accordance with Jesus' teachings, "devoting themselves to the fellowship, to the breaking of bread and to prayer" (Acts 2:42).

According to the Acts of the Apostles (Chapter 6), the deacons were the first to be called to service in the name of Christ, which meant that this "*diakonia*" also came to be written into the duties of the other levels of the priesthood. It was the deacon's task to be "the hands of the bishop" under its direction, while the priests were responsible for helping the bishop to look after and teach the flock of Christian people.

"Witness, teaching and *diakonia*" (service) were inseparable in the early church. The importance of "*diakonia*" was also acknowledged in the canons of the undivided church, such as the First Ecumenical Council of Nicaea (325). The church is sent to the world not only to preach and to save humankind but also to establish communities through which to serve the world in its material and spiritual needs. In this sense, the act of *diakonia* is equivalent to the fulfilment of the duty of the churches to help suffering people outside their membership, or to provide answers to the problems and concerns of humankind in economic, political, personal or family life. Through this kind of *diakonia,* churches enter into the world and render their witness to their Lord, evident, vivid and realistically present in practice. Without this action, a church would seem to deprived of the fundamental expression of its inner life.

This *diakonia* is neither a good moral act springing from the goodwill of a regenerated Christian, nor an expression of compassion for the misery of humankind outside the church. The care of the churches for the world is not a vehicle for an uneducated humankind. The help of the churches are not primarily as philanthropic institutions. The act of *diakonia* of the churches is ecclesial, namely it is the overflowing of the grace which binds and moves their inner life in a total fellowship. In other words, *diakonia* to the world is the echo in the world of the word of God already accomplished in the charismatic church. It is the expression of the "*ergon theou*" (the work of God) in his Holy Spirit through the "*parergon*" (the work made or produced) of humankind within the world and for the world. *Diakonia* is the other voice of the truth made and given by God to humankind as communion/koinonia. It is the act which springs out of the continuously represented event in the church.

Orthodox *diakonia* also flows from the divine liturgy in which our offerings are sanctified by Christ's offering and which requires our active "cooperation" (*synergeia*) with God in the exercise of our free will which is rooted in our common "agreement" (*symphonia*) (Matt. 18:19). *Diakonia* is therefore an expression of the unity of the church as the body of Christ. In the same way each local celebration of the eucharist is complete and universal, involving the whole of creation, and is offered for the material and spiritual needs of the whole world.

8.3. A Lutheran understanding of Ecumenical *Diakonia*

Lutheran churches emphasize that *diakonia* belongs to the church's being and identity. *Diakonia* is unfolded in every Christian's life, as a call to serve God, your fellow human beings and act as stewards of God's creation. *Diakonia* intrinsically belongs to the life of Christian congregations and communities and implies service to the local communities and wider societies. In many countries, diaconal institutions, such as hospitals, schools, and orphanages, are established and are a part of the Lutheran Church's diaconal presence in different contexts. In some countries these diaconal institutions take part in public health- and welfare-services. Finally, international diaconal organisations, offering emergency services and development aid, are a part of Lutheran ecumenical *diakonia*, and thus inseparable from the church in its essence.

Within Lutheran theology, one emphasizes that human salvation and justification before God, *coram Deo*, relies solely on Christ and not on human deeds and achievements. At the same time, the Lutheran confessions emphasise that good deeds belong to all Christian life, as a part of the Christian's sanctification and of all Christian life towards humanity, *coram hominibus*.

Hence, *diakonia* is an intrinsic part of the church's and of every congregation's life, based on God's call to be church *in* the world, not apart from the world, and to live this call in the different contexts where the church exits. Lutheran theology strongly emphasises that Christians are not only Christians within the church's worship and faith, or "God's realm", but they are called to live as responsible citizens in their respective societies, the so-called "worldly realm". Good deeds, service to the world, *diakonia*, are, according to Lutheran theology, not only a practice within the Christian community, but, based on creation theology, belonging to the world. Christians are appealed to, to serve with all people of good will for the sake of humanity, not for the sake of salvation. Lutheran theology also emphasizes that *diakonia* should never be an instrument of conversion, but has its own value and contributes to the witness about the good news in Christ.

The Lutheran World Federation emphasises *diakonia* as an intrinsic part of Lutheran ecclesiology and belonging to God's mission, the *missio Dei*: LWF member churches are called to take part in God's mission, which includes proclaiming Christ's gospel, serving the vulnerable (*diakonia*), and advocating for them.[2] *Diakonia* starts with knowledge of the context, the mapping of needs and assets, and a profound conviction that serving the poor and marginalised and serving God are inseparable. In order to serve in the world through *diakonia*, churches need to seek knowledge not only on theology, but in many different theoretical and practical fields, also from empirical studies, as an interdisciplinary endeavour. Diaconal theory and diaconal action mutually rely on each other, and the goal of diaconal sciences is to improve diaconal practice.

Many Lutheran churches employ trained deacons for the specific task of diaconal work in their congregations, and, in many churches, deacons are consecrated or ordained for service within the order of the diaconate.

Much of today's *diakonia* in Lutheran churches relates to the diaconal revival in the 18th century in Europe. This revival brought a renewed focus on *diakonia* and diaconal ministry and was strongly inspired by the earlier pietistic revivalist movement and partly in opposition to established church hierarchies, as a low-church movement. During this revival, it was emphasized that the church should revitalise its diaconal ministry, based on what was perceived as a biblical and early church understanding of *diakonia* as humble service to the needy.

2. See: https://www.lutheranworld.org/content/capacity-diakonia

Recent developments within diaconal sciences emphasize that there has been a paradigm shift within the understanding of *diakonia* from humble service, to *diakonia* as a bridge-building and empowering ministry of the church's "go-between" service in the world.

Some of the biggest Lutheran churches in the world, like the Evangelical Mekane Yesu Church in Ethiopia, have focused on the need to define the mission of the church as holistic ministry, where proclamation and service are interconnected and inseparable. This became a useful reminder for all Lutheran churches to avoid departmentalisation and a disconnection of the church's service, in for example development departments, from the regular church life in congregations.

8.4. A Reformed understanding of Ecumenical *Diakonia*

For the majority of the churches which form part the wider "Reformed" family, including many United and Uniting churches, to be Reformed is to be ecumenical. On the one hand they understand their mission and vocation as an integral part of the one ecumenical movement and Christ's universal church, and on the other hand they see *diakonia*, (love and transformative service of neighbour) as an inseparable part of God's mission and the churches' life and witness. It is not surprising that the Reformed family have played a major role in the shaping and living out of ecumenical *diakonia* as it is understood and practiced within the WCC and wider ecumenical circles.

From the time of the Reformation, a reinvigorated reading of scripture placed *diakonia* and the diaconate within the four essential offices of Christian ministry. The focus was equally on the institutional leadership in the administration of benevolence and in the direct and personal acts of service to the impoverished and suffering. For the Calvinist, both remain a permanent part of the churches' work, while the Zwingli-led stream saw that the civil authorities could and should assume responsibility for social *diakonia*. In all cases, institutional responsibility was never seen as replacing individual duty. The deacon had a responsibility to bring social responsibility, based on a reading of scripture, to the whole church. Here the Reformed contribution led to the continual focus on both individual and institutional service and, by extension, emphasis on both charity and justice. The Reformed understanding of God's mission insisted through its roots in both Old Testament and New Testament reading of scripture that loving compassion and transformative justice were inseparable.

In their local practice and contribution to ecumenical thinking, Reformed, United and Uniting churches, with others, helped shaped WCC consultations and declarations, such as the 1986 Larnaca consultation on *diakonia*. This enriched the concept to fully embrace the relationship between *diakonia* and development for justice, human rights and dignity, *diakonia* and peace, and *diakonia* and interreligious cooperation. The El Escorial Consultation on ecumenical resource sharing in 1987 also articulated the implications of prophetic *diakonia* as the practice of transformative justice that sought to overturn asymmetrical power relations within the ecumenical family.

The involvement of the wider Reformed family in the global struggles for justice, as fundamental to faith in God, was sharpened through the churches' role in combatting racism and overturning Apartheid, and in the struggle for economic and ecological justice in the face of the ravages of market driven capitalism. These struggles, largely led by churches from the global South, brought the articulation of the Belhar and Accra confessions, which inspire and provide a biblical and theological frame for the relationship between *diakonia* and justice as inseparable and unshakeable elements of obedience to God and faithfulness to the gospel of Jesus Christ. This in turn shaped the perspectives of many within the reformed community to embrace ecumenical *diakonia* as focused on systemic and structural transformation, as well as attention to integral human development and direct acts of service, love and compassion. Its character, as practised by churches, is to be contextual, compassionate, reconciling, transformative, justice-seeking and prophetic.

8.5. An Anglican understanding of Ecumenical *Diakonia*

The Five Marks of Mission, defined at the Anglican Consultative Council in 1984, aims to be a summary of what all mission is about, because it is based on Jesus' own summary of his mission:

1. To proclaim the good news of the Kingdom
2. To teach, baptise and nurture new believers
3. To respond to human need by loving service
4. To transform unjust structures of society, to challenge violence of every kind and pursue peace and reconciliation
5. To strive to safeguard the integrity of creation, and sustain and renew the life of the earth.

The third of these is clearly identified with *diakonia*. Ecumenical commitment is demonstrated by practices described in documents such as "To Love and Serve the Lord – *Diakonia* in the Life of the Church" (2012) and the Jerusalem Report of the Anglican–Lutheran International Commission (ALIC III). This document acknowledged, inter alia, that:

- *Diakonia* is deeply rooted in Scripture, an essential part of discipleship and Christian identity (Luke 4:18–19) Diaconal ministry is grounded in worship, in the sacraments of Baptism and Holy Communion, and lived out in discipleship. Through its ministry of *diakonia* the church offers a foretaste of God's kingdom
- *Diakonia* is a ministry that belongs to every believer because it is rooted in the apostolic commission that all receive in Baptism
- *Diakonia* takes the forms of prophetic witness, advocacy and empowering action, as well as compassionate care
- *Diakonia* means not only giving aid, but also confronting the concentration of power and wealth which is the cause of poverty. A diaconal church accompanies, bolsters and empowers the economically weak and vulnerable; with them a diaconal church resists abusive manoeuvres that deprive them of their basic human rights, including economic, social and cultural rights
- *Diakonia* is political in as far as it exposes structural injustice that affects people due to sex/gender, class, geography, religion and ethnic origin. The church empowers the voiceless to speak and speaks in solidarity with and for them when they cannot.

The injunctions of King Henry VIII of England in 1536 included an instruction that a poor chest should be established in every English parish. Subsequently, the 1550 ordinal retained the three-fold structure in the ordained ministry, providing for the ordering of deacons as well as priests and bishops. Accordingly, all priests and bishops are also deacons. There are also orders of permanent deacons and deaconesses, as well as pastoral care offered by lay people.

The industrial revolution in England in the late 18th and into the 19th century lead to calls for alleviation of urban poverty and destitution. Examples of responses include the creation of the Church Army in 1882, which now operates across many Provinces of the Anglican Communion, and the creation of orders of Deaconesses – such as the Anglican Deaconess Ministries (ADM) of Australia in 1891. The Deaconess orders were initially largely modelled on German practice.

Practice across the Anglican Communion varies according to need. Anglican churches and their agencies continue to be major providers of care. Examples include involvement in the campaign to eradicate Malaria from Zambia, hospitals in Nigeria and elsewhere, HIV and AIDS projects and many other projects. The Church of North India and Church of South India, created from ecumenical unions, are both members of the Anglican Communion. The Church of South India alone has more than 100 hospitals. The creation of the National Health Service in the UK in 1948 has reduced the scope for diaconal work in healthcare within the UK, yet Anglican churches continue to operate diaconal services such as care homes for the elderly. A key area of work for Anglican churches is raising awareness of the prevalence of gender-based and domestic violence, and the potential of churches to work towards its elimination, creating safe spaces, and caring for survivors of violence.

8.6. A Methodist understanding of Ecumenical *Diakonia*

Methodism started in the 18th century, with a revival movement in the Church of England led by John Wesley (1703–1791), his brother Charles (1707–1788) and others. The Wesleys were convinced that God's saving love is meant for all and that those who are saved by grace through faith will be transformed to live a holy life by the means of grace. When speaking of the means of grace, John

Wesley not only referred to the works of piety such as worship and prayer. He also identified the works of mercy as the means through which we receive God's grace. Richard Heitzenrater, in his book "The Poor and the People Called Methodists," characterised Wesley's emphasis to love God and neighbours as such:

(i) Wesley communalized the program of assistance. His people were expected to help each other in the community of faith

(ii) Wesley broadened the concept of community to include everyone, from the top to the bottom of the economic scale. No longer was there an us-and-them dichotomy

(iii) Wesley reclassified the concept of poverty. He viewed deprivation in terms of relative needs based on a sliding scale (superfluities, conveniences, necessities, extremities) with each level defined in terms of specific contexts

(iv) Wesley universalized the concept of charity, so that no one was exempt from responsibility for assisting the needy

(v) Wesley theologized the motivation for charitable activities. His basic goal in this regard was for Methodists to imitate the life of Christ. Everyone in every level of society was a child of God and deserved to be treated as such.

Today, about 80 Methodist, Wesleyan and United or Uniting Churches with a constituency of approximately 80 million people belong to the World Methodist Council. They confess in the Social Affirmation of the World Methodist Council: "We commit ourselves individually and as a community to the way of Christ; to take up the cross; to seek abundant life for all humanity; to struggle for peace with justice and freedom; to risk ourselves in faith, hope, and love, praying that God's kingdom may come." Methodist agencies have also been active in engaging with the UN Sustainable Development Goals, including with local churches and ecumenical partners.

Diaconal ministry is the ministry of all God's people. In the document "The Diaconal Plan of the United Methodist Church (UMC) in Norway" the call is expressed as such: *"Care of others is a call and responsibility for all believers through their baptism and their faith in Christ. Diaconal service, in other words, is not to be seen as a duty, but as a foundation for the Church and the individual believer. Diaconal engagement is a defining characteristic by which the Church identifies itself as the Church."*

Most churches in the Methodist tradition ordain deacons. Some, such as the Methodist Church in Great Britain, the Methodist Church in Southern Africa or the United Methodist Church, form a diaconal order "separate and distinct, though complementary" to the order of the presbyters or elders.

There are Methodist schools, hospitals, nursing homes for elderly people, and numerous kinds of diaconal institutions. Many are legally separated from the churches, but there are links, and in many countries these institutions function like outreach posts of churches.

Methodists and Wesleyans are called to live out their Wesleyan theology, which encourages them strive for personal and social holiness and to encounter Christ as they feed the hungry, heal the sick, work with (not for) the poor and care for the creation. John Wesley formulated his expectation towards the people called Methodists in the three-part formula of the General Rules: "It is therefore expected of all who continue therein that they should continue to evidence their desire of salvation, *"First: By doing no harm, by avoiding evil of every kind . . . ; Secondly: By . . . doing good of every possible sort, and, as far as possible, to all . . .; Thirdly: By attending upon all the ordinances of God"*. The order is not by chance: doing no harm and doing good is as important as prayer, worship and sacraments. Methodists ought to be known for *"faith working through love"* (Galatians 5: 6).

8.7. A Pentecostal understanding of Ecumenical *Diakonia*

Pentecostalism is a young and fast-growing movement within Christianity. There is enormous diversity within Pentecostal understandings and practices towards *diakonia*. This also reflects great diversity within the Pentecostal movement. In general, the term *diakonia* would rarely be used, but many Pentecostal Christians are involved with care programmes and relief work.

The Pentecostal World Fellowship was created in 1947, with its International Office in Kuala Lumpur, Malaysia. It has 61 representative churches, representing 33 countries. Its stated objectives include:

- SPEAK to governments and nations when and where social justice and religious rights are compromised and/or violated for the sake of the gospel
- TO FOSTER WORLD MISSIONS AND TO SUPPORT humanitarian efforts and where possible, to provide relief aid.

Sections 8 and 9 of the Pentecostal World Fellowship Statement of Faith state:

8. We believe in the church of Jesus Christ and in the unity of believers.
9. We believe in the practical application of the Christian faith in every day experience and in the need to minister to people in every area of life, which includes not only the spiritual but also the social, political and physical.

Pentecostal and charismatic churches often place emphasis on the healing power of God through prayer, yet usually in conjunction with (rather than in opposition to) conventional medical care. Pentecostal churches include a variety of groupings, including Assemblies of God. Reflecting diversity within Pentecostalism, not all Pentecostal churches are part of the Pentecostal World Fellowship. Some, but not all, challenge political and economic structures which cause poverty and injustice.

8.8. A Baptist understanding of Ecumenical *Diakonia*

Baptist churches worldwide place great emphasis on the calling of all – laity and clergy – to embrace a life of costly discipleship. The term *diakonia* is little used, but witness and service is a Baptist priority. This takes different forms, depending upon culture and context, but witness and service is core to the mission, identity and calling of all congregations which denominate as Baptist. In the UK, where Baptist witness has some of its earliest roots, 2000 congregations seek – under the guidance of Christ – to live a life of witness and service. The Baptist World Alliance (BWA) was created in 1905 and serves as a forum for collaboration. The BWA includes a development agency Baptist World Aid.

Some ministers in the Baptist tradition are ordained into specialised diaconal ministries – such as chaplains in hospitals, schools and workplace settings – but in general the church's diaconal ministry is organised within local congregations and is undertaken by the laity in a voluntary capacity, giving freely of their time and expertise. The term deacon is very familiar to all Baptist congregations. An elected diaconate, made up of minister and lay leaders, normally oversees the practical running of a local church. Typically, the diaconal work of local Baptist churches involves reaching out and caring for those on the margins of society: those who have no work or home; who suffer mental health problems; or who are abused and excluded on grounds of disability, race, or gender. Diaconal work undertaken by Baptists does not normally involve overseeing, managing or delivering state-funded social welfare services. The diaconal work undertaken is better described as complimentary to state-run welfare services. There is sometimes an element of partnership between Baptist churches and secular authorities, such as when they undertake work which is part funded or supported by the state, but most of these projects and programmes are very time limited.

In many countries, Baptist congregations have expansive multi-purpose buildings, built with the gifts of the members and strategically placed in towns and cities. These buildings are ideally situated to become havens of hospitality. Many churches share these building assets on a daily basis, by opening their doors to marginalised people, extending friendship to the stranger, and countering the isolation and destitution faced by many, with generous hospitality and safe space. In the winter season in Europe and North America, when the homeless sleep on the streets in zero temperatures, these same churches galvanize teams of volunteers to provide safe over-night shelter.

In certain situations, where freedom is denied or justice ignored, Baptists have historically felt compelled to engage in prophetic *diakonia*. In the 19th century, the conscience of Baptists was stirred to join the campaign for the abolition of slavery. Similarly, today, as the plight of refugees and victims of human trafficking worsens, a world-wide network of Baptist churches is attempting to link practical actions of solidarity with strategic networking and advocacy. Prophetic *diakonia* envisions salvation in holistic terms, combining practical and political actions by meeting victims' basic needs and at the same time, enabling victims to find their voice and addressing the roots of injustice.

8.9. A Roman Catholic understanding of Ecumenical *Diakonia*

"The Church's deepest nature is expressed in her threefold responsibility: of proclaiming the word of God *(kerygma-martyria)*, celebrating the sacraments *(leitourgia)* and exercising the ministry of charity (*diakonia*). These duties presuppose each other and are inseparable" (Benedict XVI, Encyclical *Letter Deus Caritas Est*, 25).

Throughout the centuries, the Catholic Church cared for the destitute through numerous parochial and diocesan works, as well as the engagement of religious orders, congregations and charity institutions. The history of the Catholic *missio ad gentes*, from the 16th century onward, shows how *diakonia* has been a significant element in providing credibility to the Church's message of love. At the same time, competition between Catholics and other Christian groups for new converts often turned the service of charity into a means of proselytizing, a counter-testimony of Christ's prayer "that they may all be one" (John 17:21).

Major ecclesiological developments came about with the Second Ecumenical Vatican Council (1962-1965) that emphasized the paramount importance of dialogue, including ecumenical dialogue and cooperation between the Catholic Church and all Christian churches and ecclesial communities. The Council's decree on ecumenism articulated the Catholic vision on ecumenical *diakonia* as follows: *"Before the whole world let all Christians confess their faith in the triune God... In these days when cooperation in social matters is so widespread, all without exception are called to work together, with much greater reason all those who believe in God, but most of all, all Christians in that they bear the name of Christ. Cooperation among Christians vividly expresses the relationship which in fact already unites them, and it sets in clearer relief the features of Christ the Servant. This cooperation, which has already begun in many countries, should be developed more and more, particularly in regions where a social and technical evolution is taking place be it in a just evaluation of the dignity of the human person, the establishment of the blessings of peace, the application of Gospel principles to social life, the advancement of the arts and sciences in a truly Christian spirit, or also in the use of various remedies to relieve the afflictions of our times such as famine and natural disasters, illiteracy and poverty, housing shortage and the unequal distribution of wealth. All believers in Christ can, through this cooperation, be led to acquire a better knowledge and appreciation of one another, and so pave the way to Christian unity"* (Second Vatican Council, Decree *Unitatis Redintegratio*, 12).

Progressively, the notion and the concrete experience of ecumenical and interreligious dialogue helped the evolution of Catholic missiology towards the rejection of proselytizing as a means of evangelization.

Based on the teaching of the Council, the Catholic Church better understood the importance of its commitment to a society that upholds the principles of peace, justice and the care for the needy and the neglected. The entire corpus of Catholic social teaching is currently summarized in the Compendium of the Social Doctrine of the Church (2004).

At the end of the Council in 1967, Pope Paul VI restored the ordained ministry of permanent diaconate, including among the tasks of deacons: "to carry out, in the name of the hierarchy, the duties of charity and of administration as well as works of social assistance" (Paul VI, *Motu Proprio Sacrum Diaconatus Ordinem*, 21). The Holy See also encouraged the development of an international network of Catholic organizations dedicated to charity services, in the name and under the supervision of the bishops and national episcopal conferences. The Caritas network was tasked with carrying out the church's solicitude for the poor and vulnerable at the parish, diocesan, national and international level. Today, the Caritas Internationalis confederation has 168 national members working in more than 200 countries and territories throughout the world. In recent years, the Holy See has reaffirmed the bishops' responsibility in leading charity works in their particular churches (cf. Benedict XVI, *Motu Proprio Intima Ecclesiae Natura*). This further strengthened the ties between local bishops, their national Caritas and all other Catholic institutions doing charity work.

As the official Catholic institution tasked to help those in need, Caritas actively promotes ecumenical *diakonia* at all levels of the Confederation. A particularly significant moment in this journey was on the 31st October 2016 – during Pope Francis' visit to Sweden for the commemoration of the 500 years of the Reformation – when Caritas Internationalis and the Lutheran World Federation's World Service signed a global declaration of intent to strengthen their worldwide cooperation to uphold human dignity and care for creation.

Pope Francis has championed the idea that, while the theological obstacles towards the unity of all Christians are deep and require time and efforts to be resolved, true ecumenical unity is already possible and often real in two realms: the "ecumenism of blood" and the "ecumenism of charity". In June 2018, Pope Francis visited the offices of the World Council of Churches in Geneva and, in his address, laid out his vision to the members of the Central Committee of the World Council of Churches:

> "I would also note that the work of our Christian communities is rightly defined by the word *diakonia*. It is our way of following the Master who came 'not to be served but to serve' (Mk 10:45). (. . .) The credibility of the Gospel is put to the test by the way Christians respond to the cry of all those, in every part of the world, who suffer unjustly from the baleful spread of an exclusion that, by generating poverty, foments conflicts. (. . .) Let us see what we can do concretely, rather than grow discouraged about what we cannot. Let us also look to our many brothers and sisters in various parts of the world, particularly in the Middle East, who suffer because they are Christians. Let us draw close to them. May we never forget that our ecumenical journey is preceded and accompanied by an ecumenism already realized, the ecumenism of blood, which urges us to go forward. Let us encourage one another to overcome the temptation to absolutize certain cultural paradigms and get caught up in partisan interests. Let us help men and women of good will to grow in concern for events and situations that affect a great part of humanity but seldom make it to the front page. We cannot look the other way. It is problematic when Christians appear indifferent towards those in need. Even more troubling is the conviction on the part of some, who consider their own blessings clear signs of God's predilection rather than a summons to responsible service of the human family and the protection of creation. The Lord, the Good Samaritan of mankind (cf. Lk 10:29-37), will examine us on our love for our neighbour, for each of our neighbours (cf. Mt 25:31-46). So let us ask ourselves: What can we do together? If a particular form of service is possible, why not plan and carry it out together, and thus start to experience a more intense fraternity in the exercise of concrete charity?"[3]

8.10. African instituted churches' understanding of Ecumenical *Diakonia*

The African Independent Churches (AIC), who form the membership of the Organisation of African Instituted Churches (OAIC), are movements that were founded during the latter part of the 19th century and the early 20th century. This was a time when Africa was going through rapid socio-political and economic change which resulted in cultural, political and economic domination. The founders of the AICs decided to read the scriptures in a different way which enabled them to find Christ the Liberator who did not agree with the forms of Christianity that was being propagated. These were and remain multiple visions from the grassroots and are a major motivating factor for the AICs' participation in society.

For the OAIC, it is these visions that come into play in relation to ending poverty by 2030. These AIC visions, and the efforts from multiple actors who are working for abundance of life, interact with an environment where: wanton accumulation of wealth results in gross economic inequalities; nationalism and ethnicity are becoming mobilising bases for the exclusion of the other; gender and generational inequalities make poverty more complex; there is ecological disharmony caused by unstainable production and consumption patterns; the focus is on security rather than peace. Even the efforts to deal with poverty and other issues that undermine the dignity of people and the integrity of creation are yet to rise beyond the framework of political and economic patronage. This is what motivates the OAIC to call for a liberative *diakonia*.

3. Ecumenical Pilgrimage of His Holiness Francis to Geneva To Mark the 70th Anniversary of the Foundation of the World Council of Churches. https://www.vatican.va/content/francesco/en/speeches/2018/june/documents/papa-francesco_20180621_pellegrinaggio-ginevra.html.

Liberative *diakonia* starts from the point of resourcefulness, even in situations where people seem to be in dire need. AICs, especially in local contexts, are communities that start from a point of resourcefulness even in the midst of what is looked at as poverty. The giving, sharing and caring that takes place in local contexts where the AICs minister, is in itself a prophetic witness to the world – especially to those who live economic lives of hoarding. This witness highlights that that all of us can be well when we go beyond ourselves to care for the others around us. The sharing is done out of fellowship and community building that seeks shared dignity. This kind of sharing is based on the inner motivation and a deep sense of consciousness for a community that should be well.

Liberative *diakonia* calls for processes that transcend ending poverty, to walking along-side all who have been left behind, until they break into abundance. Wholeness is at the centre. Liberative *diakonia* calls for questioning what we have been doing, in the light of whether we are dismantling the foundations on which poverty is built and sustained. Liberative *diakonia* transforms the giver/recipient frameworks. It focuses on investment in people's lives so that they can stand on their own and affirm their agency in the search and realisation of a community that is whole.

It is this value system that calls the world to order by affirming the fact that the 'The earth and all that is in it belongs to God'. This will bring us in the arena of development with humility, stewardship, and accountability to the people who for whom abundance of life must be made a reality.

8.11. Peace churches' understanding of Ecumenical *Diakonia*

The term "historic peace churches" refers to the Church of the Brethren, the Religious Society of Friends (Quakers) and the Mennonites, the collective name emerging following a conference held in Kansas, USA, in 1935. These historic peace churches are represented within the same grouping as the Moravian Church in the WCC. These churches have sought to exercise diaconal service in various forms – including in the midst of conflict. The Quakers arranged shipments of food and medicines to Cuba and North Vietnam in the 1960s and 1970s, in direct contravention of US embargoes. The Mennonite Central Committee (MCC) has provided humanitarian relief to victims of disasters and wars, including in contexts that western governments view as enemy territory, such as Iran and North Korea. The historic peace churches are committed in their diaconal work to heal the ravages of war without favouritism. An abbreviated and incomplete list of organizations carrying out diaconal work on behalf of the historic peace churches and the Moravian Church includes:

- The relief, development and peacebuilding outreach of the American Friends Service Committee and Mennonite Central Committee;
- Christian Peacemaker Teams, supported by Quakers, the Church of the Brethren, and Mennonites (among others), which aims to reduce violence and systematic injustice in areas of conflict.
- The Church of the Brethren's Global Food Initiative.
- Mennonite Diakonia Service in Indonesia
- Quaker Social Action in the United Kingdom
- The Community Outreach Ministries of the Moravian Church.

The involvement of the peace churches in ecumenical relations has a direct impact on ecumenical *diakonia*, through the sharing of personnel, resources, ideas and their commitment to peace-making in the context of diaconal service.

CHAPTER 9

Ecumenical *Diakonia* in a regional context

Photo: Paul Jeffrey/Life on Earth

9.1. Introduction

This chapter attempts to show how different socio-economic, socio-political, environmental, historic and cultural challenges can all affect approaches to *diakonia*. Issues such as conflict, political ideologies, natural disasters, wealth, poverty, the legacies of colonialism and the legal status of churches are just some of the issues that can have a direct bearing on diaconal provision. The creation of a global ethic of ecumenical *diakonia* must consider such diversity, in the overall universal context of the love of God, revealed in Christ.

9.2. Ecumenical *Diakonia* in a Latin American context

It has been said that Latin America is the most unequal region of the world and, at the same time, it is the most Christian. What does this remark tell us about ecumenical *diakonia*? Is Christianity part of the problem, part of the solution, or both?

According to Marcelo Justo, "Despite the growth of the past decade and the application of redistributive policies, Latin America continues to be the most unequal region on the planet, beaten only by a region plagued by war and famine: Sub-Saharan Africa. The social advances are unquestionable. Over the last 15 years some 100 million Latin Americans have risen out of poverty. However, the distance that separates them from the richest has barely changed. Various readings of the standard international measurement of inequality, the Gini Coefficient, seem to confirm this. According to the World Bank and the *Centro de Estudios Distributivos, Laborales y Sociales* (CEDLAS – Centre for Distributive, Labour and Social Studies), Sub-Saharan Africa has an inequality rating of 56.5, followed by Latin America with 52.9, and relatively far ahead of Asia (44.7) and Eastern Europe and Central Asia (34.7)". This inequality manifests itself in practical terms through violence, crime, powerlessness, migration, terrorism, drug abuse and trafficking, low standards of education, nourishment and health care and climate change, among others.

The majority of Latin Americans are Christians (90%), mostly Roman Catholic (69%). Membership in Protestant denominations (19%) is increasing, Pentecostalism in particular has experienced massive growth. This movement is increasingly attracting Latin America's middle classes. Anglicanism also has a long history and growing presence in Latin America. In some countries there is a growing presence of Evangelicals in political parties and governments. Indigenous creeds and rituals are practiced in countries with large percentages of Amerindians. Various Afro-Latin American traditions such as Santería, Candomblé, Umbanda, Macumba, and tribal-voodoo religions are also practiced, as well as other world religions.

This rather ambivalent scenario challenges the various churches to pursue an ecumenical *diakonia* which transforms themselves in the first place, in order to be "salt and light" (Mt 5,13-16), serving the "least of these" (Mt 25, 31-46), so to transform the various contexts, according to the values of God's kingdom of "justice and peace and joy in the Holy Spirit" (Romans 14:17).

Even when there is a very long way to go, various churches proclaim and pursue a prophetic *diakonia* that tries to comfort those in need while at the same time confronting the powers which produce such an inequality in the first place. In this regard, there is an increasing awareness and practice of this discipline in the region. There are various initiatives, such as the Empowering *Diakonia* model (which focuses on visionary, normative, need-oriented, contextual and transformative dimensions); *Diakonia* as sharing at the table; *Diakonia* following the example of Jesus, such as with the children, with the sick, with the women and with the impoverished in general. There is a rising tendency to work with ACT (Action by Churches Together) Alliance and the UN Sustainable Development Goals, in order to serve more effectively and in partnership with other FBOs, civil society and non-government organizations. Simultaneously, there are an increasing number of theological institutions that are including *diakonia* as a discipline in the curricula, as part of the *Missio Dei* (God's mission).

Latin American churches are inspired by the divine community as revealed by God as the source of power, by Jesus as the presence of God's power in the world, and by the Spirit as the outreaching of God's power, in order to serve through acts of effective love, for individual, social and ecological transformation towards the full *koinonia* of God's kingdom.

9.3. Ecumenical *Diakonia* in a Caribbean context

The Christian faith has been a dominant presence across the Caribbean for some five centuries. The earlier European philosophy which undergirded theology in the Caribbean, stubbornly postulated that the extreme suffering experienced by the indigenous Indians, enslaved African peoples and later Asian indentured servants should be borne with patience, as there would be great rewards in heaven.

This view was challenged and continues to be challenged by Caribbean theologies which recognize that human life is holistic and is shaped by systems and human interventions. The historical development of Christianity in the Caribbean has been fraught with contradictions. Thus, while the planters held the majority of the population in slavery and other forms of oppression, some representatives of the church sought to carry out acts of *diakonia*, particularly, but not exclusively in the areas of education and medical care. Although there is a valid view that the colonial intent of education was to maintain the status quo, some of the most respected educational institutions and hospitals in the region were founded and, in some cases, continue to be run by churches and their agencies.

Among the harsh realities which are part and parcel of life in the Caribbean, are varying degrees of generational poverty and inequality, hostile global economic relations, gender-based violence, human trafficking, climate change and the dispossession of large tracts of land, faced especially by indigenous peoples. These realities demand certain specific responses from the church.

Theological and Social Context for Diaconal Work

An understanding of the contemporary Caribbean has to be underscored by the knowledge that the material poverty which is seen in the region today is a product of its harsh historical foundations. While there is a strong love for the God among the peoples of the region, there are many who reject the word of God and there are many who do not actively participate in Christianity, the major religion. The need for ongoing evangelization therefore remains strong.

The social context for ecumenical diaconal work in the region is one in which economies are typically not very buoyant and the International Monetary Fund, other agencies, and governments of the major political systems of the world are part of the social fabric of the region. Thus, there are some groups which live at a very high standard, a relatively small middle class, but large numbers of persons who hover around the poverty lines. Populations are typically young, but improving health systems also support a growing percentage of older persons, many without formal pension funds.

In this setting, people have a desire to hold firmly to the God of their salvation, but the realities of life cause some, especially among the young, to veer towards hopelessness.

Notable and Influential Examples

The idea and practice of *diakonia* have been known in the region for a long time. As the various denominations were established and continue to gain strength in the region, the word of God has typically been accompanied various forms of charitable endeavours. These acts have often been aligned to the Acts of the Apostles and have become enfleshed in social activities and physical projects designed for the amelioration of human suffering and degradation.

Most denominations in the Caribbean would therefore be able to point to examples of interventions which they have made to shine of the light of Christ into the conditions in which some people exist. Two examples are offered here in summary.

The Theodora Project

Migration for the express purpose of finding a better economic reality is a feature of Caribbean life. Given the scope of the tourism in the Caribbean, it is natural that large numbers of people would expect to make their living in this sector. However, there are elements of duplicity and false promises, such as employment offers overseas, to which many fall prey. An active sex trade and entertainment culture have drawn some young and gullible people into the dragnet of human trafficking. The Theodora Skills Training Project, founded by Rev. Dr Margaret Fowler of the United Church in Jamaica and the Cayman Islands, rescues, protects and puts victims on the path to self-reliance and recovery.

The Missionaries of the Poor

The Missionaries of the Poor is a forty-year-old organization of the Roman Catholic Church in Jamaica. Founded by Father Richard Ho Lung, a Jamaican priest, it is an international monastic order served by brothers from many countries. During this period the movement has built countless homes and centres for the poorest of the poor in Jamaica and nine other countries. (https://missionariesofthepoor.org/about-mop/contact-us/)

9.4. Ecumenical *Diakonia* in a European context

The understanding of ecumenical *diakonia* in Northern and Western Europe has largely been marked by the development of the diaconal movement that emerged in Germany in the 1830s. It expressed a series of concerns that have since then been part of diaconal practice and theological reflection:

a. A call to respond to urgent social challenges caused by poverty and other expressions of human need, for instance issues of health that would stigmatize and exclude vulnerable persons. This have given diaconal action a clear identity as public action, with a mandate to defend human dignity and contribute to processes of healing and promote common good, when possible, in cooperation with public authorities.

b. A commitment to foster competence and professional skills in diaconal praxis, in the first place in order to secure quality, decency and responsibility when working with vulnerable persons. Diaconal actors became pioneers in building competent institutions and in offering professional training, and have largely impacted the development of health and social services in their countries. A particular trait of this development is the role of women, offering them new roles in church and society.

c. The diaconal movement was initiated and supported across confessional lines, and thus became a gate opener for ecumenical cooperation, and later for the ecumenical movement.

d. The founders of the diaconal movement intended to renew what they viewed as the diaconal tradition of the New Testament, in particular the ministry of deacons and deaconesses. Diaconal works have since been inspired by this tradition, above all by the example of Jesus; they have interpreted the call to *diakonia* as discipleship and service. This expresses the faith basis of *diakonia*.

Ecumenical *diakonia* in its modern and contemporary form emerged in the aftermath of the world wars, in response to the needs of refugees and others victims of war. It led to the organization of specialized agencies, such as DanChurchAid (Denmark) and Christian Aid (UK). As church-based entities, they sought ecumenical cooperation, often within the framework of the World Council of Churches, and they promoted professionalism and quality in their work within the public space. From the end of the 1950s these agencies widened their focus from European to global challenges. They engaged in development programs, and later also in issues related to justice and ecology. In many cases, mission organizations manifested a similar commitment to ecumenical *diakonia*. Changes emerged from the 1960s onwards which may be considered both as strengths and challenges in today's performance of ecumenical *diakonia*:

a. Increasing public funding implied a growing dependency on governmental/secular principles and methods. The consequence could be loosening of the ties to churches and a "NGO-fication" of the agencies and their activities.

b. Linked to this is seen a growing professionalization, very often following the logic of secular development work. This would imply less space for local churches in implementing projects, as they would often be deemed to lack the required professionalism.

c. Growing awareness of the political dimension and a more comprehensive approach in diaconal work opened opportunities for an increased focus on the prophetic dimension of ecumenical *diakonia*, and of including advocacy and public witness in all forms of its work.

Eurodiaconia, with its office based in Brussels, is a European network of 51 churches and Christian NGOs, providing social and health care services and advocating for social justice. It engages with the issues and policies of the European Union and its impact on the work of diaconal organisations.

Diversity within the European context must also be understood. Widespread secularisation in much of Europe in recent decades presents its own challenges, particularly with falling numbers in regular church attendance and the percentage of Christians in the overall population. National legislation can also have an impact: the creation of the National Health Service in the UK in 1948 effectively transferred all hospitals to state ownership and control; following the Portuguese revolution of 1974 hospitals run by church-related *misericórdias* were transferred to state control. The importance of Roman Catholic diaconal services, particularly in Southern Europe, is further described in chapter 8.9.

Russia

Russia is Europe's largest county, both geographically and in the size of the population. All church-run charities were closed after the revolution of 1917. Following *perestroika* in the 1980s, the majority of new diaconal projects were initiated and financed by western Christians. Common initiatives were developed with some Orthodox parishes, including humanitarian aid and different social fields that were prohibited to all religious organizations during the Soviet era.

The Round Table for Religious Education and Diakonia was established in 1992 by the World Council of Churches and the Russian Orthodox Church. A significant regional ecumenical diaconal initiative is the "Christian Interchurch Diaconal Council of St. Petersburg" (founded by the Orthodox, Catholic and Lutheran churches). Since 2008 it has worked as the "*Diakonia*" charitable foundation.

The majority of the Russian population (up to 80%) identifies itself with the Russian Orthodox Church. The document *"On the principles of organization of social work in the Russian Orthodox Church"* (2011) emphasizes that "the social service of the Church may not be suppressed or restricted by religious, national, state and political or social frameworks." It emphasises the need for the "exchange of experience with foreign charitable organizations, including volunteer undertakings, analysis and use of the experience of other Christian denominations, which are more developed in the sphere of social service for historical reasons". Whilst not necessarily copying Western models, opportunities for co-operation and mutual understanding with other countries and churches exist.

9.5. Ecumenical *Diakonia* in an African context

Diaconal work in Africa is vibrant in the context of rapidly-growing churches in many countries. Churches exercise diaconal ministry in a variety of ways and expressions, including using different terminologies to name what they do. Historically, many churches are well known for their diaconal services through schools, hospitals & clinics, agricultural rural projects including digging of bore holes, development services, women's and gender empowerment, and livelihood skills building. Whereas many of these are organized at the national denominational headquarters, diaconal ministries are also carried out through national, sub-regional and regional councils of churches (Fellowships of Councils, All Africa Conference of Churches (AACC) and Organization of African Instituted Churches (OAICs)). These include ministries for refugees and migration, civic education, independence and liberation struggle movements, advocacy for peace building, climate justice, economic justice, gender justice and interreligious dialogue. Significant diaconal ministries are carried out by church groups, especially by the women and youth.

As a whole, Africa is endowed with natural resources, diversity of cultures, traditions and religions and a vibrant youthful population which are wellsprings of opportunities. However, these also create considerable challenges for churches and ecumenical institutions, not the least diversity in denominational and linguistic traditions and interreligious and ethnic conflicts. Furthermore, despite the huge diaconal commitment of the churches and ecumenical partners, unequal distribution of resources at the national level, weak governance, violence and ongoing exploitation of natural resources by powerful governments, and multinationals (with the backing of the small clique of leaders in the continent), thwart effective stewardship of the richness of Africa.

Since the creation of the All Africa Conference of Churches in 1963, the challenge of delivering effective diaconal care has been a major issue for the organisation and its members. Overall, the level of commitment from African churches and diaconal agencies is enormous – yet also reflects large challenges and opportunities to care and serve in Christ's name.

Francophone

French-speaking Africa has notable Christian and Muslim communities. France granted independence to almost all of its former African territories in the early in 1960s, yet often retained considerable economic, political and social interests in the region.

The Fellowship of Christian Councils and Churches in West Africa (FECCIWA) is one example of a space for experiencing ecumenical *diakonia*. It works for sustainable peace, respecting human rights, freedom of expression for people and their participation in every decision concerning them. FECCIWA contributes to the improvement of the living conditions of the populations in 13 countries. Its anti-corruption campaign in schools in West Africa has allowed for the training of peers in young schoolchildren. Another example is the advocacy campaign for food security among government institutions in ECOWAS and in churches: "Eat what you grow and grow what you eat". This has helped to make churches take food security policy to heart by integrating food security and agricultural policy into their development plans, with the commitment of the youth and women's movements.

Lusophone

Angola, Cabo Verde, Guinea-Bissau, Mozambique and São Tomé & Príncipe were formerly ruled by Portugal, with a resulting impact on the cultures of these nations – notably the continuing legacy of the Portuguese language. Unlike the UK, Belgium and France, Portugal resisted demands for decolonialization in the 1960s, leading to wars of liberation. The "Carnation Revolution" against the dictatorship of Salazar and Caetano took place in Portugal on 25th April 1974, rapidly leading to independence for each of Portugal's African colonies.

This legacy left these nations amongst the poorest in the world, although recent exploitation of mineral resources (notably oil in Angola) is starting to change the situation – though with little impact for the poorest. Lack of state resources for healthcare and educational provision places a major onus on diaconal agencies and development agencies to facilitate services, such as clinics. Christianity (notably Roman Catholicism) is the majority religion in each of the nations. In absence of other functioning public services, the responsibility on religious communities to provide basic care and welfare is considerable.

Anglophone

There are 24 countries in Africa with English as official language, because they were colonised by Britain. The South African democratic elections of 1994 marked a new era of political liberation in Africa. The churches in Anglophone Africa played a prominent role in achieving democratic political rule. The churches have continued to strive for economic independence of African countries. Founded in 1980, the Fellowship of Christian Councils in East and Southern Africa (FOCCESA) – renamed FOCCISA in 1999 -has championed ecumenical *diakonia* work especially with a focus on peace building, monitoring multinational mining companies and monitoring how governments are using money. The ecumenical bodies have provided leadership in health and healing, especially HIV and AIDS and malaria, resisting gender-based violence and child marriages through the Tamar Campaign using contextual bible studies.

9.6. Ecumenical *Diakonia* in an Asian context

Christianity is a minority faith in the majority of Asian countries. Nevertheless, Asia includes some very large churches (in terms of membership), numerous smaller churches and an active diaconal commitment in many nations. The Christian Conference of Asia was inaugurated in 1959. Reflecting the diversity within Asia, this section will look at approaches to *diakonia* in the contexts of China, East Asia, South Asia and Australasia respectively.

China

China's opening up and reforms after 1978 have given Chinese churches more opportunities to engage in ecumenical *diakonia*. The China Christian Council was established in 1980 and includes a Social Services Ministry, providing capacity building courses at provincial level and the overseeing of care for the elderly.

As early as 1985, Bishop K. H. Ting established the Amity Foundation as an NGO that would enable Chinese Christians to contribute to China's development. Ting strongly believed that love is the primary attribute of God and that *diakonia* is a way of expressing God's love in action. As such, it was an integral aspect of Christian mission. It would make Christianity better understood and accepted in China, and overcome the stigma of being a "foreign religion" that had been a product of Western imperialism.

In a situation of extreme poverty that confronted Chinese society in the 1980s and 1990s, the symbols for *diakonia* were often the five loaves and two fishes. Chinese Christians often saw their role as providing for both the spiritual and the physical nourishment of fellow human beings. As Chinese churches emerged from the Cultural Revolution, Christians shared what they had with one another, even though they were poor. As their numbers and resources began to grow, they started kindergartens, orphanages, health clinics and homes for the elderly in response to the immense social needs around them. These were often on a very small scale, as religious organizations were barred from providing social services until 2003.

The establishment of Amity in 1985 offered a platform for the ecumenical sharing of resources with churches overseas. It was an opportunity to develop a new kind of postcolonial relationship that centred on equality, mutual respect and mutual consultation. This "new beginning" of an ecumenical *diakonia* nurtured mutual learning, equality and friendship. It was accepted that the Amity Foundation was an independent Chinese organization that upheld the three principles of self-management, self-propagation and self-financing. The ecumenical sharing of resources meant that all partners were equal, whether they were contributing finances, expertise, labour or service. Chinese Christians have also emphasized "servant-hood" and humility in diaconal practice. This keeping of a low profile and emphasis on participatory development has often impressed local governments and helped transform mindsets.

From the 1990s onwards, Amity engaged in development work in rural areas that emphasized water systems, renewable energy, preventive health care and HIV and AIDS prevention work. Local churches in different areas have moved on to larger scale projects, seeking professional training to improve their services that include elder care facilities, hospitals, and care for people living with disabilities. Today, as the challenges of climate change, the growing wealth gap and pollution confront Chinese society, there is a growing understanding that *diakonia* should be a channel for the advocacy of sustainable and inclusive development and that it requires interreligious and intercultural cooperation to be effective.

East Asia

Globalization has brought about tremendous economic growth in East Asia, yet there is suffering. There is a widening gap between the rich and the poor due to growth and competition in the market. The "mammonism" of the corporate giants has profound and detrimental social consequences. Environmental degradation, such as dam construction, deforestation, the disaster at the Fukushima nuclear power station in Japan (2011) and the market-driven process of industrialization, can have social, political and economic consequences. Cultural commodification, high tech media and communication markets have caused an erosion of traditional East Asian culture in terms of identity, values and sensibility. The aesthetic world of beauty and spiritual world of mystery is destroyed by the commercialization and commodification of cultural heritages and creation. Religion can also be misused for division, such as suppressing gender justice and enforcing racism. Religious fundamentalism is rising and religions as oppressive institutions become intensified in the vortex of political and market ideology.

There are increasing tensions between people's democracy movements and authoritarian regimes in East Asia. Geopolitically, the Cold War is not yet over in East Asia, most graphically illustrated by the division of the Korean peninsula. This has profound consequences for families divided by the partition, plus the wider regional context and the need to preserve peace and seek reconciliation.

In all of these contexts, *diakonia* must take initiatives for economic justice, for direct participation and intervention in the market process, and for economic actions for sustainable life.

Fullness of life is in jeopardy from globalization regimes in East Asia; this danger comes from unlimited greed for power and money. In this context, *diakonia* is seeking an alternative vision for life in conviviality, fullness and security. Jesus as the suffering servant is the *Diakon* of life. Immanuel (God dwells among the living) is the partnership between God and all living beings. It is the focal point of *diakonia* to raise all living beings as subjects of conviviality. In Asian traditions, there are rich religious, cultural and philosophical resources of new life. Addressing this, in the context of such religious and cultural diversity, are major missiological and theological tasks for Asian Christian communities in their praxis of *diakonia.*

South Asia

South Asia includes India, Pakistan, Bangladesh, Nepal, Bhutan and Sri Lanka. When Britain left in 1947, the separate independent nations of India (majority Hindu) and Pakistan (majority Muslim) were created – a partition on the basis of religion. More than half of India's Muslim population left for Pakistan. The aftermath of the partition was devastating, with many thousands of people killed on both side of the border in the name of religion.

Christianity in South Asia is, in general, a small minority. Christians in India constitute about 2.5% of the population (approximately 28 million). The National Council of Churches in India (NCCI) was constituted by the Protestant and Orthodox churches in India in 1914. The then Prime Minister of India, Jawaharlal Nehru, requested that the Indian churches intervene in the aftermath of partition. The NCCI set up an *ad hoc* relief committee which eventually became the Churches Auxiliary for Social Action (CASA), one of the largest faith-based national humanitarian aid and development organisations. The NCCI includes Anglicans, Reformed, Methodists, Baptists, Lutherans and Orthodox (including the Mar Thoma Church). The Church of South India and the Church of North India (united Anglican, Congregationalist, Methodist and Presbyterian) are the largest. The churches also own a significant number of educational institutes and hospitals.

India has witnessed a rise of Hindu nationalist parties, notably the Bharatiya Janata Party (BJP) which came to power in 2014. There has been a sharp increase in attacks against minorities in India, particularly Muslims. The region is also affected by terrorism. Sri Lanka has endured ethnic conflict between the Tamil and Singhalese population and terrorist bombings in churches and hotels in March 2019 claimed hundreds of victims. A far-right group emerging in Bangladesh has led to killing of several intellectuals, artists and peace activists. The countries of the Indian subcontinent are thus intertwined in their problems, which are often closely connected with religion. Furthermore, both India and Pakistan possess nuclear weapons.

The Indian subcontinent is unique in the heinous practice of casteism or "untouchability". Certain communities, merely because of their descent and work (menial jobs), are discriminated against for ongoing generations, including atrocities against people of so-called lower castes or Dalits (untouchables). The Indian church is predominantly a Dalit and indigenous people's church.

Australasia

Australia and New Zealand have particular contexts, as countries with longstanding indigenous populations, a majority population from European immigration over recent centuries and more recent immigration from East Asia. Cities such as Sydney, Melbourne and Auckland are now large, prosperous, cosmopolitan and multicultural, but not without pockets of poverty and social problems. Environmental and geographic issues, including New Zealand's vulnerability to earthquakes and vast distances between communities in the Australian Outback, add to the complexity. Diaconal agencies, such as *Diakonia* UCA in Australia, respond to these multi-faced challenges. The next global Assembly of the Diakonia World federation was supposed to have been held in Darwin, Australia, in 2021 but had to be cancelled due to COVID-19..

9.7. Ecumenical *Diakonia* in a Middle Eastern context

The emergence of new challenges and crises with all their implications have deeply affected the life and the mission of the churches. This calls them to witness in an increasingly complex situation in the world and to respond to the changing times by being up to date and relevant in terms of program, structure and action.

The fall of Soviet regime and the end of the Cold War, the American supremacy in technology, military power and economy, 9/11 and the war on terrorism, the limited role of UN as an international actor in the world order and the failure to become a catalyst between warring countries, were all factors contributing to wars, conflicts and destabilization worldwide.

For decades, ethnic wars and persecutions in Iraq, Syria, Israel, Palestine, Lebanon and the Arab uprising highlighted divisions within Islam, divisions within ethnicities (such as Arabs, Turks, Iranians, Kurds and Baluchs), between Shi'a and Sunnis, generating hatred and violence, producing waves of refugees, poverty, unemployment and exodus of populations from their country of origin. Populations in the Middle East are worn out with bloodshed and violence; the economy is drained as corruption infects public life; the social fabric of old civilizations is torn apart with the spread of abuse of human beings and human rights.

More than 18 million migrant workers – around 4 million Palestinians, 2 million Iraqis and 5 million Syrians refugees in addition to 2 million internally displaced persons in Iraq and 6 million in Syria– face human rights violations, resulting in feelings of frustration, despair and anguish. These create a new era and challenge in the life of the churches, necessitating immediate political action on the international, regional and local levels.

To resolve this tumultuous situation, churches have had to understand the systems created by governments and the structures governing the Middle Eastern social, economic and political systems. Churches have had to familiarize themselves with new and complex situations of economic globalization, and effects of capitalism which are forcing people into wars, violence and conflict situations. They had to reconsider the Biblical principles which stress values of inclusion, human dignity and brotherly coexistence, a vision that will discern the reality and will release new energy. For change and transformation to happen, churches have to cultivate a new quality of *diakonia* in all its dimensions: spiritual, material, preventive and prophetic: *diakonia* that is directed to individuals, groups, and institutions, for local, regional, national or international needs and situations.

A new vision of ecumenism must emerge to envisage a global ecumenism that reflects, works and acts together for the betterment of the human condition: a global ecumenism that enhances dialogue, collaboration and common action. Only such ecumenism can strengthen the churches' prophetic ministry and reconciliatory engagement.

It is the responsibility, therefore, of the individual Christian and church to react to concrete situations of suffering and injustice, to react to governments, raise their voices to live by the values of the kingdom, like Stephen did in Acts: "I see the heavens opened and the Son of Man standing at the right hand of God." (Acts 7:56) They have to translate the gospel message into concrete service.

"I have observed the misery of my people who are in Egypt, I have heard their cry on account of their taskmasters. Indeed, I know their sufferings. I have come down to deliver them" (Ex 3:7-8). In a similar way God's incarnation in Jesus happened in particular social, economic, political, religious and cultural context that shaped his ministry.

Democracy, justice, equality and freedom cannot be imposed with hatred and blood. Nor can human rights for millions of refugees and migrants be established through instigating fear of the stranger, discrimination or detentions. It has to be defined through a humanity based on faithfulness to God and Christ – *diakonia* in the three dimensions of its mission: transformation, reconciliation and empowerment.

9.8. Ecumenical *Diakonia* in a Pacific context

In the context of the Pacific Islands facing the impact of climate change and the increasing attention of extractive industries, *diakonia* as care for creation has been a focus of Pacific churches since the inception of the Pacific Conference of Churches in 1961.

Diaconal approaches to Pacific issues are a resonance between the Christian principles of justice, care for creation, and a preferential option for the vulnerable and marginalised in our communities and an indigenous understanding of people as part of the land, sea and sky, as well as the practice of reciprocity and community.

In the context of economic globalisation – with an extractive and consumer driven form of development that reduces creation to economic resources – the WCC document, "*The Island of Hope – An Alternative to Economic Globalisation,*" developed through global ecumenical consultations at the dawn of the 21st Century remains a valid articulation of the Pacific form of *diakonia*, in which:

> Spirituality, family life, traditional economy, cultural values, mutual care and respect are components of the concept of the Island of Hope which prioritises relationships, celebrates quality of life and values human beings and creation over the production of things. The Island of Hope is an alternative to the project of economic globalization which entails domination through an unjust economic system.

The ethics of "The Island of Hope" are based on the deep respect for the whole community of life. It fosters a culture of sharing and caring, based on justice. Its values reflect God's care for creation and Christ's teaching to love one another and do justice to the poor.

For the Pacific churches, approaching the end of the second decade of the 21st Century with increasing and more predatory system of economic extraction and more intensive acquisitiveness, militarization and consumerism, the Island of Hope needs to be revisited as a model of abundance at a time when the scarcity model is the dominant narrative.

Currently described as the "Reweaving of the Ecological Mat," by the Pacific Conference of Churches and Pacific Theological College, this form of *diakonia* continues the call to serve God and not Mammon, by continuing to rethink development and offer alternative forms of development that serve creation by promoting the wellbeing of humankind and environment.

In the context of the climate crisis, the recent report by the Intergovernmental Panel on Climate Change on Oceans and the Cryosphere added science analysis to the lived reality of Pacific Island communities, who are at the forefront of climate change.

The Pacific Ocean, viewed traditionally as the source of life, as mother and as an integral part of Pacific identity, is currently under threat from climate change. Increasing heat and acidification is destroying the fragile marine eco-systems and reducing the phytoplankton that produce 50% of the oxygen breathed on this planet. Climate change is also seen as a threat due to rising seas, loss of food sources and salt-water inundation and storm surges. Extreme weather patterns, from cyclones to droughts and floods, also are becoming part of the Pacific climate change experience.

In this context, the diaconal approach for Pacific churches to communities who are among the lowest producers of greenhouse gasses, is to continue to advocate for care for the ocean, as part of care for creation. Pastoral responses need to be prepared for communities who experience devastation of land and sea, are facing forced up-rootedness and displacement and for those Pacific communities who will be called to receive these uprooted sister and brothers from other island nations and coastal areas, so that this experience can be one of exodus rather than exile.

9.9. Ecumenical *Diakonia* in a North American context

Christian religious practice and its diaconal expression on the North American continent is, like much of the population of both Canada and the USA, transplanted from other soils and contexts. This includes those whose traumatic passage was shaped by enslavement.

The historic religious and diaconal culture of North America was predominantly shaped by the faith commitments of immigrants from Europe, including Great Britain. Along with European Protestant, Anabaptist and Catholic refugees fleeing persecution or economic hardship in their "old country", came the faith-informed social commitments of those growing theological traditions.

While universal public education, basic health care, public hospitals and orphanages, the social security networks and various programs intended to provide food and housing security to those living in poverty have long been understood to be core commitments of the social contract between citizens and their governments, it was the faith practice of those who settled North America from elsewhere that began the work and set the tone for how free, self-governing peoples should care for the "least among them". The church has continued a prophetic witness and engaged its practical presence in extending such care, both in cooperation with governments, and sometimes, in the difficult margins where political choices and the failure of public morality have left many behind.

The church's historic diaconal contributions have not been uniformly positive ones. In both Canada and the USA, policies of marginalization and genocide toward indigenous peoples were supported by the church, and aided by misguided efforts to provide education and access to indigenous children. In the name of Christ, and in the guise of traditional diaconal outreach, indigenous children were removed from their homes, communities and families, and sent to boarding schools where they were systematically stripped of their heritage, language and customs.

In Canada, the report of the Truth and Reconciliation Commission has been welcomed with regard to its truth-telling about the history and accountability that all Canadians have to indigenous communities. The pace of implementation has been disappointingly slow. There is still a huge concern about missing and murdered indigenous women whose cases are not getting the attention and investigation that they should.

In the United States, the repudiation of the Doctrine of Discovery and a confessional turn toward repairing historical harms done to indigenous peoples have been primarily a church-led effort. This calls on the US government to acknowledge its own culpability and take responsibility for its role in the destruction of indigenous peoples' lives, habitats, livelihoods and culture.

2019 marked the 400th year since the first enslaved person was put on North American soil. The legacy of enslavement in the Americas is another grave failure of the prophetic diaconal witness of the church. Recognizing complicity and the twisting of bible and theology to support this evil, the church is gaining strength and voice as a partner in acknowledging the historical and ongoing destructive power of racism, white supremacy, and the historic and continuing role in supporting policies of colonial oppression, both political and economic. In the US, the voice of the black church, lifted in lament and prophetic challenge and the continuing grace-filled willingness of the black church to engage with white culture and challenge the white church, is a powerful diaconal expression impelling us toward self-examination, confession, reparation and reconciliation.

As historic, European-rooted Christian traditions wane in numbers and influence in both Canada and the United States, faith traditions from Africa, Asia, the Middle East and Latin America, both Christian and not, are gaining adherents and a more visible presence in the public face of faith and the practices of *diakonia*. While youth in general continue to leave the church and organized faith expressions, the churches that seem to be attracting young people are, by and large, those engaged in caring for and strengthening their local community, committed to creation care and climate action, and engaged in justice-seeking social movements.

The Nature of Ecumenical Diakonia in North America

The landscape of Christian diaconal work in North America is as varied as its churches and communions. Unlike much of Europe, where church diaconal work on the large scale is significantly government church-tax supported and administered by professionals, or Africa, Asia, and Latin America, where local congregations and their members bear the largest share of financial and social responsibility for supporting those in need or distress, social support systems and diaconal expressions in North America are a patchwork of ecumenical, denominational, congregational, state, non-governmental and philanthropic partnerships.

Towards the end of the 20th century, the powerful ecumenical movements of earlier decades and their supporting churches suffered declining membership, with financial consequences. At the same time, church members and citizens alike, increasingly exposed in "real time" through media and social media to the unfolding of disasters and the experience of suffering of their neighbours, began to demand that their churches and denominations provide ways for members to practice the compassion of Christ in a more direct and personal way. Thus, the local practices of church members toward their immediate neighbours expanded to a broader engagement both in domestic and international diaconal service.

The North America Forum of ACT Alliance is one important convening body for shared diaconal practice for both Canada and the United States. Canadian members of the Alliance further coordinate their efforts and their access to governmental grants to maximize impact and witness to the unity of Christ's presence. In Canada, the changes in government policy and practices with regard to international grants for development are pushing towards giving fewer and larger contributions. This has resulted in more cooperation between denominational agencies in submitting joint proposals to access government funding for their development and humanitarian assistance programs.

In the United States, where domestic disaster response is a part of diaconal outreach, Church World Service, once the primary unified expression of diaconal practice for mainline Protestants in conciliar relationship, now serves as a convening body for some denominational disaster and refugee response partners to share best practices, discuss emerging needs, and coordinate their domestic and international efforts.

National Voluntary Organizations Active in Disaster (NVOAD) and its regional and state subgroups, gathers all willing actors in domestic disaster response in order to provide coordination and resource sharing across the entire voluntary responder community. It is also a platform for ecumenical and interfaith coordination with other secular voluntary organizations and has the additional value of attracting non-traditional and non-mainline faith groups into its membership, increasing the collaboration of evangelicals with Catholic, Orthodox and mainstream Protestant diaconal actors.

Xenophobia and the refusal of responsibility for responding to the urgent needs of the millions of people on the move are the most pressing and troubling issues confronting diaconal communities in North America. Political and economic crises in Latin America, the restriction of refugee movement into Europe, and the perceived favourable future for migrants seeking to emigrate to North America have made the crisis in the Americas one of the most painful in the northern hemisphere. Meanwhile, in the US, political power is held by anti-migration factions and racism further fuels the fear and anger dominating the US response to the urgent crisis at the border with Mexico.

Among the members of the North America ACT Forum, coordination with colleagues and the fora in Latin America and the Caribbean are an emerging strategy to address these challenges and the needs of migrants. Efforts to respond as effective diaconal practitioners to this great global crisis of the 21st century are inspired by humanitarian corridors in Europe and informed by listening to the voices of those on the move.

CHAPTER 10

The Way Forward

Photo: Paul Jeffrey/Life on Earth

10.1. Introduction

Ecumenical *diakonia* is facing a number of challenges, as described in chapter 7. The new social and political landscape calls for churches, diaconal agencies and the ecumenical movement to reconsider structures and practices and jointly to work out new strategies and innovative practices that respond to today's challenges.

Diaconal agents represent a long record of pioneering practice, both with regard to delivering health and social services and to engagement in development work. Innovation is therefore not to be considered a threat; rather it is an opportunity for applying new insight, building new relations, and developing better methods of work.

This final chapter aims to indicate some key areas of strategic planning and innovative action. It points at some crucial issues that require attention and that represent opportunities for strategizing ecumenical *diakonia* in view of "the signs of the times" (Matt 16:3).

10.2. Recognizing the *kairos* moment

When discerning "the signs of the times," *diakonia* seeks to apply its theological insight. Social and political changes that cause concern in a secular perspective, because of their possible negative consequences may be judged an opportunity for renewal and transformation in perspective of faith. In theological language, there may be a *kairos* moment, a time loaded with promises of a new and better future.

This is how committed Christians in South Africa interpreted the time of apartheid and their struggle to overcome it. The *Kairos Document,* published in 1985, interpreted this time of deep crisis as "a moment of truth" and of confessing hope. It aimed to develop a prophetic theology that would enable Christians to analyze the context in which they were living and to interpret "this *kairos*" (Luke 12:56) in light of the coming of God's kingdom. The document offered new insight into biblical texts and questioned the segments of the church that either supported the apartheid system, or preferred to remain silent in face of oppressive rule and so maintain the status quo. The *kairos* moment thus included the critical question of what it takes to be church in times of crisis, to reflect theologically, interpreting the signs, and to perform diaconal action that announces hope with justice and peace.

This challenges churches, agencies and ecumenical bodies to:

- Facilitate space for interdisciplinary reflection on "the sign of the times" and for developing tools for interpreting theologically contemporary challenges as "moments of truth and hope"
- Deepen the understanding of prophetic *diakonia*, facilitating opportunities of sharing experiences and insight from diaconal practice
- Provide faith accompaniment to diaconal actors who work in situations of deep social and political unrest.

10.3. Affirming *diakonia* as a shared vision and mandate

This document affirms the ecumenical understanding of *diakonia* as an integral dimension of the church's nature and mission. Chapter 4 presented the theological basis of this view, drawing insights from different confessional traditions and reflecting learning processes within the ecumenical movement. It affirmed the trinitarian dimension of *diakonia*, which means seeing it as an expression of the triune God's salvific care for creation and humanity. It also underscored its ecclesial dimension, which means a call to all churches and Christians to engage in God's holistic mission of healing, reconciliation and transformation. In addition, it emphasized the prophetic dimension of *diakonia* as a vocation to defend human dignity, resist evil, and promote justice and peace.

Ecumenical *diakonia* expresses the shared vision of churches, agencies and ecumenical bodies and their shared mandate to act together. This challenges them to:

- Affirm this shared vision and mandate in strategic planning, working documents and communication work;
- Articulate the distinctiveness of *diakonia* as faith-based and rights-based action
- Recognize initiatives that enhance the coordination of diaconal work, such as the ACT Alliance and other ecumenical bodies, as an integral dimension of the ecumenical movement and as an expression of the shared mandate to engage in *diakonia*
- Enhance mutual recognition of roles and mandates, seeking coordination and cooperation whenever possible.

10.4. Affirming the diversity of gifts

Diakonia embraces diversity as richness and opportunity. Chapter 6 has described some of the many gifts that churches and diaconal agencies possess and that are important resources for diaconal engagement. It includes tangible and intangible assets. It also points to the fact that some of these assets may be ignored or underestimated when ecumenical *diakonia* is implemented, especially the gifts of ordinary people who reside on of the margins of society.

Agents of ecumenical *diakonia* will benefit from acknowledging the complementarity of diaconal resources and linking more actively to the rich variety of gifts and assets. Ecumenical *diakonia* should develop professional approaches and methods that give due space to *diakonia* "from below" and to the insights and skills of local congregations and their members.

Ecumenical *diakonia* affirms the complementarity of diaconal competence of churches, agencies and ecumenical bodies. This challenges them to:

- Build awareness regarding the diversity and complementarity of diaconal assets and competence
- Become involved in processes of mapping diaconal assets, both tangible and intangible
- Develop networks, strategies and methods of mobilizing local diaconal assets in activities of ecumenical *diakonia*
- Share knowledge and best practices related to this issue, and include this material in professional training.

10.5. Affirming justice as a priority

Diakonia is rights-based action, advocacy and public witness related to just causes are integral parts of diaconal action. Chapter 5 presented some of the just causes in today's world that challenge ecumenical *diakonia*, such as economic justice, climate justice, gender justice, health justice, and not least, the issue of just peace. It has concluded that justice must be a priority cause in the strategic planning of ecumenical *diakonia*, with more attention given to its prophetic mandate.

Diaconal agents understand justice both as a theological and a socio-political issue. The first relates to the biblical message of God's saving justice, which calls all to engage in defending the dignity and the rights of the poor and oppressed. The second affirms the importance of establishing legislation that defends human rights and of opting for approaches that address people in vulnerable situations as rights-holders and those in power as duty-bearers.

Ecumenical *diakonia* affirms justice as a priority for churches, agencies and ecumenical bodies. This challenges them to:

- Include advocacy and public witness in all diaconal action and activities
- Build competence and share experiences related to working for justice; deepen interdisciplinary reflection on justice and prophetic *diakonia*

- Strengthen coordinated efforts of advocacy and public witness; join forces in ecumenical campaigns related to justice issues
- Accompany local churches in their efforts to strengthen public witness and advocacy competence.

10.6. Strengthening structures of shared action

Ecumenical *diakonia* presupposes structures that facilitate the smooth running of its work. Today ecumenical agencies work closely together with local partners, either bilaterally or multilaterally. Chapter 7 presented some of the challenges that face such cooperation. It points to the need for strengthening the structures of shared diaconal action.

This challenges churches, agencies and ecumenical bodies to:

- Deepen the concept of partnership in ecumenical *diakonia* through interdisciplinary reflection on practice
- Collect and share examples of best practices
- Strengthen structures of shared action in strategic and planning documents
- Strengthen collaboration within and between regional and national ecumenical councils and ACT forums.

10.7. Strengthening networks of cooperation

The role as agents of civil society and the mandate to engage in advocacy and public witness urge actors of ecumenical *diakonia* to build alliances and networks of cooperation. This includes working with secular organizations, governments, with the private sector, and with people of other faiths. The overarching goal of this strategy is to contribute to the building of just, participatory and sustainable societies with equal access to the common good.

This challenges churches, agencies and ecumenical bodies to:

- Develop strategies and share experiences on how to share resources, build alliances and participate in networks
- Strengthen the capacity of local churches to engage in civil society and join networks of advocacy and public witness
- Develop strategies for building alliances with civil society and with governments when working toward the Sustainable Development Goals
- Focus on *diapraxis* as an approach and method in ecumenical *diakonia*; share resources, both financial and human, as well as knowledge and best practices on *diapraxis*, and include this material in professional training.

10.8. Strengthening communication

Good cooperation within ecumenical *diakonia* requires robust structures and effective channels of communication. Without these, misunderstanding may create tensions and confusion regarding the roles of different actors and the principles of working together (cf. chapter 7.4).

For this cooperation to be effective between ACT Alliance, regional and national ecumenical councils and local churches, structures must be put in place that enable access to relevant information for all involved partners, offer a space for exchanging experiences and views, and for verifying opportunities for cooperation. The WCC has a unique role to promote such communication that goes beyond mere sharing of information, but seeks to provide safe space for mutual advice, for cultural self-reflection, and for reflecting on working styles, such as how to accommodate each other when engaged in ecumenical *diakonia*.

This challenges churches, agencies and ecumenical bodies to:

- Develop a culture and working style of mutual respect and recognition in all working relationships
- Establish effective channels of communication with regional and national ecumenical offices
- Develop strategies for improving communication related to regional and national ACT forums
- Develop strategies for communicating with non-member churches, civil society, the public and the private sector, and with all people of good will.

10.9. Strengthening diaconal capacity

Ecumenical *diakonia* requires competent practitioners at all levels. Chapter 6 presented elements of what constitutes diaconal professionalism and pointed to examples of formal diaconal training. Diaconal capacity includes ability to articulate the distinctiveness of diaconal practice, as faith- and rights-based action. It aims to develop insight that connects theory and practice, is interdisciplinary in its approach and methodology, and is socially relevant and innovative. The contemporary challenges described in chapter 7 urge agents of ecumenical *diakonia* to invest in diaconal training at different levels, including diaconal practitioners, in particular those in leadership positions, pastors and church leaders, and lay Christians engaged in diaconal work.

Training for *diakonia* in local churches, specialized ministries and agencies is currently developed at very different levels depending on the history, socio-political circumstances and structural frameworks available for civil society organizations. In some churches, organization for diaconal institutions was not possible at all (for instance during the period of the Soviet Union). In other churches there are small scale diaconal activities possible within local churches, but no larger diaconal institutions yet. Some churches are in circumstances where it is possible to receive partial state support for Christian social diaconal services rendered on behalf of the churches, in other settings this is not possible at all. These differences are mirrored by very different levels of diaconal training and education for Christian social services. There are settings with strong and established schools, colleges or universities of applied sciences for diaconal sciences and social work, whereas in other settings there are almost no institutes of training and education available.

Recent years have however seen a significant rise of interests and motivations for training capacities and curriculum model development in *diakonia* studies from churches in various contexts. It belongs to the core tasks of the ecumenical movement in the 21st century to enrich and facilitate diaconal learning and education in as many churches and different settings possible. This will allow each local church to find access to appropriate training resources for strengthening diaconal capacity and to get engaged in mutual exchange, cross-border education and ecumenical partnership programs for diaconal learning, which demands a common major commitment of diaconal agencies, development agencies, mission agencies and educational networks.

This challenges churches, agencies and ecumenical bodies to:

- Include capacity building in *diakonia* in their strategic and programmatic plans
- Offer training opportunities for joint training and learning for employees and leaders, strengthening their diaconal competence
- Elaborate and provide relevant training material
- Encourage theological seminaries and other relevant institutions to include *diakonia* in their curricula and training programmes.

Producing diaconal and developmental capacity building will also include a substantial reconsideration of priorities of development agencies, with the goal of increased funding to be made available for study, training and scholarships projects in this area. These should aim to explore the integral relationship between theology and development, theology and ecumenical *diakonia* discourse, and theology and ecumenical social ethics, thereby enhancing the capacity building of churches in *diakonia* and strengthening their work in social services. A dissociation of theology from *diakonia*, development and social ethics would thus be detrimental to the effectiveness and distinctiveness of delivery of services. Social change is only sustainable if it includes norms, values and ethical concepts.

10.10. Diaconal practice and code of conduct

Codes of conduct aim to raise ethical awareness and guide behaviour. Such codes are not merely words; rather, they exemplify the fundamental principles and values of working together.

Most professions have developed ethical standards for their work. Diaconal agents involved in humanitarian aid subscribe to the Code of Conduct that the International Red Cross and Red

Crescent Movement and NGOs in Disaster Relief elaborated in 1992. It contains ten principle commitments, among them these:

- Aid is given regardless of the race, creed or nationality of the recipients and without adverse distinction of any kind. Aid priorities are calculated on the basis of need alone
- Aid will not be used to further a particular political or religious standpoint
- We hold ourselves accountable to both those we seek to assist and those from whom we accept resources.

Accountability is a fundamental value in diaconal work, as it is in all actions of the church. Churches and agencies may have established their own code of conduct. ACT Alliance has adopted a *Code of Good Practice* that sets out common values, principles and commitments that will shape the humanitarian, development and advocacy work of ACT members. Its overarching principles state that each member of the ACT Alliance commits to:

- Acting in ways that respect, empower and protect the dignity, uniqueness, and the intrinsic worth and human rights of every woman, man, girl and boy
- Working with communities and individuals on the basis of need and human rights without any form of discrimination, ensuring that the capacities and capabilities of communities are considered at all times, and especially targeting those who suffer discrimination and those who are most vulnerable
- Speaking out and acting against those conditions, structures and systems which increase vulnerability and perpetuate poverty, injustice, humanitarian rights violations and the destruction of the environment
- Working in ways that respect, strengthen and enable local and national-level capacity
- Not using humanitarian or development assistance to further a particular religious or political partisan standpoint
- Upholding the highest professional, ethical and moral standards of accountability, recognising our accountability to those with whom we work, to those who support us, to each other, and ultimately to God
- Meeting the highest standards of truthfulness and integrity in all of our work, and
- Endeavouring not to act as instruments of government foreign policy.

ACT Alliance has also established a *Code of Conduct Policy* for the staff of all ACT members for the prevention of misconduct, including corruption, fraud, exploitation and abuse, including sexual abuse.

Such codes aim to raise ethical awareness and ensure safeguarding vulnerable persons, in particular women and children. This is in particular the case in situations of asymmetrical relations, when diaconal workers exercise economic, social and even religious power in working with persons in vulnerable situations. The risk of abusing power must be taken seriously by establishing relevant measures of prevention. Standard procedures of including codes of conduct at all levels of diaconal work will increase the awareness of this issue and provide tools for reaction when needed.

This challenges churches, agencies and ecumenical bodies to:

- Establish routines that include codes of conduct with the purpose of raising ethical awareness and guiding behaviour in all forms of diaconal work
- Offer training opportunities for diaconal workers regarding ethics and professional behaviour
- Provide space for partners in ecumenical *diakonia* to reflect on shared values and norms
- Initiate a process of elaborating basic principles of working style that guide the way we engage and collaborate in ecumenical *diakonia.*

10.11. The Environmental Crisis and Ecodiakonia

The environmental crisis affecting planet earth could place severe strains on diaconal provision, as well as other social services. Potential crises include as access to safe drinking water, loss of habitat, rising sea levels and pollution-related illnesses. Some are already looming, such as the existential threat to some Pacific island nations. Future action should include an advancement of the concept of "*Ecodiakonia*" – exploring the close relationship between diaconal care and the environment in the context of climate change.

10.12. Summary

Diakonia often assumes the role of "go-between." This chapter has pointed to a number of challenges that urge ecumenical *diakonia* to engage in innovative reflection and practice and to develop strategies and plans that affirm the shared mandate of churches, specialized agencies and ecumenical bodies. The tasks of affirming and facilitating mutual relationships, of coordinating diaconal action and of strengthening practices of cooperation are a vital expression of the role of "go-between."

The spirituality of justice and peace must permeate ecumenical *diakonia*, its structure, its theoretical framework and its practice. It is a spirituality that in faith recognizes justice and peace as God's gracious gifts, as liberating good news to all humankind, and it empowers us to join in the ecumenical Pilgrimage of Justice and Peace.

ADDENDUM

The Diaconal Work of the Churches in the Context of COVID-19

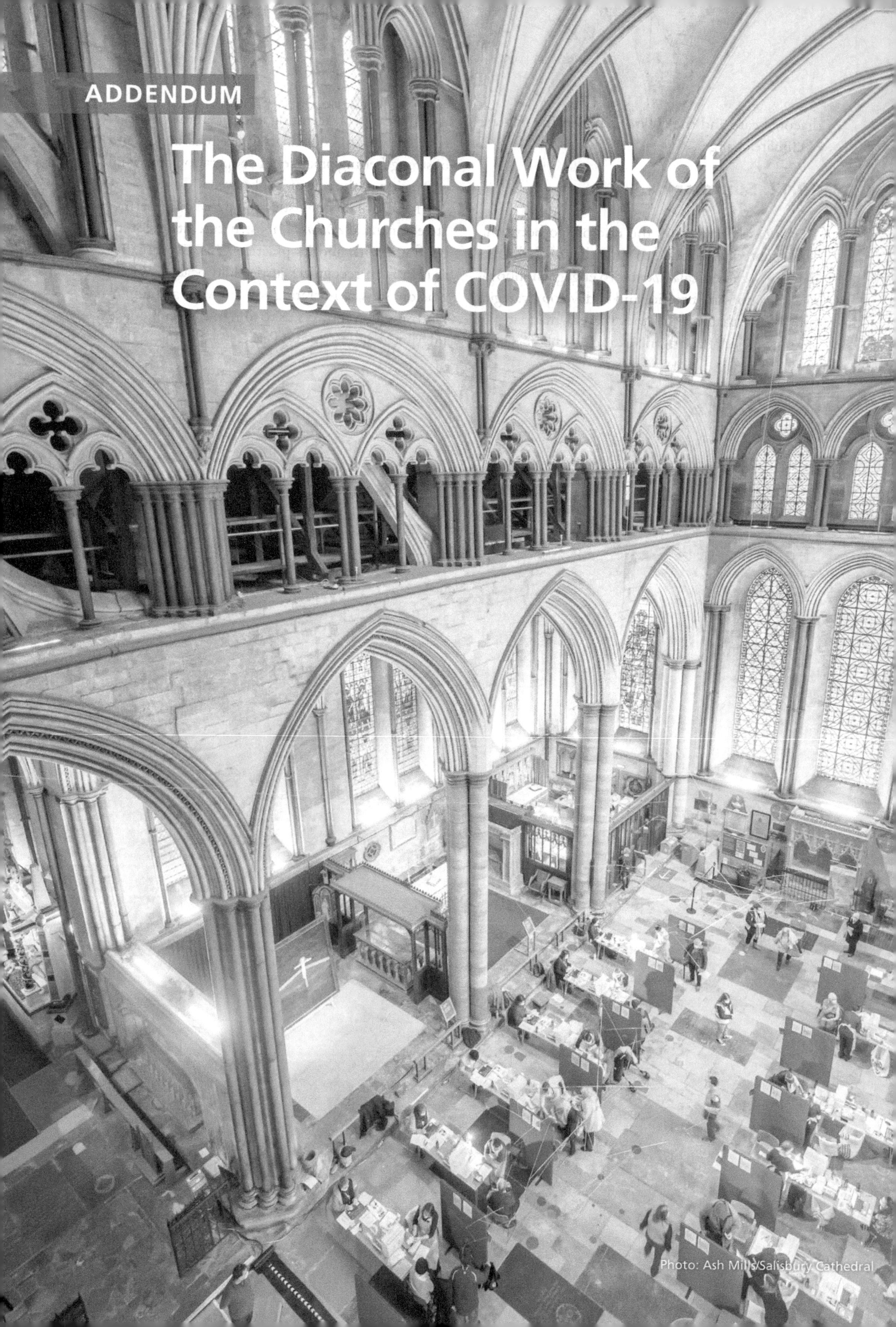

Photo: Ash Mills/Salisbury Cathedral

Rationale

On 11 March 2020, the World Health Organization (WHO) declared COVID-19 a pandemic. The pandemic has demonstrated the fragility of our world and has laid bare risks ignored for decades, including inadequate health systems, gaps in social protection, structural inequalities, environmental degradation, and the climate crisis. Entire regions that were making progress towards eradicating poverty and narrowing inequality have been set back years in a matter of months.[4]

The Bible (New Revised Standard Version) records the words "health" 37 times, "disease" 88 times, "compassion" 80 times, and "care" 163 times. In response to God's command to love and to serve, churches are called to respond to people's suffering:

"Then the righteous will answer him, 'Lord, when was it that we saw you hungry and gave you food, or thirsty and gave you something to drink? And when was it that we saw you a stranger and welcomed you, or naked and gave you clothing? And when was it that we saw you sick or in prison and visited you?' And the king will answer them, 'Truly I tell you, just as you did it to one of the least of these who are members of my family, you did it to me.'" – Matthew 25:37–40 (NRSV)

This document aims to show the impact that COVID-19 is having on the diaconal work of churches and church-related organizations by (1) setting out the social, economic, and theological contexts and (2) highlighting practical examples internationally, thereby helping churches and their partners to work for good practices in their diaconal responses and to better advocate for those most in need.

The protection of life can be described as a vector of grace. Diaconal services of churches and church-related organizations have been striving to respond to this unprecedented crisis. Resources (human, physical, and financial) are under severe constraint in many countries, yet the words of Matthew 25:37–40 do not permit inaction. Issues of justice, equity, and alleviation of poverty, which directly impact on needs, expectations, and demands for diaconal services, must not be neglected in the face of the new challenges that COVID-19 creates. While the need for succour and assistance have increased globally, the ability of churches and communities to act has been hampered because of restrictions on gathering, working, and responding. Nevertheless, this crisis has also offered inspiring responses from our faith communities to chart the way forward and bring healing and transformation with love, faith, hope, courage, and persistence.

This document is arranged in two parts: the first section is an overview of the current situation, and the second section shows some examples of diaconal work from around the world.

Section 1: Overview

As of 23 October 2021, more than 243 million people had been infected with COVID-19, and the global death toll was almost 5 million.[5] Whilst the majority of patients have recovered, the human cost

4. Antonio Guterres, "UN Secretary-General's Nelson Mandela Lecture: 'Tackling the Inequality Pandemic: A New Social Contract for a New Era,'" 18 July 2020, https://www.un.org/sg/en/content/sg/statement/2020-07-18/secretary-generals-nelson-mandela-lecture-%E2%80%9Ctackling-the-inequality-pandemic-new-social-contract-for-new-era%E2%80%9D-delivered.

5. "COVID-19 Dashboard," Johns Hopkins University of Medicine Coronavirus Resource Center website, https://coronavirus.jhu.edu/map.html.

Photo: Sean Hawkey/Life on Ear

of the pandemic has been – and continues to be – severe and tragic; every death represents a tragedy of incalculable loss to family and friends. In many cases, an individual's death may lead to a loss of income for a family with consequent implications of increasing poverty, including potentially depriving people of home, livelihood, healthcare, and food. The number of people facing acute food insecurity was expected to rise to 265 million in 2020, an increase of 130 million from 2019 because of the impact of COVID-19.[6] This is happening in a context in which nearly 690 million people (8.9 per cent of the global population) go hungry each day and night, and 2 billion people (26.4 per cent of the world population) experience a combination of moderate and severe food insecurity.[7] The situation is adding a burden for the 1.8 billion people who currently have to depend on a source of drinking water contaminated by faeces (23 per cent of the global population) and the 2.5 billion people who lack access to improved sanitation (35 per cent of the global population).[8] COVID-19 has proven to be much more than a health crisis. While the impact varies from country to country, the pandemic has created social and economic disruption that has increased poverty, especially in contexts where the informal economy is widespread. Already, vulnerable groups have been the most impacted.

The pandemic has also shown the frailty and inadequacy of the global economic system. Countries already struggling with limited resources are now even more acutely affected. The hubris of modernity and ideas of unlimited progress have been shattered. The COVID-19 pandemic follows almost exactly a century after the global influenza pandemic.

6. "WFP Chief Warns of Hunger Pandemic as COVID-19 Spreads (Statement to UN Security Council)," World Food Programme website, 21 April 2020, https://www.wfp.org/news/wfp-chief-warns-hunger-pandemic-COVID-19-spreads-statement-un-security-council.

7. "The State of Food Security and Nutrition in the World 2020," Food and Agriculture Organization of the United Nations website, http://www.fao.org/3/ca9692en/online/ca9692en.html.

8. Lisa Guppy and Kelsey Anderson, *The Global Water Crisis: The Facts (Hamilton, Ontario: United Nations University Institute for Water, Environment and Health, 2017),* https://inweh.unu.edu/wp-content/uploads/2017/11/Global-Water-Crisis-The-Facts.pdf.

Churches and church-related organizations attempt to respond as effectively as possible through their diaconal and health services. In many cases, the limited diaconal infrastructure (financial, infrastructure, human) is severely stretched, particularly in the world's most economically disadvantaged countries. Due to social confinement measures, many countries report dramatic increases in domestic violence cases, including intimate partner violence and sexual abuse. The home has become a place of fear for many women and children, with restrictions of movement, financial constraints, and generalized uncertainty emboldening perpetrators and providing them with additional power and control.[9]

The inability of many children to participate in formal education – particularly where computer and communications facilities are absent – may lead to long-term educational disadvantage and consequent lack of essential skills for future employment. The closure of schools due to the pandemic also is causing 370 million children (of the 1.3 billion who are out of school) to miss school meals and is limiting their access to nutritious food and health support schemes. For many children, these are the only meals they can count on.[10]

Despite the challenge of COVID-19, diseases prevalent in the global South – such as Sahel meningitis, Lasse fever, Ebola and malaria – must not be overlooked. In many countries of the global South, it is not only the disease and its medical and health-related impacts causing concern and heavy social costs; even more impactful are the side effects of approaches such as lockdowns that are often enacted without close consideration of the social and economic consequences. In Nigeria, hundreds of schools were closed, prices for daily food increased four to six-fold, and part of the population is effectively threatened by starvation. This may take a heavier toll than the immediate health-related repercussions of the pandemic. The COVID-19 pandemic also reduces

9. "Joint Statement by the Special Rapporteur and the EDVAW Platform of Women's Rights Mechanisms on COVID-19 and the Increase in Violence and Discrimination against Women," 14 July 2020, UN Human Rights Office of the High Commissioner, at: https://www.ohchr.org/EN/NewsEvents/Pages/DisplayNews.aspx?NewsID=26083&LangID=E.

10. "WFP and UNICEF Joint Response to COVID-19," World Food Programme website, https://www.wfp.org/school-health-and-nutrition.

global media coverage of other serious problems. Sharing responsibilities and insights in an ecumenical *diakonia* network of equal partners might also require a deliberate effort to provide counter-information and allow all churches to share their own stories of suffering and resurrection.

The COVID-19 pandemic has highlighted the comparative paucity of vaccine research and manufacturing in the global South. Dependency on importing medicines presents major supply, logistical, and financial challenges, as highlighted by the African Vaccine Manufacturing Initiative (AVMI).[11]

The effect on the targets set by the UN Sustainable Development Goals (SDGs) 2015–2030 cannot yet be measured or envisaged. However, the world is not on track to achieve the ambitious 2030 sustainability agenda, not to mention the internationally agreed climate agreements and environmental goals for 2050. It is only likely that pandemics such as COVID-19 will be repeated or even reoccur more often should the global community fail in the SDGs agenda. Churches and all people of goodwill cannot allow the SDGs to be forgotten or downplayed.

1. Theological Reflections

The pandemic is an unprecedented event in the contemporary era, emphasizing the fragility and vulnerability of human existence.

a. One Body

We cannot overcome the crisis in isolation. We can only cope with the pandemic if we stand together in solidarity and remember the message of St Paul in 1 Corinthians 12:12 that we are "one body."[12] Solidarity should go beyond the local context as the pandemic dramatically impacts vulnerable populations in every society. It is crippling the lives and livelihoods of societies and countries already disadvantaged socio-economically. Therefore, assistance, empowerment, advocacy, and accompaniment have to be boosted.

b. Complexities Implied in "Service" and "Solidarity"

Jesus' parable of the Good Samaritan (Luke 10:25-37) helps us to reflect on the question "Who are we called to love and care for?" and offers guidance about the complexities implied in the terms "service" and "solidarity." Jesus tells this story in the context of the command to love one's neighbour. The person who stopped and helped was a Samaritan – coming from a community that had been in dispute with Jesus' community about religious identity, the correct way to worship, and the right to participate in political matters for centuries. In the context of the pandemic, the parable is an invitation to reflect on the need to transcend boundaries in one's service to, and solidarity with, the suffering. It is also a call to overcome the negative assumptions we may hold and recognize with humility and gratitude that the "other" may show us the true meaning of service and solidarity.[13]

c. Mending the Broken Relationship between God, Humanity and Creation

Psalm 104:14-18 reminds us that God bestows life, satiety, and sustenance on all creation – plants, animals, and all forms of life – not exclusively on humanity. Intact living spaces for biodiversity are crucial not only for each living organism but also for human beings. Unfortunately, the situation in the world today is dire and indicates a rapidly deteriorating disruption of this relationship, demanding urgent transformation. Healing and transformation are needed to ensure that justice and dignity are brought to our relationships with each other, with creation, and with the environment.[14]

The pandemic is an urgent call for new reflection on how to mend the disturbed balances between

11. African Vaccine Manufacturing Initiative website, https://www.avmi-africa.org.

12. "Dr Beate Jakob: 'We are One Body,'" 15 April 2020, World Council of Churches, at: https://www.oikoumene.org/en/press-centre/news/dr-beate-jakob-we-are-one-body.

13. "Serving a Wounded World in Interreligious Solidarity: a Christian Call to Reflection and Action During COVID-19 and Beyond," 27 August 2020, World Council of Churches and Pontifical Council for Interreligious Dialogue, at: https://www.oikoumene.org/resources/documents/serving-a-wounded-world-in-interreligious-solidarity-a-christian-call-to-reflection-and-action-during-covid-19-and-beyond.

14. Manoj Kurian, "The Broken Relationship Between Humanity and Creation," *NCC Review 140:5 (June 2020), 233–243,* https://seafile.ecucenter.org/f/5bef62a4751349baae78/?dl=1.

humanity and nature and between technological civilization and ecology. The destruction of wild habitats, trade in wild animals, and climate change all increase interactions with nature that expose humans to a wide range of animal diseases[15] to which we have little resistance and which can become the basis for new pandemics. Over the last 30 years, approximately 60–70 per cent of the new diseases that emerged in humans had an animal origin. Three to four new infectious diseases emerge each year, most of which originate from wildlife,[16] of which COVID-19 is only the latest after other epidemics, including Ebola, severe acute respiratory syndrome (SARS), avian flu and Zika. The need to protect biodiversity and a sufficient number of zones for wildlife unused by humans is one of the essential lessons of this global pandemic. A key theological challenge is to reinterpret the relationship between ecology, health, and sustainable development. The "One Health"[17] approach proposed by the UN and WHO has become important for many actors. All these considerations have direct implications for planning an effective diaconal response.

d. Misleading Theologies

The pandemic also facilitates the spreading of many false ideologies and highlights a need for churches to be clear on key themes of the gospel. This means rejecting (1) exploitative theological projections and the instrumentalization of the virus to instigate fear, (2) stigmatization of the vulnerable, and (3) the conceptualization of virus infection as God's punishment or wrath on certain groups or as a sign of the end times. However, many churches also realize that COVID-19 and other deadly diseases that have been around in non-Western contexts for many decades pose serious pastoral and theological questions that cannot be easily dismissed. Churches need to revisit ancient eschatological and apocalyptic texts and images, interpreting them responsibly, to find a way to speak meaningfully to human hopes as well as anxieties and fears.

Since October 2019, the All Africa Conference of Churches (AACC) has organized annual symposiums addressing misleading theologies. This initiative aims to promote relevant contextual theology in the face of a proliferation of different theologies and misinterpretation of scripture leading to false doctrinal teachings and practices. Such action is of critical importance in the context of health and healing, especially in response to new challenges resulting from COVID-19.[18] The WCC has also produced relevant material, such as the Bible study "Telling Unwelcome Truths: True and False Prophecy."[19]

e. Restoring Intergenerational Justice

Many of the measures to fight the COVID-19 pandemic have been enacted at the expense of children and young people. Often, young people have felt restrictions during lockdown periods most severely. Young people have often been affected by ill-equipped e-learning that substitutes regular programmes from their educational institutions. Young people and children have been adversely affected by the closure of kindergartens, schools, and universities. A huge educational gap, that cannot be overcome, risks impacting the maturing and education of a whole generation, with especially serious consequences for the children of migrants and refugees. Therefore, developing child-friendly concepts of protection and hygiene and respect for the educational rights of children and the rights of those in need of care and protection (particularly older people) are major questions for many churches. How can we grapple with the theological challenge that a sizable part of the world's population lives unsus-

15. Kate E. Jones et al., "Global Trends in Emerging Infectious Diseases," *Nature 451 (2008), 990–993*, https://doi.org/10.1038/nature06536.

16. *COVID 19: Urgent Call to Protect People and Nature (Gland, Switzerland: World Wide Fund For Nature, 2020)*, https://c402277.ssl.cf1.rackcdn.com/publications/1348/files/original/FINAL_REPORT_EK-Rev_2X.pdf?1592404724.

17. "One Health," World Health Organization website, 21 September 2017, https://www.who.int/news-room/q-a-detail/one-health.

18. World Council of Churches, "African church conference tackles misleading theologies in faith and healing." https://www.oikoumene.org/news/african-church-conference-tackles-misleading-theologies-in-faith-and-healing.

19. Pauline Wanjiru Njiru, "Telling Unwelcome Truths: True and False Prophecy," 12 August 2020, World Council of Churches, at: https://www.oikoumene.org/resources/documents/telling-unwelcome-truths-true-and-false-prophecy-bible-study-by-pauline-wanjiru-njiru.

tainably in terms of environmental and financial resources? Such contemporary lifestyles may be at the expense of the future chances for a decent life of younger generations. Are older generations entitled to sacrifice the well-being of their daughters and sons? This has to be seen in the context of the biblical sources that tell us that Jesus' sacrifice for humanity is done "for all time" (Heb. 10:11-14)?

2. The Pandemic's Effect on Churches, Church-Related Development Agencies and Diaconal Agencies

Churches and Christian faith-based organizations (FBOs) provide spiritual counselling, prayer services, accompaniment, and comfort for those suffering and dying. Demand for diaconal services in response to the pandemic may, however, increase at the exact point when funding and income are under the greatest pressure.

Dr Mathews George Chunakara, general secretary of the Christian Conference of Asia, said, "Although the inequity that persists in many forms is worrying and of great concern, we must continue to preserve our hope and move forward. . . . As the surge of COVID-19 continues to cause serious concern, we are hard-pressed but not distressed, we are perplexed but not destroyed. Let us strengthen our collaborations and accompaniment at every level – among churches and councils, [civil society organizations] and FBOs, states and non-state actors – as we move forward towards recovering and rebuilding from the worst effects of the global pandemic."[20]

The pandemic has had a severe impact on the life and work of the church. There has been disruption to common prayer, with a consequent negative impact on sacramental life and pastoral services to the community. For many traditions, this is an appalling blow, for which an online presence is a poor substitute or no substitute whatsoever. Many local congregations have had to pioneer new forms of being present through digital means of communication: sending words of consolation, orientation, and encouragement to their members; providing networks of mutual support in neighbourhoods; and organizing common prayer in alternative forms, in open spaces outside, or through video clips. However, such provision may be of limited or no impact where there is little access to expensive new technology.

Where available, public funding for diaconal services and development aid is likely to come under increased pressure due to reduced tax revenues in many countries as a result of economic downturn and increased unemployment. The government of the United Kingdom (UK) has also announced a cut in its overseas aid budget from 0.7 per cent to 0.5 per cent of its gross national income.[21]

Church collections have diminished in many countries, sometimes due to the curtailment of Sunday services. An unintended and very unwelcome consequence of the pandemic for churches may be a reduction in services and work related to public theology, social ethics, global mission, and ecumenical cooperation. The income of some Christian nongovernmental organizations (NGOs) in Europe is under acute pressure, with inevitable negative consequences for services, employment, outreach, development work, and – most regrettably of all – the potential beneficiaries (agents of change) of such work in some of the world's poorest countries. The word "beneficiary" is, however, problematic because it can give a false impression of people merely waiting to receive help from elsewhere. In practice, much work is already being done – often with very meagre resources.

3. Work of the World Council of Churches and ACT Alliance in Supporting Diaconal Work

Both the World Council of Churches (WCC) and ACT Alliance are active in addressing the pandemic. The WCC and ACT Alliance aim to give practical advice and coordination to their members and partners. Above all, the aim is to protect life.

20. "WCC–CCA Joint Asia Regional Consultation Urges Churches to Deepen Accompaniment amidst COVID-19 Pandemic," Christian Conference of Asia website, 8 June 2021, https://www.cca.org.hk/news-and-events/wcc-cca-joint-asia-regional-consultation-urges-churches-to-deepen-accompaniment-amidst-covid-19-pandemic/.

21. Patrick Wintour, "Foreign Office Minister Resigns as Sunak Cuts Aid Budget," *The Guardian, 25 November 2020,* https://www.theguardian.com/global-development/2020/nov/25/uk-foreign-aid-budget-cut-chancellor-announces.

The WCC does not claim to be a pioneer in this work but has gained experience that has enabled it to respond. The WCC produces information and resources, but it is not the place of the WCC to offer advice. The WCC is not able to offer direct financial aid but can offer help in other ways, including online resources through the WCC website. These include documents, publications, and now webinars and podcasts, such as the webinar "COVID-19 Vaccination: How Churches Can Ensure that Stateless People Are Not Left Behind"[22] and a podcast addressing death and dying during the pandemic.[23] The WCC has developed programmes to build leadership capacity for *diakonia* and sustainable development in partnership with several regional ecumenical organizations, notably in Africa[24] and Asia.[25]

On 13 October 2021, the Rev. Prof. Dr Ioan Sauca, acting general secretary of the WCC, gave an address on the pandemic, the WCC, and global health at a meeting of the WCC, the Evangelical Church in Germany (EKD), the German Federal Foreign Office, and the TransAtlantic Network.[26] The WCC has a longstanding work programme on health and healing that includes both mental and physical health. The programme focuses on congregational roles in churches that promote health, which primarily deals with prevention, awareness-raising around social determinants of health, advocacy, and pastoral accompaniment. When they understand the dynamics, local congregations (with their various groups such as women's fellowships, youth groups, choirs, and so on) are often best suited to offer home-grown, cost-effective solutions. Such work includes preparedness and awareness of emergency planning and following biblical principles on watching for the signs of the times. The WCC has produced the handbook, *Health-Promoting Churches Volume II: A Handbook to Accompany Churches in Establishing and Running Sustainable Health Promotion Ministries,* to accompany churches in establishing and running sustainable health-promotion ministries.[27]

At the start of the pandemic, the WCC released the online publication *Health and Hope: The Church in Mission and Unity*, a collection of previously published articles that resonate with the worldwide struggle amid the COVID-19 pandemic.[28] Further WCC publications have been produced that focus particularly on equipping churches to respond to the challenges brought by the COVID-19 pandemic. The resource *Ecumenical Global Health COVID-19 Response Framework* lays out care parameters.[29] The joint publication *Serving a Wounded World in Interreligious Solidarity: A Christian Call to Reflection and Action during COVID-19 and Beyond* was produced with the Pontifical Council for Interreligious Dialogue.[30]

22. "Webinar: 'Covid-19 Vaccination: How Churches Can Ensure that Stateless People Are Not Left Behind' – Speakers," 15 March 2021, World Council of Churches, at: https://www.oikoumene.org/resources/documents/webinar-covid-19-vaccination-how-churches-can-ensure-that-stateless-people-are-not-left-behind-speakers.

23. "WCC Podcast Deals with Death and Dying," 15 December 2020, World Council of Churches, at: https://www.oikoumene.org/news/wcc-podcast-deals-with-death-and-dying.

24. "WCC Seminar in Mozambique Shows Vital Role of *Diakonia," 20 June 2019, World Council of Churches, at:* https://www.oikoumene.org/news/wcc-seminar-in-mozambique-shows-vital-role-of-diakonia.

25. "WCC Contributes to Capacity Building in *Diakonia and Development in Asia," 9 December 2019, World Council of Churches, at:* https://www.oikoumene.org/news/wcc-contributes-to-capacity-building-in-diakonia-and-development-in-asia.

26. "Rev. Prof. Dr Ioan Sauca: The Pandemic, the World Council of Churches, and Global Health," 13 October 2021, World Council of Churches, at: https://www.oikoumene.org/resources/documents/rev-prof-dr-ioan-sauca-the-pandemic-the-world-council-of-churches-and-global-health.

27. Mwai Makoka, ed., *Health-Promoting Churches: Volume II (Geneva: WCC Publications, 2021),* https://www.oikoumene.org/resources/publications/health-promoting-churches-volume-ii.

28. "WCC releases 'Health and Hope' online publication as a resource amid COVID-19 pandemic," 3 April 2020, World Council of Churches, at: https://www.oikoumene.org/news/wcc-releases-health-and-hope-online-publication-as-a-resource-amid-covid-19-pandemic.

29. "Ecumenical Global Health COVID-19 Response Framework," 13 August 2020, World Council of Churches, at: https://www.oikoumene.org/resources/publications/ecumenical-global-health-covid-19-response-framework.

30. *Serving a Wounded World in Interreligious Solidarity: A Christian Call to Reflection and Action During COVID-19 and Beyond (Geneva: WCC Publications; Vatican City: Pontifical Council for Interreligious Dialogue, 2020),* https://www.oikoumene.org/resources/publications/serving-a-wounded-world-in-interreligious-solidarity.

Healing the World: Eight Bible Studies for the Pandemic Era invites Christians to wrestle with their fear, grief, and uncertainty from within a biblical perspective.[31] A special issue of the WCC journal *The Ecumenical Review*, further focused on the pastoral and theological challenges posed by the pandemic.[32]

The WCC Ecumenical HIV and AIDS Initiatives and Advocacy (WCC–EHAIA) promotes HIV competence among churches and works with theological institutions to integrate and mainstream HIV into theological curricula as well as to address the root causes of the HIV pandemic. Experience from this work can also help inform the diaconal response to COVID-19 through the many lessons learned from dealing with HIV and AIDS. The WCC's convening role has been fundamental in sustaining the continuing focus on the HIV response despite other pressing priorities. Churches can be influential institutions because they are deeply rooted in communities worldwide. They can be a force for transformation – bringing healing, hope, and accompaniment to all people affected by HIV as well as COVID-19. The WCC–EHAIA programme has demonstrated the efficacy of linking grassroots, national, and regional actors with international decision- and policymakers.[33]

Experience has demonstrated that where women are primarily responsible for cooking and procuring food, an increase in food insecurity places them at heightened risk for violence. The increase in sexual and gender-based violence (SGBV) during the pandemic has led UN Women to describe this as the "Shadow Pandemic."[34] The WCC addresses SGBV through its Just Community of Women and Men[35] programme, notably the Thursdays in Black campaign that aims to promote a world without rape and violence.[36]

Through the Churches' Commitment to Children programme, the WCC advocates for the protection and welfare of children through projects at local, national, and global levels, including cooperation with UNICEF. This is critical during COVID-19 when exploitation of children and loss of educational opportunities through school closures are of serious concern. The aim is to promote child protection, child participation, and intergenerational climate justice.[37] The Out of the Shadows campaign also includes online resources for ending sexual violence against children.[38]

A COVID-19 support group of WCC staff was established to support the work of churches during the first year of the pandemic. As well as providing a coordinated response, the group has developed resources, including prayers, practical information, sample questions and answers (Q&A), podcasts, and more.[39]

The spiritual dimension of the work of churches is of crucial importance, underpinning all other work. The WCC publishes spiritual resources such

31. *Healing the World: Eight Bible Studies for the Pandemic Era (Geneva: WCC Publications, 2020)*, https://www.oikoumene.org/resources/publications/healing-the-world.

32. "Ecumenical Review Focuses on 'Christ's Love in the Midst of Pandemic,'" 4 February 2021, World Council of Churches, at: https://www.oikoumene.org/news/ecumenical-review-focuses-on-christs-love-in-the-midst-of-pandemic.

Further information about the WCC's work on health and healing is available online at https://www.oikoumene.org/what-we-do/health-and-healing.

33. Further information about EHAIA is available online at https://www.oikoumene.org/what-we-do/ehaia

34. "The Shadow Pandemic: Violence against Women during COVID-19," UN Women website, https://www.unwomen.org/en/news/in-focus/in-focus-gender-equality-in-covid-19-response/violence-against-women-during-covid-19.

35. "Just Community of Women and Men," World Council of Churches website, https://www.oikoumene.org/what-we-do/just-community-of-women-and-men.

36. "Statement on the Dual Pandemics of COVID-19 and Sexual and Gender-Based Violence," 23 April 2020, World Council of Churches, at: https://www.oikoumene.org/resources/documents/statement-on-the-dual-pandemics-of-covid-19-and-sexual-and-gender-based-violence.

Further information is available online at https://www.oikoumene.org/what-we-do/thursdays-in-black.

37. "WCC's Engagement for Children," World Council of Churches website, https://www.oikoumene.org/what-we-do/wccs-engagement-for-children.

38. Material on this campaign is available at https://www.oikoumene.org/what-we-do/wccs-engagement-for-children/out-of-the-shadows.

39. These resources are available online at https://www.oikoumene.org/resources/covid-19-resources.

as prayers and Bible studies internationally.[40] One such recent WCC publication is titled *Voices of Lament, Hope, and Courage: A Week of Prayer in the Time of the COVID-19 Pandemic.*[41]

Major challenges in other areas also impact the response to COVID-19, as highlighted in the context of the difficulties in reaching the ambitions of the SDGs – particularly in addressing poverty (SDG 1). The WCC is working in areas such as clean water (SDG 6) through the Ecumenical Water Network[42] and food security (SDG2) through the Ecumenical Advocacy Alliance,[43] including participation in the UN Food Systems Summit.[44]

ACT Alliance and its members have responded to the COVID-19 pandemic in various ways, including issuing an appeal.[45]

There have been a growing number of global health crises in recent decades, and the rise of global travel and mass tourism has accelerated the spread of viruses and pathogens. The COVID-19 crisis was not entirely unexpected; however, global pandemics are the most complex crises to plan for in terms of emergency response. Firstly, the humanitarian infrastructure is not designed for scaling up at a global level. Secondly, urban agglomerations and informal settlements as well as refugee "mega camps" (such as those in the Darfur region in Sudan and Cox's Bazar in Bangladesh) have grown tremendously in the past decades, creating ticking time bombs when it comes to a health crisis like the COVID-19 pandemic.

40. "COVID-19 Resources," World Council of Churches website, https://www.oikoumene.org/resources/covid-19-resources.

41. The publication is available online at https://www.oikoumene.org/resources/publications/voices-of-lament-hope-and-courage.

42. "Ecumenical Water Network," World Council of Churches website, https://www.oikoumene.org/what-we-do/ecumenical-water-network.

43. "Ecumenical Advocacy Alliance," World Council of Churches website, https://www.oikoumene.org/programme-activity/ecumenical-advocacy-alliance.

44. "At Webinar on Food Systems, "the Times Are Too Dire to Not Speak Truth,"" 11 October 2021, World Council of Churches, at: https://www.oikoumene.org/news/at-webinar-on-food-systems-the-times-are-too-dire-to-not-speak-truth.

45. Further information about the ACT Alliance response is available online at https://actalliance.org/covid-19/.

Taking in the recommended approach as discussed in the Inter-Agency Standing Committee (IASC)[46] and other global humanitarian coordination bodies, ACT Alliance's response to COVID-19 has taken a multisectoral approach complementing the work led by the WHO and governments. The ACT Alliance response has focused on providing communities with immediate support and prioritizing water, sanitation, and hygiene (WASH) activities,[47] cash support, awareness-raising, and prevention of SGBV.

In designing the "Total ACT Alliance Response" plan, ACT Alliance followed the overall principles set out by IASC in its draft "COVID-19 Global Humanitarian Response Plan":

- Maximize the complementarity and synergies between ongoing responses and plans.
- Ensure flexibility to adjust the responses and targets to the fast-evolving situation and needs.
- Build on existing coordination mechanisms.
- Ensure full respect for humanitarian principles.
- Ensure inclusion of all people – notably vulnerable, stigmatized, hard-to-reach, displaced, and mobile populations who are frequently left out of national plans or who are inadequately included in such plans.

ACT Alliance issued a rapid response fund (RRF) call to its members, leading to 21 projects in 18 countries worldwide. The widespread effects of COVID-19 have also affected donor countries, resulting in reduced financial support for the humanitarian sector, including FBOs. ACT Alliance has produced a pamphlet highlighting the importance of the role of FBOs during epidemics and pandemics, which provides some recommendations to donors:

a. A localized and locally-led, multisectoral approach is most effective.

Faith leaders and actors keep building resilient and prepared communities and play a key role in strengthening capacity at the local level. Donors

46. Inter-Agency Standing Committee website, https://interagencystandingcommittee.org/.

47. "Water, Sanitation and Hygiene (WASH)," UNICEF website, https://www.unicef.org/wash.

and humanitarian agencies should engage local communities and faith leaders and actors to ensure contextualization and reception of behavioural messages and practices, shifting the weight from the international to the local response.

b. It is important to adopt a holistic approach.

The mix of theological and technical support provided by faith leaders and faith-based actors enabled communities to engage holistically to challenge the superstitious beliefs and fears around Ebola. Clinically accurate government messaging lacked a connection with people's worries and could not create a tipping point of behavioural change. The use of religious texts and the trust communities had in their faith leaders helped change minds and hearts, and provided hope and spoke to the heart of the community identity. The Ebola crisis ultimately led to the strengthening of relationships between the WCC and ACT Alliance and the WHO; such cooperation is highly desirable to effectively and rapidly reach many communities globally – thus aiding the humanitarian and diaconal response.

c. Faith-based actors work will be essential both in the delay and mitigation phases of COVID-19.

During the Ebola crisis, faith-based actors played a key role in channelling medically appropriate messages using the local language. Thousands were trained to support humanitarian and medical efforts. In the delay phase of COVID-19, the implementation of safety measures during gatherings, burials, and religious functions will help slow down the contagion. Faith-based actors' access to the excluded and marginalized, the disabled, and those with low literacy, and the trust they have developed with the communities will contribute to making sure that no one is left behind. During the mitigation phase, religious and traditional leaders will help reduce stigma and support the survivors of COVID-19.

d. Faith-based actors and faith leaders must be included in response planning.

During the Ebola response, there was an initial delay in engaging faith leaders, who then proved instrumental in curbing the epidemic and ensuring a fast recovery. Faith leaders and actors must be involved in the planning and design phase as they have unparalleled knowledge of the local needs and challenges, have the trust of locals, and can quickly promote the behavioural changes needed to contain the spread of the virus.

e. Faith-based actors must receive appropriate funding to help reach communities worldwide.

The role of faith-based actors during a health crisis cannot be underestimated. Donors must establish practical entry points for faith-based organizations and actors to participate meaningfully in coordination and decision making on both COVID-19 response and recovery and wider humanitarian, development, and peace efforts at national and sub-national levels.

f. Faith literacy among humanitarian staff must be strengthened.

Humanitarian and development agencies must challenge the perception that staff, especially at field level, have of faith leaders, and take advantage of the literature around Ebola, HIV, and other epidemics to strategically partner with faith and traditional leaders and actors to increase access to communities.

The COVID-19 crisis has challenged both the WCC and ACT Alliance, yet both have sought to utilize their resources as effectively as possible in response to the pandemic.[48]

A WCC document, *COVID-19 and Sexual and Gender-Based Violence* was developed.[49]

4. The Challenge of Practicing Diakonia *in the Face of Physical Distancing*

The care of one human being for another often requires physical presence. For diaconal workers, such as staff in care homes for the elderly, this is very challenging in the context of COVID-19. The cost, practicality, and availability of personal protection equipment (PPE) must also be considered – particularly in the world's poorest countries. Early in the pandemic, there were acute shortages of PPE in many countries, creating additional risks for staff and service users.

The alleviation of loneliness, particularly amongst older people living alone, is a major aspect of diaco-

48. More information on the WCC's response to COVID-19 is available online at https://www.oikoumene.org/resources/covid-19-resources.

49. It is available at https://www.oikoumene.org/sites/default/files/File/31032020_COVID-19and%20SGBV.pdf

nal service in many countries. The absence of human contact can also contribute to mental health issues. Many diaconal services (and other social-care services) have been unable to provide such services due to restrictions on the size of gatherings.

Where diaconal services are closely connected with other church activities, particularly common prayer and prayer groups, the ability to provide such care is restricted. In the absence of reliable communications, many in need of diaconal care may be unknown to providers.

5. Diakonia *in the Context of Unemployment*

The economic and social impact of the pandemic is also contributing to the exacerbation of loss of work and adding to the vulnerability of people's livelihoods. This is occurring in a context in which 2 billion workers – more than 60 per cent of the world's workforce – are in informal employment.[50] (In Africa, 80 per cent of the workforce hold informal employment.) Most of them do not have access to a social safety net to fall back on if there is a disruption to their livelihoods. This has several implications for a diaconal response:

a. **The direct impact on individuals and their dependants who face loss of income.** In the absence of state-funded or insurance-related benefits, the loss of income can potentially result in destitution and even starvation. The response could even become one of disaster relief.

b. **The effect of unemployment on mental health.** The sense of loss of dignity and self-worth due to unemployment can have a devastating impact on individuals – including increased risk of alcoholism, drug abuse, suicide, self-harm, and violence (including women and children becoming victims). Diaconal services can be at the forefront of trying to help such individuals.

c. **The effect on funding for diaconal services.** Unemployment can also lead to the loss of state revenue from taxation, with – in many cases – a direct effect on funding of social services, ironically, when the demand and need for diaconal services are likely to increase considerably.

50. *Women and Men in the Informal Economy: A Statistical Picture, 3rd ed. (Geneva: International Labour Office, 2018),* https://www.ilo.org/wcmsp5/groups/public/---dgreports/---dcomm/documents/publication/wcms_626831.pdf.

6. Online Ministries

Online diaconal services may be of help to some, particularly where there is easy and affordable access to technology. Likewise, online common prayer has been appreciated by millions of people globally. Nevertheless, millions more have little or no access to such technology – particularly in the world's poorest communities. The danger of exacerbating the division between the rich and the poor is therefore even greater during the pandemic.

7. Medical and Public-Health Perspectives of the COVID-19 Pandemic

Why has COVID-19 spread so far and so fast? Firstly, it is a virus new to humans, and our bodies do not have the necessary specific immunity against it. Secondly, it is easily transmissible from person to person through respiratory droplets, surfaces, and possibly through the air. Thirdly, infected persons can pass on the infection to others for many days before they feel sick themselves or without feeling sick at all. Fourthly, the world is now highly interconnected with much travel within countries and across continents.

While many people only suffer a mild illness, COVID-19 can cause life-threatening illness in people who are elderly, have weak immunity (e.g., people with HIV or cancer), or have pre-existing diseases (e.g., diabetes or lung and heart disease). In the absence or the delay of vaccination, prevention is the only tool to stop this pandemic. Prevention measures include physical distancing, hand and respiratory hygiene, and isolation (quarantine) of people who are sick or suspected to be infected. Even healthy, low-risk people should follow these strict measures to protect the weak and vulnerable.

The source of the transmission to humans and the medical and socio-economic consequences of the pandemic have been topics of much speculation, accusation and counteraccusation, conspiracy theories, and trustworthy as well as fake medical science. COVID-19 has uncovered gaps in health systems that were hitherto masked and has also highlighted how health is not the preserve of the medical sector. The existing global politico-economic system is largely responsible for the socio-economic fallout of COVID-19 and, therefore, should be reviewed with honesty and courage.

Values of love, compassion, solidarity, and justice have motivated people of faith all over the world to positive action. The question is how churches can deploy their health assets amid today's challenges of pandemics, climate change, and the unequal distribution of resources, not least health-related ones. The WCC, through its work on health and healing, has a role to play in promoting good practice and utilizing the assets of churches to promote health.[51] Church hospitals and Christian health associations (CHAs) play a vital role; many hospitals – both in economically developed and developing countries – are run by churches or diaconal institutions. The Rev. Dr Fidon Mwombeki, general secretary of the All Africa Conference of Churches (AACC), writes:

> "It is well known that in Africa, churches contribute a large portion of health services, especially in remote and rural areas. In this way, churches are using their medical facilities as frontline responders. We thank God that so far, the virus is mainly in large cities in Africa. But the trend is clear that it spreads even to the countryside. Churches are seriously preparing their facilities to be capable and available for helping those who will need treatment and care. Many of these facilities are not adequately equipped or supplied. Churches need additional capacity to be ready for this major task."[52]

8. Vaccination

Churches can play a key role in encouraging vaccination. This can, for many, help to break barriers of suspicion. Church leaders have acted as Vaccine Champions.[53] The WCC has collaborated with UNICEF on promoting World Immunization Week.[54] Prof. Dr Sauca said: "As COVID-19 vaccination programmes are being rolled out, religious leaders of all faiths play a critical role in sustaining public trust in health authorities and services, as well as in the approved vaccines themselves. As a Christian fellowship, it is our duty and moral obligation to publicly challenge rumours and myths and confront them with facts. While moral and ethical concerns also loom over vaccine access and distribution practices, we must take up responsibility and advocate for what is right from a medical, ethical, and human rights perspective."[55]

The development of a vaccine against COVID-19 has taken place with unprecedented urgency. Whilst most commendable and welcome, this also raises questions as to why diseases virtually absent in the global North, such as malaria, have not been treated with a similar effort. Until all are vaccinated, irrespective of nationality, the risk of COVID-19 and variants remains a lethal reality to the entire world.

As Christians, the gospel principle of love of neighbour is essential to our understanding of common humanity. By early 2021, almost all wealthy countries had started widespread vaccination campaigns, with considerable debate about prioritizing age and risk groups. This has been primarily due to the purchasing power of such countries. The WHO and Gavi, the Vaccine Alliance, have together created the initiative COVAX[56] to facilitate the availability of vaccines to the global South. Yet, vaccinations are happening at a much slower pace than in the global North and have often barely commenced as of October 2021. The preponderance of vaccine research, development, and production in the global North has also highlighted the comparative paucity of the pharmaceutical sector in the global South. Pastor Peter Noteboom, general secretary of the Canadian Council of Churches, said: "In this pandemic, what better way to love the Creator God and to love your neighbour than to get vaccinated, advocate for vaccination for all, and contribute time and money to ensure everyone around the world has access to vac-

51. "Dr Mwai Makoka: Harnessing Religious Health Assets for a Better Post-COVID World," 13 October 2021, World Council of Churches, at: https://www.oikoumene.org/resources/documents/dr-mwai-makoka-harnessing-religious-health-assets-for-a-better-post-covid-world.

52. Fidon Mwombeki, "Faith Responses to COVID-19: Listening to Representatives of Religious Communities," All Africa Conference of Churches website, 30 April 2020, https://www.piron.global/en/fidm-04-2020-featured-actors/.

53. "Vaccine Champions," World Council of Churches website, https://www.oikoumene.org/resources/covid-19-resources#vaccine-champions.

54. "Simple Vaccination Message: 'Do to Others, What You Want Them to Do to You,'" 29 April 2021, World Council of Churches, at: https://www.oikoumene.org/news/simple-vaccination-message-do-to-others-what-you-want-them-to-do-to-you.

55. "Vaccine Champions," WCC.

56. "COVAX," Gavi website, https://www.gavi.org/covax-facility.

cines? The COVID-19 virus does not discriminate. Our response must also not discriminate. We must make vaccines available for everyone everywhere."[57]

9. Potential Long-Term Implications

During the tsunami disaster in 2004, build back better (BBB) strategies emerged in the process of recovery. This aimed to build back better societies and help religious communities become more resilient to potentially reoccurring risks. The ecumenical movement can help promote some common elements for a global strategy to build back better in the recovery and reconstruction of social systems and communities within the still-ongoing pandemic. The challenge is having to stop patterns of thinking based on the assumption that one day the pandemic will be over, and that we can only then embark on a genuine process to rebuild our societies to be more resilient, to follow more integrated One Health approaches, and to be better prepared in an alternative model of development. We are faced with the task of conceptualizing strategies to build back better our health systems, nutrition systems, and social security systems whilst the pandemic is still ongoing.

Long term BBB priorities will need to include the need to tackle poverty, food security, greener ways of living, and attention to health – both physical and mental. A global movement for ecumenical dialogue on BBB strategies is required, leading to more resilient and healthier societies and religious communities while still coping with the heavy impact of the pandemic.

10. Summary of Section 1

As of late 2021, the response to the pandemic is still mainly a medical one, with widespread vaccination programmes in the wealthiest countries combined with emergency actions and government restrictions. The failure to share vaccines equitably is a scandal that churches must continue to highlight.

The diaconal response must focus on alleviating human need and human suffering, as well as assisting with medical services – including facilitating vaccinations. The diaconal response will therefore be a long-term one, with the pandemic continuing to make its tragic impact felt for many years to come. Diaconal care for those who have been traumatized or lost loved ones may be required for many decades.

57. "Vaccine Champions," WCC.

The global economic impact of the pandemic may well result in increased unemployment, with damaging implications (for both finances and self-esteem) for those out of work and with consequences for wider society. The viability of some diaconal providers raises serious concerns, particularly when demand for services is expected to grow. There is, however, an opportunity to build back better and address the structural economic and social injustices exposed by this pandemic. Churches and church-related agencies must plan for a long-term diaconal response to the pandemic; an effective response must include ecumenical and international collaboration. The challenges of tackling poverty, climate change, and food insecurity, and giving attention to mental as well as physical health are major challenges for all in the coming decade, including the churches.

The opening of this document mentions healing and transformation with love, faith, hope, courage, and persistence. It is tempting to regard COVID-19 as an overwhelming problem, but this can too easily become an excuse for inaction. In 1 Corinthians 13, St Paul reminds us that we are called to faith, hope, and love. In addressing the implications of COVID-19 and in all the tribulations of life, the church, trusting in the grace and mercy of God, is and must remain a place of constant prayer, lament, and hope.

Prayer

We remember before God those who have died, and we pray that God's love will surround all who mourn them, now and always:[58]

Gracious God,
as we remember before you the thousands
 who have died,
surround us and all who mourn with
 your strong compassion.
Be gentle with us in our grief,
protect us from despair,
and give us grace to persevere
and face the future with hope
in Jesus Christ our risen Lord.
Amen.

58. "Archbishops Invite Nation to Join Them in Daily Prayer from this Evening amid Covid-19 Pandemic," 1 February 2021, The Church of English website, https://www.churchofengland.org/news-and-media/news-and-statements/archbishops-invite-nation-join-them-daily-prayer-evening-amid. *Prayer from The Church of England.*

Photo: Paul Jeffrey/Life on Ear

Section 2: Examples

The Response of the Churches: How Do We Serve the People?

Dr Mwombeki writes:

> "Churches are taking practical actions to support government systems and through direct diaconal services. The churches have the widest presence in both rural and urban areas. Churches have become teaching points for people on the importance and how to wash hands and the use of sanitizers. At the same time, many churches have launched localized diaconal services, providing food and other necessities to the very vulnerable families, particularly because African governments are not structured to even know the identity of the most vulnerable or even how to serve them. Congregations have collected and distributed food and cleaning materials to the vulnerable in their communities."[59]

Below is a very small selection of practical examples of the diaconal response worldwide.

Argentina

The pandemic has been affecting Argentina at a time of great socio-economic fragility, food emergency, and national debt crisis. According to official data, at the end of 2019, 35.5 per cent of the population were living below the poverty line, and in the capital, Buenos Aires, 40.5 per cent live in poverty. Inspired by the biblical parable of the loaves and fishes (Matt. 14:14-25), the Evangelical Methodist Church of Argentina (IEMA) and the Regional Ecumenical Advisory and Service Centre (CREAS) developed an initiative for cooperation and ecumenical *diakonia* called "Bread and Fishes for the Sustainability of Life," which bears witness to faith and life abundant in Jesus.

Faced with the rapid spread of COVID-19, this cooperation aims to support families and communities affected by the public health, economic, and social crisis generated by the pandemic in Argentina, thereby ensuring food security. Between May and July 2020, food and care were provided for 665 families, 104 tonnes of food and sanitary and biosecurity items were delivered in 20 communities. The support of 60 volunteers facilitated this. Such solidarity aims to unite people: despite lack of money, there is life abundant (see John 10:10).

China

This report is based on an interview with the Rev. Shen Zhanqing, director of the church and social service unit of the Amity Foundation.

In China, Hubei Province and its capital city Wuhan were at the epicentre of the COVID-19 outbreak, and churches, like all other organizations, were severely affected. The lockdown began at the end of January 2020, and the suspension of large gatherings made normal visits impossible. There were infected pastoral workers and believers who needed treatment. There were many people in need of spiritual care and support in addition to the need for PPE. Despite great difficulties and challenges, Christians in Hubei and local congregations put funds and energy into countering the epidemic. Common prayer was shared on social media. Pastoral duties were performed online or through phone calls. Whenever possible, pastors visited elders and those without access to technology and help.

The China Christian Council and the Amity Foundation shared information and worked closely together. Churches donated 16 million Chinese yuan (2.3 million US dollars) to the foundation for its relief work, their largest single contribution to date. Church members assisted in procuring supplies and checking quality and safety. Christian entrepreneurs made donations in kind. Local congregations actively cooperated with the foundation to distribute disinfectant, equipment, and protective gear to smaller hospitals, local communities, and nursing homes. Seminaries participated in similar activities, responding to local needs.

In the countryside, life has been difficult for those left behind. Christians have become more concerned about their neighbours' needs and responded actively. Zhanqing said that if Christians were known previously to "read the bible and pray" in the course of the fight against COVID-19, their social activism and warm-hearted services demonstrated the "sharing of unconditional love." The church's active efforts have aimed to put into practice the belief that God is love. According to Zhanqing, the Amity Foundation should help nurture the ability of those in local congregations to serve the community so that the church will become a "church that serves," and its members will personify "love that walks."

59. Mwombeki, "Faith Responses."

Egypt

The majority of Egypt's population of over 100 million is Muslim, but the Coptic Orthodox Church (COC) has a substantial and longstanding presence in the country. The Bishopric of Public, Ecumenical, and Social Services (BLESS) was established in 1962 as part of COC. BLESS has a leading role in providing diaconal services to poor and marginalized communities throughout Egypt.

BLESS developed an action plan in response to the pandemic, guided by humanitarian principles as well as inclusivity, gender, protection, and community engagement principles. The objectives are to:

- Provide immediate, life-saving assistance; food; hygiene; and sanitizing supplies to people with the greatest needs in line with national priorities.
- Promptly disseminate knowledge and raise awareness on key measures to avoid being infected with COVID-19, particularly among children, women, people with disabilities, youth, and vulnerable groups.
- Empower duty bearers and caregivers to provide adequate assistance and ensure the protection of vulnerable groups.
- Address psychosocial needs for the targeted communities and groups, particularly those who lost loved ones.
- Counteract the spread of rumours, misconceptions, and stigma related to being a COVID-19 victim.

Challenges include:

- Funding for humanitarian action not keeping pace with the scale of need, leading to situations of high and prolonged distress
- Fear of infection transmission that can occur for those in charge of work in the field during the response to the pandemic
- Poor access to digital tools and platforms and insufficient digital competencies

Germany

Diakonie Deutschland is the social welfare service of the mainline Protestant churches in Germany. It is a major provider of care services such as residential care for the elderly. As such, COVID-19 has had a major impact on operations, expenditure, and income. Different regulations must also be followed in the different federal states. Detailed information (in German) about the work of Diakonie Deutschland to address the pandemic is available online at https://www.diakonie.de/coronavirus-hilfe-und-infos.

The diaconal care facilities have drawn up emergency plans and adhere to the health authorities' applicable hygiene and safety measures. A particular challenge for diaconal work was and is the need to reduce social contacts. A lack of PPE resulted in a number of infections in the early days of the pandemic. Since residents of older people's homes belong to at-risk groups, there were particularly severe incidents of mass illness and death in some diaconal institutions. Since then, sufficient PPE for staff as well as patients were obtained. It is a difficult balance between the protection of residents and nursing staff on the one hand and the quality of life and self-determination of residents and their relatives on the other.

Despite the need to reduce social contact, many people have shown helpfulness and solidarity. Local diaconal offices and local congregations, together with others, have set up neighbourhood support networks.

As well as providing diaconal services within Germany, Diakonie Deutschland – through the organization Diakonie Katastrophenhilfe – provides humanitarian aid worldwide. It is also supported by ACT Alliance member Brot für die Welt (Bread for the World).

India

The 30 member churches of the National Council of Churches in India[60] have been active in responding to the challenges posed by the pandemic. They have been providing a range of services:

- Foodgrains, groceries, and food parcels, and support for community kitchens benefiting people living in poverty and migrant workers
- Shelter for homeless people in schools and other church buildings
- PPE for vulnerable communities
- Awareness-raising campaigns across India
- Psychological support to the isolated and

60. *"NCCI Constituents Responding to COVID-19," National Council of Churches in India website,* https://ncci1914.com/02-03-04-constituent-response/.

the poor, and care for older persons and the marginalized

- Mobilization of hospitals and dispensaries to respond to specific healthcare needs raised by the pandemic, in close collaboration with the state health services

Indonesia

Indonesia faces multifaceted challenges from COVID-19, not only in terms of health, economics, and unemployment but also in education. The Indonesian government is encouraging distance learning, but this creates difficulties for students unable to afford a smartphone or other computer access. This has the effect of widening the educational and, ultimately, the economic gap between rich and poor. Other natural disasters are compounding the need for diaconal services, yet churches, including ecumenical and interfaith initiatives, are actively working in the majority-Muslim country to respond to needs.

Kenya

Churches have reacted to the pandemic through their diaconal services and adherence to and awareness-raising about government guidelines (such as suspending common prayer and encouraging hygiene practices). Given that churches can often reach rural and even remote communities more effectively and comprehensively than almost any other organization, the authority and responsibility of the church are of critical importance in combating the pandemic.

Christian Aid – a member of ACT Alliance – has a longstanding record of working in Kenya. During the pandemic, it focused on providing clear health information about COVID-19 and minimizing the impacts of lockdown. In collaboration with the Kenyan government, partner organizations coordinate awareness-raising campaigns in local languages about how the virus can be caught and spread. Christian Aid sets up handwashing points and guides people to hotlines and healthcare facilities when they become sick. They are campaigning to ensure that rural communities continue to receive vital goods and services and provide a range of advice and support for women at increased risk of physical and sexual violence during lockdown.

Middle East

Upon the outbreak of the pandemic, the Middle East Council of Churches reacted quickly to co-operate with governmental and non-governmental organizations to help vulnerable people and share knowledge of good hygiene practices at family and community levels. The MECC organized activities to raise the awareness of COVID-19 among vulnerable refugees and internally displaced persons (IDPs), trained staff, provided Personal Protective Equipment (PPE), and adhered to World Health Organisation protocols (such as physical distancing).

The MECC launched a special appeal to its partners to meet the needs of people through the provision of hygiene materials, unconditional cash assistance, and distribution of guideline brochures. It facilitated the provision of basic needs through distribution centres, supplemented in some cases by door-to-door distributions. In coordination with security advisors, the MECC also conducted a risk analysis for activities – especially in places with large numbers of affected people. Additionally, the organization began issuing a weekly COVID-19 report – shared with partners and published online.

A specific example is the Greek Orthodox Patriarchate of Antioch and All the East (GOPA). The University of Balamand, owned by the Patriarchate, opened a major vaccination centre on the premises of the University in Lebanon. It administered many thousands of doses of the vaccine to Lebanese and Syrian people. The Department of Ecumenical Relations and Development (DERD), founded in 1994 and affiliated with GOPA, has been working to assist the destitute population in Syria during and after the war. These needs have been further exacerbated by COVID-19.

UK

Many churches are being used as vaccination centres, including some historic cathedrals.[61] The state-run National Health Service (NHS) is the principal

61. "Blackburn Cathedral Now Hosts One of New COVID-19 Mass Vaccination Centres," Blackburn Cathedral website, https://blackburncathedral.com/blackburn-cathedral-now-hosts-one-of-new-covid-19-mass-vaccination-centres/. *Blackburn Cathedral (Church of England) is one of the cathedrals in the UK being used as a vaccination centre.*

healthcare provider in the UK, but some church-run institutions provide diaconal care. One example is CrossReach, the social-care service of the Church of Scotland. It is a major provider of care services, such as residential care for the elderly, and its staff have had to adapt to the challenges of COVID-19. The risk posed to staff has meant that some services have had to be temporarily suspended, such as the Tom Allan Centre in Glasgow that provides confidential counselling.[62].

Zambia

The Council of Churches in Zambia (CCZ) has permitted the use of its David Livingstone College of Education in Livingstone as a quarantine facility by the government. The Rev. Emmanuel Yona Chikoya, CCZ general secretary, said, "We have worked with the Zambia Conference of Catholic Bishops and the Evangelical Fellowship of Zambia.... We have issued pastoral statements to the nation calling the church to follow and abide by government guidelines regarding the fight against COVID-19."[63]

DIAKONIA World Federation

Compiled from reports sent by the Rev. Sandy Boyce, president of DIAKONIA World Federation and a deacon of the Uniting Church in Australia.

The pandemic has had an enormous impact on those already vulnerable and struggling for survival. In response, the executive committee of DIAKONIA World Federation (Diakonia Weltbund e.V.) decided to release funding from the DIAKAID budget for quick response grants to support projects initiated by member associations to respond to the challenges and turmoil arising from the pandemic.

Individual member associations have offered financial support for projects in other countries. The deaconess community Bethesda in Basel, Switzerland, maintains its commitment to diaconal work, even though the small community of 20 elderly sisters is no longer able to conduct projects of their own. The three projects outlined below indicate their generous and practical support to vulnerable people.

In collaboration with Connexio, the humanitarian and development agency of the United Methodist Church in Switzerland, the Bethesda sisters have offered emergency aid and focussed on alleviating the suffering of vulnerable people and food insecurity. In Argentina, food packages have been distributed to people in slum areas who have lost their income because of quarantine measures. In North Macedonia, protective clothing and disposable tableware were purchased to continue meal delivery and home-care ministries for elderly and sick people. In the Democratic Republic of Congo, pastors' families, whose income had diminished to the extent that they could no longer live on it, each received a big sack of cornmeal. Thanks to the love in action of the Bethesda sisters, thousands of people have been helped quickly and efficiently.

The Bethesda sisters have also funded relief work undertaken by Osteuropa Mission Schweiz (OEM – Eastern Europe Mission Switzerland), an independent Christian relief agency that advocates for ethnic minorities and the socially disadvantaged and is committed to fighting poverty that impacts the most vulnerable. OEM church members have prepared soup for needy people on the streets. As the food packages were distributed, the church members prayed with the people and blessed them.

The Bethesda sisters have also supported relief efforts in the Philippines in collaboration with the Onesimo Bulilit Foundation, an FBO working among street children and their families and at-risk young people in Manila. It helps young people whose lives in the slums or on the streets are filled with hopelessness. During the COVID-19 lockdown, Onesimo has distributed food packages to thousands of families. Despite the pandemic, about 400 young people are still cared for in the community-based programs in the slum churches. As schools have been closed, the young people rely on alternative school systems such as those provided by community-based programs. Many of the slum churches have no computer or internet provider. They were so thankful for financial support so that the young people could continue their training through online learning.

In Winnipeg, Canada, a diaconal minister of the United Church of Canada serves as the community minister at St. Matthews Maryland Community

62. Further information is available online at https://www.crossreach.org.uk

63. "Knowing COVID-19 was on its way, Africa's churches prepared", World Council of Churches website, 7 May 2020, https://www.oikoumene.org/news/knowing-covid-19-was-on-its-way-africas-churches-prepared

Ministry, an outreach that provides support to and builds community alongside some of the most vulnerable people in the city. When COVID-19 first emerged, most support programs had to be cancelled. The team provided a pick-up food service for the first months of the pandemic, which saw a doubling of demand from approximately 70 to 150 meals per day.

The Methodist Deaconess Order Fiji had to deal with the impact of both COVID-19 and Cyclone Harold in April 2020. They could provide groceries for two deaconesses serving in the outer islands. After their houses had been blown down, some neighbouring families had taken shelter with the deaconesses. The order also provided food for vulnerable people on the street. In addition, the deaconesses learned that children in most of the Methodist schools had come to class without lunch because most of their parents had been laid off from work. The deaconesses serving in schools were encouraged to work with teachers and parents to recognize the students' plight and provide lunch packs.

During the pandemic, a hospice chaplain and member of the Lutheran Diaconal Association in Michigan in the United States of America has continued to be at the bedsides of those near the end of their lives. In the hospitals, the hallways are empty, and there are no visitors and no routine procedures, but the units themselves are overflowing and busy with lonely patients. The deaconess's ministry has become one of praying for COVID-19 patients in isolation rooms, using nurses' phones in the hallways, and comforting and reassuring their loved ones by phone. She recounts that recently she sat at the bedside of a dying patient and held the phone while his daughter and then his son and then his wife each called and said their goodbyes.

The pandemic and resulting lockdown, social isolation, financial stress, and insecurity about the future have taken a toll on mental health and emotional well-being. A deacon in Australia invited her congregation to consider ways to support people in their neighbourhood. The responses were creative and addressed the need for community connection despite the requirement for social isolation. After talking to a local cafe owner who deals with overwhelmed, anxious, and stressed customers, the church responded with donations to a pay-it-forward programme to supply coffee to people through the cafe. Teenage shop assistants who continued to work despite the stress caused by abusive customers and the threat of COVID-19 were appreciative to be acknowledged with the gift of boxes of chocolates provided to local supermarket staff. Schoolteachers and other school staff who were expected to continue to work despite the lockdown were experiencing stress as they tried to juggle face-to-face learning and the challenges of transitioning to online learning. The church gave packs of well-being cards to the teachers of four schools to help them focus on caring for themselves as well as their students. The church also delivered activity kits so families could do crafts with their children at home and displayed the results on the windows and doors of the church buildings. While there was no church in the building due to lockdown, the church found creative ways to be in the community, bringing some joy and welcome respite to those living with stress, anxiety, and financial uncertainty due to the disruption brought about by COVID-19.[64]

64. Further information is available online at http://www.diakonia-world.org/.

Contributors

Reference Group on Ecumenical Diakonia (2015–2018):

Rev. Professor Dr Kjell Nordstokke (Convener), Church of Norway
Dr Agnes Abuom, Moderator of the WCC Central Committee, Anglican Church of Kenya
Rev. Dr Sushant Agrawal, Moderator of ACT Alliance Governing Board, Church's Auxiliary for Social Action (CASA), Baptist, India
Rev. Cornelia Füllkrug-Weitzel, Bread for the World, Protestant Church in Germany (EKD)
Rev. Professor Beverley G. Haddad, Anglican Church of Southern Africa
Rev. Dr Carlos Ham, Presbyterian-Reformed Church in Cuba
Dr Karen Nazaryan, Armenian Apostolic Church (Mother See of Holy Etchmiadzin)
Ms Pauliina Parhiala, ACT Alliance, Evangelical-Lutheran Church of Finland
Ms Zo Ramiandra Rakotoarison, Malagasy Lutheran Church, Madagascar
Rev. Rolf Steffansson, Finnish Evangelical Lutheran Mission (FELM), Finland

Reference Group on Ecumenical Diakonia (2018–2022):

Dr Agnes Abuom, Moderator of the WCC Central Committee, Anglican Church of Kenya
His Eminence Metropolitan Professor Dr Gennadios of Sassima, Vice-moderator of the WCC Central Committee, Orthodox – Ecumenical Patriarchate
Rev. Dr Sushant Agrawal, Church's Auxiliary for Social Action (CASA), Baptist, India
Rev. Dr Henriette Hutabarat-Lebang, Gereja Toraja Indonesia (Reformed)
Rev. Dr Laurie Kraus, Presbyterian Church (USA)
Rev. Cibele Kuss, Lutheran Foundation of Diakonia, Brazil
Dr Hani Riad, Bishopric of Public, Ecumenical and Social Services (BLESS), Orthodox, Egypt
Ms Corrie van der Ven, Kerk in Actie / ACT Alliance, Netherlands
Ms Miriam Weibye, Church of Scotland
Rev. Professor Dr Dietrich Werner, Bread for the World / Protestant Church in Germany (EKD), Germany

Other contributors (not already listed in the Reference Groups):

Dr Souriya Bechealamy, Middle East Council of Churches
Mr Davide Bernocchi, Caritas Internationalis, Roman Catholic Church
Rev. James Bhagwan, Pacific Council of Churches
Rev. Dr Myra Blyth, Baptist Union of Great Britain
Rev. Sandy Boyce, Uniting Church in Australia / Diakonia World Federation
Mr Ghassan Chahine, Middle East Council of Churches
Dr Theresa Carino, Amity Foundation, China
Monsignor Pierre Ciambo, Caritas Internationalis, Roman Catholic Church
Rev. Dr Stephanie Dietrich, Lutheran World Federation
Rev. Ted Dodd, United Church of Canada / Diakonia of the Americas and Caribbean
Rev. Dr Chris Ferguson, World Communion of Reformed Churches
Ms Nina Hallak, Middle East Council of Churches
Rev. Fifamé Fidèle Houssou-Gandonou, Protestant Methodist Church of Benin
Rev. Professor Dr Jooseop Keum, Presbyterian Church of Korea
Very Rev. Professor Dr Jack Khalil, Greek Orthodox Patriarchate of Antioch and all the East
Rev. Dr Vladimir Khoulap, Russian Orthodox Church (Moscow Patriarchate)
Ms Kerstin Kollander, ACT Alliance

Rev. Nicta Lubaale Makiika, Organisation of African Instituted Churches

Mrs Jennifer Martins, Caribbean and North American Council on Mission (CANCOM)

Mr Alain Epp Weaver, Mennonite Central Committee, USA

Bishop Rosemarie Wenner, United Methodist Church

WCC Staff:

Professor Dr Isabel Apawo Phiri, WCC Deputy General Secretary

Rev. Dr Dong Sung Kim†, WCC Programme Executive

Rev. Dr David Marshall, WCC Programme Executive

Rev. Dr Nyambura Njoroge, WCC Programme Executive

Dr Fulata Lisungu Moyo, WCC Programme Executive

Ms Athena Peralta, WCC Programme Executive

Rev. Dr Martin Robra, WCC Programme Executive

Rev. Matthew Ross, WCC Programme Executive (Secretary to the Reference Group since 2018 and Editor)

Mr Dinesh Suna, WCC Programme Executive

Photo Descriptions and Credits

Cover

Photo credit: Paul Jeffrey/Life on Earth (2017)

Evelyn Nkhambule, her grandson Jesse on her back, stirs chilies she has spread out to dry in the sun at her home in Edundu, Malawi. Families in the village have benefited from intercropping, crop rotation, and composting practices they learned from the Malawi Farmer-to-Farmer Agro-Ecology project within a program of the Livingstonia Synod of the Church of Central Africa Presbyterian.

Executive summary, p. 9

Photo credit: Paul Jeffrey/Life on Earth (2011)

Fishers in Gaza unload a net from a fishing boat before dawn. Since the Israeli military imposed a naval blockade in 2007 they have been limited to fishing just three nautical miles from their coastline. Despite having 40 kilometers of coastline and a long tradition as fishers, many fishers are unemployed and the people of Gaza are forced to import fish from Israel. As fishing close to shore mostly involves the harvest of immature fish, biologists warn of a negative impact on fish stocks in the region.

Introduction, p. 13

Photo credit: Paul Jeffrey/Life on Earth (2021)

Cape Blanco lighthouse on a coast of Pacific Ocean in Cape Blanco, Oregon, United States.

The History of Ecumenical *Diakonia*, p. XX

Photo credit: Albin Hillert/WCC (2016)

Pottery at the Anaphora Institute, a Coptic Orthodox retreat and educational centre located north-west of Cairo, Egypt.

Diakonia in today's polycentric ecumenical movement, p. 36

Photo credit: Albin Hillert/ Life on Earth (2019)

Market day at the Minawao camp for Nigerian refugees in the Mokolo, Cameroon, when refugees and host communities gather to sell and buy goods. The Minawao camp in the North region of the country hosts some 58,000 refugees from North East Nigeria, who are supported by the Lutheran World Federation, together with a range of partners.

Theological Reflection on *Diakonia*, p. 42

Photo credit: Paul Jeffrey/Life on Earth (2019)

A girl acolyte prays as she holds a candle during Catholic Mass in St Ignatius, Guyana. St Ignatius is an Amerindian village in the Upper Takutu-Upper Essequibo region of Guyana, originally founded by Jesuit priests.

The Changing Landscape of Diaconal Action, p. 53

Photo credit: Albin Hillert/WCC (2018)

40-year-old Deab Abu Malik herds his sheep in the Jordan Valley on the West Bank in Occupied Palestinian Territories. Volunteers of the World Council of Churches Ecumenical Accompaniment Programme in Palestine in Israel accompany shepherds in many parts of the West Bank, providing an international presence known to have a mitigating effect on confrontations between Israeli settlers and the Palestinians. Accessing their lands regularly is vital for the communities and their herds.

The Distinctiveness of Diaconal Practice, p. 67

Photo credit: Sean Hawkey/Life on Earth (2012)

Khady Waylie, a cotton farmer in Sitaoulé Banandding, Senegal, throws freshly picked cotton onto a heap. The harvest is a celebration that marks the end of a season's hard work. Khady grows cotton that is certified Fairtrade and exported by FNPC, the National Federation of Cotton Producers.

Contemporary Challenges, p. 78

Photo credit: László Lehel/HIA (2022)

Distribution of aid on the Easter weekend at the Orthodox Church of the Nativity of the Blessed Virgin in Borodyanka, Ukraine. Consisting of food and hygiene products, aid is provided by Hungarian Interchurch Aid, member of the ACT Alliance. Russia's war of aggression in Ukraine has caused death and suffering on a dramatic scale, leaving at least 15 million people in urgent need of humanitarian assistance and protection. Over a quarter of Ukraine's population have fled their homes, with nearly two-thirds of the children in Ukraine now displaced.

Ecumenical *Diakonia* in a confessional context, p. 87

Photo credit: Paul Jeffrey/Life on Earth (2014)

Hien Nguyen, a Catholic nun from Vietnam, lights candles at the interfaith service at St. Paul's (Anglican) Cathedral in Melbourne, Australia. The memorial service for those who have died of HIV and AIDS-related causes involved several delegates to the 20th International AIDS Conference. The service came following a march through Melbourne demanding an end to stigma and discrimination against those living with the virus, and a candlelight service in a nearby plaza.

Ecumenical *Diakonia* in a regional context, p. 97

Photo credit: Paul Jeffrey/Life on Earth (2017)

A woman operates a traditional loom to weave cloth in Kalay, a town in Myanmar.

The Way Forward, p. 109

Photo credit: Paul Jeffrey/Life on Earth (2017)

Enjoying relative peace for the first time in years, a boy lays out the framework for the thatched roof of a hut. A peace process that began in 2006 has brought hope to the two million people in northern Uganda who were displaced by the long war with the Lord's Resistance Army. In the village of Amuca, families have returned and are harvesting crops, building homes, and enjoying the first peace they've had for more than 20 years.

The Diaconal Work of the Churches in the Context of COVID-19, p. 116

Photo credit: Ash Mills/Salisbury Cathedral (2021)

Amidst the COVID-19 pandemic, a mass vaccination centre was set up in Salisbury Cathedral, United Kingdom. Hour upon hour, from classical to show tunes, musicians of the Cathedral were playing to people while they were receiving their vaccination shots. An album of music played for the vaccinations was later recorded, called Salisbury Meditations, to raise funds for the NHS.

p. 118

Photo credit: Sean Hawkey/Life on Earth (2012)

Social distancing sign in London, as people are adapting to the restrictions and measures related to the COVID-19 pandemic.

p. 130

Photo credit: Paul Jeffrey/Life on Earth (2011)

A child peeks from behind the door into their house in Batey Bombita, a community in the southwest of the Dominican Republic whose population is composed of Haitian immigrants and their descendents.

9782825418062